British Classics Outside England

British Classics Outside England

The Academy and Beyond

Judith P. Hallett
Christopher Stray
editors

BAYLOR UNIVERSITY PRESS

Cover Design by Nicole Weaver, Zeal Design

Library of Congress Cataloging-in-Publication Data

British classics outside England : the academy and beyond / Judith P.
Hallett and Christopher Stray, editors.
    p. cm.
  Based on papers presented at a conference held June 2005 in Hay-
on-Wye.
  Includes bibliographical references and index.
  ISBN 978-1-60258-012-1 (pbk. : alk. paper)
  1. Classical philology--Study and teaching--Great Britain--History-
-19th century--Congresses. 2. Classical philology--Study and
teaching--Great Britain--History--20th century--Congresses. 3.
Classical philology--Study and teaching--United States--History-
-20th century--Congresses. I. Hallett, Judith P., 1944- II. Stray,
Christopher.

  PA78.G5B75 2008
  480.941'09034--dc22
                              2008011911

Contents

Introduction

British Classics Outside England

ᴓ—Judith P. Hallett and Christopher Stray

This collection of essays grew out of several papers presented at a conference on classics in nineteenth- and twentieth-century Britain held in Hay-on-Wye in June 2005. As the town of Hay-on-Wye lies on the border between England and Wales, it was a particularly apt location for discussions about the transmission and impact of classics across borders. The essays in this book, like the papers from which they developed, explore the impact of British classics—the study of Greco-Roman antiquity, with an emphasis on the classical Latin and Greek languages—beyond the borders of England itself, during the nineteenth and twentieth centuries, both inside the academy as specialized scholarship and teaching and outside the academy as a mode of social and cultural formation. Their explorations focus on a variety of educational and cultural institutions, as well as on several important individuals.

One way to look at the spread of classics beyond England is to see it as a twofold process of cultural colonization. The expansion of British culture to the Empire, and its role in maintaining imperial authority, is a phenomenon with which we are familiar, especially with the export of young men from Balliol College, Oxford, to rule the colonies as Platonic guardians (Symonds 1986). Classical antiquity was routinely drawn on for analogical justification of British rule, though English literature, hardly taught in its home country, in the Empire itself became a classical literature promoted by the conquerors and seized on by some of their colonial subjects.[1] Less well known, and certainly not in the same context, is the role of classics as part of an "internal colonialism" through which the social, political, and cultural authority of England over Scotland, Wales, and Ireland was maintained.[2] A major bulwark of this colonialism was provided by the prestige of Oxford and Cambridge, especially the former, whose curriculum was dominated by classics as that of Cambridge was by mathematics (Stray 2007). The colleges of the two ancient universities had close ties to specific regions outside of England: at Oxford, Jesus College took students from Wales, while Balliol received students from Glasgow (called "Snell exhibitioners" because they were funded by a bequest from John Snell). It was common for students from the provinces to take a bachelor's degree at their home university and then to migrate to Oxbridge for a second (also bachelor's) degree. J. A. K. Thomson, the subject of chapter 7, took degrees first at Aberdeen and then at Oxford; other Aberdeen classicists to follow similar routes included John Strachan, Peter Giles, Robert Neil, and James Adam.[3]

It is worth emphasizing (although the topic lies beyond the purview of the present volume) that this process of internal colonialism also took place inside the boundaries of England itself. The regional ties to Oxbridge colleges mentioned above applied within England as well. Furthermore, when new universities were founded in London and Durham in the 1820s and 1830s, and in Manchester, Birmingham, Liverpool, and elsewhere in the second half of the nineteenth century, the pattern of migration to Oxbridge continued.[4] In addition, the students who migrated had usually been taught by professors whose own training had been at Oxford or Cambridge.[5]

The picture sketched above may suggest a colonial system secure in the confidence of its own superiority. The reality is more complicated. The major threat to such confidence in the nineteenth century was the overwhelming reputation of German scholarship. The sheer size of the German professorial establishment, together with its reputation for industry and professionalism, daunted many English scholars. In comparison, the elegant scholarship of their own compatriots, focused as it was largely on composition in Latin and Greek, seemed an amateur enterprise, although pride could be taken in belonging to the country of Bentley and Porson. Not until Hugh Munro's edition of Lucretius appeared in 1864 was it felt that England could produce work to rival the Germans (and Munro was Scottish by birth).

In the middle of the nineteenth century, classical scholarship in the United States began to shake off its "colonial" dependence on English models by turning to German higher education for guidance and inspiration.[6] Basil Lanneau Gildersleeve (1831–1924), the subject of Ward Briggs's essay in this volume, played an important part in this challenge to the hegemony of English classical scholarship in Anglophone North America. Gildersleeve founded the *American Journal of Philology*, edited Pindar's Olympian and Pythian *Odes*, and coauthored a widely used book on Latin grammar. The first classicist inducted into the American Academy of Arts and Letters, he received his training in Germany and implemented a number of German academic practices after arriving at the Johns Hopkins University in Baltimore as its first faculty appointment in 1875.

Nevertheless, the faults inherent in the German system—among them niggling pedantry, inaccuracy, overspecialization, lack of literary background, and an absence of the innovative approaches that had characterized the work of Germans previously—became increasingly apparent toward the end of the nineteenth century. At the same time, British classical scholars began to produce exciting new work both in traditional philology and in cross-disciplinary research, such as that of the so-called "Cambridge Ritualists."[7] In response, Gildersleeve and other American classicists "oscillated" (to use Gildersleeve's own word) back to appreciating the contributions of British scholarship.

The conflicted attitude among American classicists toward both their English and their German scholarly models is memorably illustrated by Paul Shorey's address on the occasion of the American Philological Association's fiftieth anniversary in 1919 (Shorey 1919). In seeking to provide "a little more justice to American scholarship than it usually receives either from Americans themselves or from foreigners" (34), Shorey (1857–1934), the first professor of Greek at the University of Chicago, characterizes English scholarship as "brilliantly amateurish" (48) and German philology as tending toward "the abuse of conjecture and the pyramiding of hypothesis" (44).[8] His conclusion—a tricolonic comparison of R. C. Jebb (1841–1905), professor of Greek at Cambridge, Ulrich von Wilamowitz-Moellendorff (1848–1931), professor of Greek at Berlin, and Gildersleeve—leads to a poetic prophecy, addressed to both England and Germany, that "we shall outstrip you both when time is ripe" (58–61). Shorey's predictions were by no means fanciful. Over the course of the twentieth century the United States has come increasingly to the fore as a major world center of classical scholarship. Some might, in fact, argue that Britain currently occupies a colonial position relative to its ex-colony where both teaching and research on classics are concerned.[9]

In addition to singling out Jebb as a paradigmatic representative of British classical scholarship, Shorey's 1919 address makes frequent mention, both laudatory and critical, of another luminary on the British classical and cultural scene in the early twentieth century: Gilbert Murray (1856–1957), who had assumed the Regius Professorship of Greek at Oxford in 1908. Murray enjoyed both renown and influence in the United States as well as in the British Isles. Indeed, he figures in all three of the essays in this volume focused on American classicists, those by Briggs on Gildersleeve, Barbara F. McManus on Grace Harriet Macurdy, and Judith P. Hallett on Edith Hamilton, as well as in McManus's essay on the Scottish J. A. K. Thomson and Eleanor Irwin's on the Welsh Kathleen Freeman.

Murray's role in spreading British classics beyond Britain involves a more expansive, boundary-crossing, definition of classics itself. His translations of Greek drama served as the texts of professional productions by such theatrical legends as Harley Granville-Barker, Dame Sybil Thorndike, and Max Reinhardt; Murray himself was sufficiently recognizable to the theater-going public to be caricatured by George Bernard Shaw as Adolphus Cusins in *Major Barbara* (1905). Efforts to communicate with audiences outside the small enclave of classical scholars by Gildersleeve, Hamilton, Thomson, and Freeman owe much to Murray's example.[10]

Murray's student Gilbert Highet (1906–1978), Anthon Professor of Latin at Columbia University, an emigré to the United States from Glasgow (where Murray himself held the chair of Greek from 1889 through 1898) via Oxford, did much to bring British classics to American shores. He could also look to Murray as a model for his far-reaching endeavors in popularization and consequently labored to burnish Murray's image in the U.S. classics community.[11] Although Highet is not the subject of a separate essay in this volume, the essays on Hamilton and Thomson prominently feature him, documenting his influence on the former, and comparing his work on the classical tradition to that of the latter.

The theme of internal and external colonialism also figures in several of the essays in this volume, which explore the differing and complex responses "beyond England" to the heritage of British classics. Interwoven with this theme are issues of gender, social class, and regionalism. For example, the number of professional women classicists in the United States at the turn of the century made it more difficult for male classicists in America to assert their equality with their British and German counterparts, thus creating intense pressure on the women to downplay their gender and write and act like "honorary males" (McManus 1997, 20–35). Ironically, as McManus shows in chapter 6, it was her strong ties to England that enabled Grace Macurdy to escape this pressure, since as an American she did not pose a threat to the British classics establishment.

Hallett's essay shows that Edith Hamilton readily capitulated to such pressure. She notes that although Hamilton was educated and employed at all-female institutions and shared her bed and life with two women, Hamilton's social circles during the years of her intellectual celebrity were mainly composed of men. What is more, Hamilton's writings on Greek antiquity say virtually nothing about the women who inhabited ancient Athens. Nor do they discuss the legendary Greek female poet Sappho, whose words and image have certain resemblances to Hamilton's own. Hailed on her ninetieth birthday as an "honorary Athenian," Hamilton was an honorary male as well. Not surprisingly, the British scholars and writers that she invoked to enhance her intellectual credibility were also men.

A focus on individual classicists, shared by several of the essays in this volume, has multiple benefits in an investigation of this kind. Our volume reflects upon the solitary and collective efforts of various men and women in research and teaching, reading and writing, about an interdisciplinary area of academic endeavor that encompasses language, literature, history, and material culture. It considers how their efforts affected a variety of audiences—local, national, and international, inside and outside the academy. Their stories therefore serve as a salutary reminder of how their specific personal experiences as well as their general sociocultural circumstances helped to shape not only their own lives but also their chosen discipline and profession, as well as the world around them. These essays look at their individual subjects as historical embodiments of social developments, using analytical and critical as well as narrative and biographical frameworks.

Both Gildersleeve and Hamilton, for example, suffered major losses for which their careers furnished recompense, emotional in one case and financial in the other: the former owing to the defeat of the South in the U.S. Civil War; the latter owing to her father's alcoholism and bankruptcy, which necessitated that his four unmarried daughters (unlike their female cousins) seek gainful employment rather than remain home as companions to their mother. Hamilton's forty-year relationship with Doris Fielding Reid, a female former student nearly three decades her junior, also provided her with uncritical support and admiration for her writing and for her decision to ignore the protocols and publications of academic specialists when reenvisioning and reinterpreting classical antiquity. The thirteen-year age difference between Macurdy and her longtime male companion Thomson, as well as the transatlantic dimension of their companionship, may well have contributed to their productivity as scholars and to their willingness to pursue new directions in their scholarship.

The first part of this volume is devoted to British classics beyond its English heartland: in Scotland, Wales, and the British Empire. Mick Morris discusses the role of classics in nineteenth-century Scotland, when a distinctive tradition of scholarship, teaching, and social access to knowledge was proudly claimed in "North Britain." In his influential book *The Democratic Intellect: Scotland and her Universities in the Nineteenth Century* (1961), George Davie reasserted this claim by locating it in the context of a new wave of Scottish nationalism. Morris, a long-term resident in Scotland whose full-scale treatment of nineteenth-century Scottish classics is forthcoming, offers a fresh assessment not only of the evidence for the provision of classical learning in Scotland, but also of Davie's provocative thesis. Morris's chapter deals with classics at both secondary school and university level, thus providing the first comprehensive assessment of the subject. In the nineteenth century, Scotland, which had joined the United Kingdom in 1707, still preserved its own educational and legal systems; in a sense it can be seen as a cultural fifth column within the Union, assimilated yet distinct.

If little has been written on classics in Scotland, the literature on Wales is even sparser—especially in English. Ceri Davies's survey of the relationships between Classics and Welsh national identity in the nineteenth century therefore represents a welcome and accessible treatment of this theme. His account focuses on the reports of three English educational commissioners (the "Blue Books" of 1847), whose generally disparaging description of Welsh schools was embellished with denunciations both of the use of Welsh and of the morals of its speakers. At the time of the Chartist movement, the dissemination of English was seen by the political establishment as a civilizing process which might work to defuse radicalism. The reaction in Wales was fierce, and among its results were the founding of schools, university colleges, journals, and competitions, all of which featured writing on classics, including translations of Greek tragedy. The language issues in Wales centered on two vernaculars, English and Welsh, and the politics of culture involved their relationship both with each other and with the classical languages. The role of Welsh in a sense combined that of classical and vernacular: similar to and yet interestingly different from the role of Persian and Sanskrit in India, and from that of Gaelic in Scotland.

Eleanor Irwin's chapter also deals with Wales, but moves into the twentieth century to consider the life and work of a pioneering woman classicist, who is also mentioned toward the end of Davies's account. Kathleen Freeman was one of the few women to teach the subject at university level. Combining serious scholarship with a concern for the general reader, her work is notable for the unusual topics that it treats as well as for the imaginative forms in which it was published. Freeman managed to develop a conventional academic career without the dramatic difficulties faced by Grace Macurdy; she also led a parallel literary life as an author of detective fiction. Her classical publications include studies of philosophy and law; in her work on Greek city-states she looked beyond the inevitable duo of Athens and Sparta. Her concern for outreach was manifested in the leading role she took in reviving, after the Second World War, the moribund Philosophical Society of England. All in all, this is an unusual life and career that offers a striking and instructive contrast to the others discussed in this volume.

The last chapter of this section deals with the role of classics in the examination for the Indian Civil Service. Central to this topic, as Phiroze Vasunia shows, is the grand plan instigated by Benjamin Jowett, Master of Balliol College, Oxford, to send British (and particularly Oxford) graduates out to govern the British Empire. Vasunia discusses both the workings of the examination system and the role of classics in it. He also considers the obstructions put in place when the colonials themselves attempted to win places in the governing elite. Both internal and external colonialism feature in Vasunia's analysis: while Oxford and Cambridge dons struggled to revise the examination rules to favor their own graduates, both sought to exclude men from elsewhere in Britain. Through this history there also runs an interesting tension between the ideology of merit-based appointment and the concern to exclude those who were not white and English.

The second part of the book accords center stage to the interactions between the study of classics in the United Kingdom and that in an ex-colony, the United States. In an article on German scholarship published in 1915, Gilbert Murray included a list of leading classical scholars in the English-speaking world. Among those he singled out was Gildersleeve. Ward Briggs's essay begins by examining the role that Gildersleeve's complicated family and personal history played in his evolving attitude toward Britain and the British. Briggs then turns to Gildersleeve's experiences with individual British scholars, highlighting a visit to the U.K. (including Ireland) in 1880, during which he assessed a number of classicists as potential colleagues for his own institution. Gildersleeve's role as editor of the *American Journal of Philology* (*AJP*) is by itself enough to make him a significant figure in the development of Anglo-American classical scholarship. But as readers of his "Brief Mention" columns in *AJP* will know, he also combined learning with an engagingly personal style.

Barbara McManus's account of Grace Harriet Macurdy's life serves as an interesting contrast to the earlier chapter on Kathleen Freeman. Both women sought to make their careers in a scholarly and institutional world dominated by males. Each successfully established herself as both a teacher and an author. But unlike Freeman, Macurdy benefited from the protective academic environment offered by the independent women's colleges that flourished in the United States at this time. Her own career, however, was almost derailed by the resentment harbored by a member of her own sex: Abby Leach, her own head of department at Vassar, and a well-known figure in the U.S. classics establishment. Macurdy's links with British scholarship date back to her initial correspondence with Gilbert Murray in 1906, six years after she returned from studying in Berlin with two legendary German scholars, Wilamowitz and Hermann Diels. But these ties were strengthened considerably by her close friendship with Murray's protégé, J. A. K. Thomson. McManus, who is preparing a full-length biography of Macurdy, insightfully contrasts this professional relationship with that between the British scholars Jane Harrison and Francis Cornford.

Thomson, the other half of this "odd couple," is the subject of McManus's second contribution. A path-breaking student of classical reception with a special interest in English literature, he was rescued by Murray's support from the dismal prospects which would have otherwise followed his mediocre Oxford degree. Among the opportunities Murray's patronage opened up for him were teaching posts in the United States, first at Harvard and then at a women's college, Bryn Mawr. It was at this stage of his professional life that his relationship with Macurdy, begun earlier by correspondence, came to loom large. Thomson was eventually appointed to a chair at King's College, London, with Murray again acting as *deus ex machina*. Although he is now virtually forgotten, McManus's essay argues that Thomson deserves to be recognized for his contributions to the now burgeoning field of classical reception studies. Thomson's works have far more in common with current research in that area than the better known works of Gilbert Highet, who enjoyed an illustrious career as both a Columbia University classics professor and a media celebrity. Thomson's story also provides a privileged glimpse of how a British classicist viewed, and learned from, his experiences in the United States.

The final contribution, by Judith P. Hallett, explores the long life and writing career of another influential popularizer, Edith Hamilton, whose books and essays on classical civilization achieved staggering—and, as Hallett argues, perhaps not entirely deserved—success for much of the twentieth century. *The Greek Way*, first published in 1930, continues to be a bestseller; *Mythology*, which appeared twelve years later, has attracted an even wider readership. In her essay, based partly on interviews with Hamilton's friends and family, Hallett traces the ways in which Hamilton compensated for her lack of scholarly credentials and legitimated herself as an American public intellectual, with the Kennedy family among others, by identifying with "the best of Britain." In so doing, Hallett uncovers a remarkable story worthy of the Greek myths retold by Hamilton herself.

The chapters by McManus, Irwin, and Hallett illustrate, *inter alia*, that issues of gender are often important in the scholarship whose history we survey in this book. Underlying the movements of English domination and resistance to England in the U.K. was a further level of gender repression: in Scotland, for example, we hear of the "lad of parts" (a poor boy whose talent enabled him to rise through schooling) but not of the "*lass of parts*." Only in the account of the Indian Civil Service do we glimpse the theme of feminization, in the denial of virility to the males of subordinate races. A future task might be to focus more specifically on the ways in which gender interacts with regionalism and colonialism (and indeed with social class, race, and religion) in the forging of professional identities and intellectual priorities in the field of classical studies. The reader will notice that large parts of the British Empire go unmentioned; another future task, then, is to extend the analysis to Australia, Canada, New Zealand, and South Africa. In all these countries classics has been and is being taught, and university departments flourish. In each of them, the content and justification of the subject has been developed through interaction between British traditions and local influences. In the case of Canada, the British influence has interacted both with French academic and cultural traditions and with those from the United States (Goff 2005; Hardwick and Gillespie 2007).

The editors wish to thank David Gill and Anton Powell for their roles in the Hay-on-Wye conference from which this volume emerged, Barbara McManus for her immense help with editing its component parts, and Ward Briggs for elucidating American attitudes toward German classical scholarship "back in the old days." Chris Stray would like to dedicate this volume to Sir Moses Finley (1912–1986), an exile from the U.S.A. who found, and greatly enriched, a new academic home in the U.K. Judy Hallett would like to dedicate it to Jonathan Walters (1948–2004), who—as the *Res Gestae* of Augustus might have put it—*alis immortalibus per Oceanum ad solis occidentis regionem usque ad fines nostras navigavit.*

We would also like to thank the following for permission to quote from materials in their collections: the Blegen Library, American School of Classical Studies at Athens; the Schlesinger Library, Radcliffe Institute for Advanced Studies, Harvard University; Special Collections, Vassar College Libraries; Alexander Murray; and Caroline Skinner O'Neil; Princeton University Library for permission to quote from the Edith Hamilton Collection.

Judith P. Hallett
Bethesda, Maryland

Christopher Stray
Swansea, Wales
July 2007

Part I

BRITISH CLASSICS OUTSIDE ENGLAND
Scotland, Wales, and the Empire

Chapter 1

The Democratic Intellect Preserved

Scotland and the Classics 1826–1836

∽—Mick Morris

The Tweed is one of the broadest rivers in the world.
—T. R. Glover[1]

There exists currently no published history of the teaching of classics in nineteenth-century Scotland, yet Scotland's ancient universities have had a notable tradition in the teaching of Latin (in Scotland named "Humanity"), and this language, together with Greek, was a compulsory part of any undergraduate's course of studies in the period in question.[2] Major classical scholars such as Richard Jebb, Gilbert Murray, and Lewis Campbell all made distinguished contributions as teachers in Victorian Scotland, but their efforts have gone largely unrecorded. Added to this, the major reforms of education witnessed in Britain in the nineteenth century invariably were tested first in Scotland. The attempts at reform discussed in this chapter, for example, long predated the reform of Oxford (the Oxford University Act was passed in 1854). These interventions consistently seemed to represent a very serious, radical, and possibly harmful challenge to what, many Scots felt, was their own distinctive and separate tradition in education, both in their schools and in their universities.

13

These attempts to introduce change were quite deliberately intended to have a very direct impact on the teaching of the ancient languages. Government investigators invariably found large differences between one Scottish university and the next; for example, the curriculum in Latin and Greek at Aberdeen seemed markedly different from that, say, at Glasgow.[3] As there was no Scottish gold standard on the classical curriculum, they fell back on the English model, Oxford. The Scottish universities were made to aspire in Latin and Greek to the standards applied on the banks of the Isis. This process began in 1826 when the reforming Home Secretary Robert Peel decided, after being informed that "certain Irregularities, Disputes and Deficiencies have incurred in the Universities of Scotland calculated to impair the utility of those Establishments,"[4] that a comprehensive official government investigation should be initiated.

On 31 August 1826 the commissioners appointed by the Crown to investigate the Scottish universities met for the first time in Edinburgh. The work of this royal commission represents not just the first government investigation into the work of Britain's universities but also one of the most comprehensive descriptions of the work and culture of a nation's universities ever produced in Britain. When, after much delay, the evidence they had collected was presented to parliament, in 1837, it consisted of four folio volumes of evidence totalling nearly 2,000 pages. The commissioners had called, and in some cases recalled, one hundred eighty witnesses, including every professor. They had made nearly five hundred specific requests for written evidence; they also made a close examination of every extant legal document connected with these institutions, from their medieval charters of foundation onwards.[5] But the commission was not just dramatic in its scale of investigation, but also in its recommendations. When its *Report* appeared in 1831, six years prior to the four volumes of its *Evidence*,[6] it recommended nothing less than the complete overhaul of Scotland's ancient universities; the creation of a new type of university governance; the foundation of a new Scottish university campus, in Dumfries;[7] and finally, the imposition of a uniform Scottish university curriculum in classics. This final decision would make the formation of a national, federated "University of Scotland," with the five ancient universities under one umbrella—an overt ambition of the commissioners—much more easily achieved in the near future.[8] The radicalism of these proposals, then and now, needs little underlining. Peel, who always took a keen interest in Scottish educational affairs,[9] must have felt reform was at hand, but his hopes turned to dust: no part of the commission's reforms was made flesh. The questions that must be asked are: why in "an age of reform" did such concerted and repeated attempts by "the powers that be" fail so lamentably? Why in Scotland did governments of both the Tory and Whig persuasions so palpably fail to make their case?

SCOTLAND'S UNIVERSITIES IN THE 1820s

In 1820 England had two universities, but so did Aberdeen: King's College (1495) and Marischal College (1593). The five Scottish universities, with the exception of St Andrews, were situated in city centers: Adam Smith could, in the 1760s, walk across the road from Glasgow College and lunch with the "Tobacco Lords" in the merchant city and talk trade; David Hume, a decade earlier, could leave his home in the Lawnmarket and walk the two hundred yards to meet and drink claret with his friends from Edinburgh University. There were no religious barriers or entrance tests imposed at admission. Classes were large, a hundred fifty not being unusual, and these institutions were non-collegiate: students, like their professors, were part of the landscape of the city. Classes for the five key subjects were cheap to enter, a fee of three guineas being the norm for a session's study.[10] Above all else, the four-year program of study owed more to Europe than to England. The pattern was usually not to graduate: neither David Hume, who matriculated at the University of Edinburgh at age ten,[11] nor Adam Smith, who entered Glasgow at age fourteen, bothered with what they, and other Scottish students, saw as an expensive and irrelevant ceremony. Another factor at work was the Scottish suspicion of what they often saw as the potential for spiritual corruption in attending an English university: far from home, surrounded by Episcopalian temptations any son of Scotland might, in a collegiate environment, soon lose the true faith of his native land.[12] This applied particularly to Oxford.[13]

Scottish professors occupied an especial and distinguished place in the culture of these cities: when Sir Daniel Keyte Sandford, professor of Greek at Glasgow College, died in 1838 the corporation and the whole university processed with the coffin down High Street to the Bromielaw (Glasgow's main dockside). As the boat carrying his coffin and all his Greek students sailed down the Clyde to the Isle of Bute for his interment, all the ships on the Clyde had their flags at half-mast out of respect to the scholar who was passing by on his last journey. Similar scenes were witnessed when in 1895 Edinburgh's flamboyant professor of Greek, John Stuart Blackie, was taken to his final place of rest at Dean Cemetery: Princes Street was packed with a silent crowd.

But all was not well with the university system: in the eighteenth and nineteenth centuries professorial chairs, in the absence of any pension, were openly bought and sold; for example, Andrew Dalzel bought the chair of Greek at Edinburgh for £300 in 1772. In the absence of any pension aging Scottish professors had only one asset to sell to secure their old age in their increasing infirmity, the post itself.[14] Professors appointed their successors. One family, the Monros, held the chair of anatomy and surgery at Edinburgh for 120 years.[15] They were known, unsurprisingly, as "Monro Primus, Secundus and Tertius." The University at St Andrews happily awarded medical degrees without teaching any medicine. One man, John Lee, managed to be simultaneously, in 1820, a minister at the Canongate Kirk in Edinburgh, a professor at St Andrews (church history), and finally a professor at Aberdeen (moral philosophy)—two universities separated by ninety miles. Corruption, mismanagement of endowments, and naked nepotism seemed to be the charge brought against these institutions by the wider Scottish community.

THE "MYTH" OF MOBILITY: GEORGE DAVIE
AND "IAN MACLAREN"

Any analysis of Scottish university education in the nineteenth century has to examine two separate but related issues: the controversy over the concept of the "democratic intellect" and the truth (or otherwise) of the portrait often given in Scottish Victorian history and fiction of the "lad of parts." Both terms have become a form of educational shorthand used in quite complex arguments over the nature of learning in Scotland and how access is granted to, or withheld from, the higher reaches of that learning. It is fair to say, too, that both terms have often been reduced to mere slogans, of either praise or abuse, in this debate. Thus it is necessary to look briefly at the genesis of both terms.

The most noted modern analysis of Scottish universities in the nineteenth century is George Davie's *The Democratic Intellect: Scotland and her Universities in the Nineteenth Century* (1961).[16] The book grew out of Davie's interest, as a professional philosopher, in the Scottish school of common-sense philosophy. As he worked on the background to this topic, he discovered "the story behind the story."[17] In this book Davie presented a radical reinterpretation of the course of Scottish intellectual life in the Victorian period. Far from seeing the period as one of general progress and improvement in Scottish university education, he describes the period as one in which a series of government attacks were made on every distinctive feature of Scotland's five ancient universities: the governance, curriculum, finances, degree structure, and system of appointment were all "reformed." The Act of Union (1707) had dismantled Scotland's parliament but left in place her unique legal system and also her established church. Davie suggests that the third element that made Scotland distinct from England was her universities:

> The Scots gave up their political and economic independence but retained the right to follow their national usage in religion, law and education. In education, especially, the two countries continued to develop in independence of one another, and it would not be too much to say that, during the century following the Union, the educational system of Scotland became more and more unlike that of England at the very time when, in other respects, the country was becoming increasingly anglicised.[18]

To maintain a sense of difference in the Union between two partners of such unequal economic strength the Scots could and did insist on guarding their "language"[19] but their most visible form of superiority over England was their university system: they had many more and they were in most cases the envy of Europe. Davie laments the English forces that altered Scottish university governance and curriculum, the changes recommended so forcibly by the three royal commissions of 1826, 1858, and 1889. The Commissioners were usually lawyers or Scottish aristocrats who were, to a man, Anglophiles: Davie describes them as "a group of influential Scots who wished to impose Southern standards."[20] In this long and bitter debate the Scots saw education as "[t]he chief forum of resistance to Southern encroachment, and . . . a rallying point for national principle, which could still bring together the dissident religious factions."[21] The prime targets for the 1826 commissioners were the faculties of arts at Glasgow, Kings, Marischal, St Andrews, and Edinburgh; for Davie the commissioners were determined to dislodge philosophy from its preeminent place in Scottish undergraduate studies. In Davie's eyes the Scottish universities saw the study of Latin and Greek as a vital link to a European tradition, but not, as in English public schools and Oxford, preeminent amongst all branches of learning. The Scottish undergraduate would study science, philosophy, and mathematics as well, and they would be of equal importance. The legislation enacted in the nineteenth century produced a situation where

> the Scots abandoned the attempt to regulate the higher education of their country according to their own ideals. Hitherto they had been striving to introduce into their universities the specialism required by modern life in a form suited to their hereditary ideas of education—namely as courses to be taken only after the student had gone through a general education distinguished from other countries by the prominence given to the teaching of philosophy.[22]

By the end of the nineteenth century Scotland's universities offered both specialist and generalist degrees, but the former were far more prestigious and therefore more popular. The central place of philosophy in the Scottish arts curriculum had vanished, too.[23]

Davie's chapter on the 1826 commission is entitled, unsurprisingly, "The First Assault" and he identifies heroes and villains as the evidence is presented to the commissioners: Scots like Jeffrey, Hamilton, and Jardine defending the Scottish generalist approach whereas others, like Williams,[24] Sandford,[25] with his "Oxonian outlook,"[26] and most of the commissioners were

> quite out of sympathy with national tradition and strongly favoured a policy which would give priority to an immersion in detail and which, indeed, would perhaps not merely postpone but abolish altogether the introduction of generalities.[27]

George Davie exhibits a well-established grouping in Scottish intellectual life: socialist, republican, and internationalist. His closest friend was the poet Hugh MacDiarmid, a man of similarly forthright views. A colleague of Davie's on the campus at Edinburgh was Hamish Henderson, a poet, folklorist, and cofounder in 1951 of the School of Scottish Studies at that university.

Davie's book caused a stir when it was published and was reviewed favorably by, among others, C. P. Snow, Herbert Butterfield, and David Daiches. The book was broadly applauded and welcomed across the political spectrum in Britain.[28] What gave the book then and now its prominence in Scottish life, and made the work's title such a resonant rallying cry, were the cultural and political events occurring in Scotland in the 1960s.[29] The fortunes of the Scottish National Party were reviving across the country, and in 1967 they returned their first member of parliament (MP) in twenty years to Westminster; seven years later the number of nationalist members of parliament had risen to eleven.[30] In Glasgow and more especially Edinburgh major public campaigns were launched to save the architectural heritage of both cities. Interest in Scotland's role in the European Enlightenment was a growing area of historical research and publication.[31] Davie's book, and especially its title, appealed to those looking for a positive sense of Scottish identity, and this appeal remains to this day.

The term "lad of parts" first appeared in print in one of the "classics" of the Kailyard School of nostalgic nationalist literature, Ian MacLaren's *Beside the Bonnie Briar Bush* (1894). This very sentimental but immensely successful novel deals with the travails of its hero, George Howe, poor but academically very able, who manages, with the help of the local dominie (schoolmaster), to gain a bursary (scholarship) at university. He succeeds brilliantly at the college and gains a "double first" but his efforts have left him fatally weakened, and he returns to his village to die. The lad of parts describes the poor but gifted young boy (there was, of course, no "lass of parts"), who through his own hard work and Scotland's egalitarian education system gains access to university and the world of the professions, while never forgetting his humble roots. Ian MacLaren was the *nom de plume* of a Free Church of Scotland minister, Reverend John Watson. Thus at the very moment when the door was being closed on the bright but impoverished Scottish aspiring university scholar, due to the introduction of university entrance examinations, he makes his entrance into Scottish popular fiction.

R. D. Anderson has pointed out how useful this myth of the lad of parts was, both to those who were politically conservative and also to those who regarded themselves as radicals. To the deeply conservative, as many Victorian professors were, this myth illustrated how

> individual mobility was a safety valve which preserved social stability and allowed the best minds in the poorer classes to be absorbed into the system. According to Simon Laurie, the leading Scottish educationalist of the late nineteenth century, the kind of opportunity provided by the traditional parish schools "makes the clever poor contented, and thus saps the foundations of Socialism."[32]

For those who held a more open and inclusive view of Scottish society this paradigm represented

> an ideology of meritocracy. At best this meant equality of opportunity and democratic elitism rather than egalitarianism, and it was a standard part of liberal individualist thinking. If there were no barriers to the rise of ability, if exceptional individuals could find an outlet for their talents, then inequality rested on merit rather than birth or wealth, and a class-based and hierarchical society was given moral justification. The elites of a capitalist society were held to be open as those of the ancient regime had not been, and the ideology of individualism was one of the forms in which the class values of the bourgeoisie were transformed into eternal laws of nature and reason.[33]

It would be, however a very grave mistake to regard this vision, however sentimental and politically loaded, as simply untrue; the Scots were familiar with too many examples within their nation. A very famous example, David Livingstone, would have been made known to millions of readers from the pages of that most popular of Victorian manuals of improvement, *Self-Help*:

At the age of ten Livingstone was sent to work in a cotton factory near Glasgow as a "piecer." With part of his first week's wages he bought a Latin grammar, and began to learn that language, pursuing that study for years at night school. He would sit up conning his lessons till twelve or later, when not sent to bed by his mother, for he had to be up and at work in the factory every morning by six. In this way he plodded through Virgil and Horace. . . . In this way the persevering youth acquired much useful knowledge. . . . He supported himself during his college career entirely by his own earnings as a factory workman, never having received a farthing of help from any other source.[34]

The author of *Self-Help*, Samuel Smiles, himself a Scot,[35] clearly believed that many of his noted countrymen like James Watt, the surgeon John Hunter, and the geologist Hugh Miller demonstrated, like Livingstone, the opportunities that opened up in Scotland to the thrifty, able and hardworking. Smiles's book was an immense and worldwide sensation:

The book was a remarkable success. Twenty thousand copies were sold in the first year; fifty-five thousand by the end of the five years; a hundred and fifty thousand by 1889 and over a quarter of a million by 1905. These sales far exceeded those of the great nineteenth-century novels. What was more remarkable, however, was the book's popularity when translated into other languages. It appeared in Dutch and French, Danish and German, Italian and Japanese, Arabic and Turkish and "several of the native languages of India."[36]

To this needs to be added the observation that in many a parish school and a local pulpit Scots could see, in the dominie or the minister, evidence that one of their own, a man from sometimes a very humble background, had made the journey successfully to university and had become their schoolmaster or their clergyman.

It is perhaps best to see terms like "the democratic intellect" and "the lad of parts" as part of a very complicated post-Enlightenment process whereby Scots, both at home and those displaced by the diaspora, attempted to give themselves some sense of national identity at a time of extreme social, political, and ecclesiastical turmoil. At its worst this process could certainly produce a great deal of mawkish fiction and song, which seemed to feed an almost unlimited appetite.[37] Yet there was a much more serious dimension to this process of manufacturing a national identity that includes the life and public works of men like Reverend Thomas Chalmers,[38] Livingstone and "the world's richest man," Andrew Carnegie. Added to this there was and still is the impact of the writings of men like "the Wizard of the North" (Sir Walter Scott), Carlyle, Ruskin, and Robert Louis Stevenson. This process may be best illustrated by turning to a man who was a poet, politician, and imperial administrator but above all else the most popular and influential historian of his day, Lord Macaulay.[39] Early in his magnum opus, *The History of England from the Accession of James II*, comes this passage:

> The administration of Scotland was in Scottish hands; for no Englishman had any motive to emigrate northward, and to contend with the shrewdest and most pertinacious of all races for what was to be scraped together in the poorest of all treasuries. Meanwhile Scottish adventurers poured southward and obtained in all the walks of life a prosperity which excited much envy, but which was in general the just reward of prudence and industry. Nevertheless Scotland by no means escaped the fate ordained for every country that is connected but not incorporated with another country of greater resources.[40]

"WHAT EXACTLY DO YOU DO?"
THE WORK OF A SCOTS PROFESSOR

Before the two-year interrogation of witnesses began, the royal commission sent a circular letter to the chairmen of every presbytery in Scotland, the aim being to find out the current state nationally of the parish schools. In this questionnaire, issued on 28 August 1826, all were urged "to make the earliest possible return." Amongst questions asked were: How many years have any of the teachers attended a university? How many pupils at present study Latin? How many study Greek? What Greek grammar is taught? What Latin and Greek classics are read? The returns from 906 parish schools provide a snapshot of the education received by the lad of parts in 1826. The commissioners also invited comments from anyone concerned with matters relating to the Scottish universities.[41]

Although the commission was intended to investigate the national picture in university education, it could be argued that Edinburgh was the main focus and that this was, in many ways, a royal commission of inquiry into the capital's university. The statistics paint the picture: Edinburgh College ("college" not "university" was the preferred ancient Scottish usage) was the home of the inquiry, and here it was that ninety-seven days of meetings took place out of a total of a hundred six; of eighty-three witnesses called at Edinburgh, far in excess of elsewhere,[42] forty-four were employed by the university; and the evidence published as a result of the Edinburgh questionings is by far the most detailed and comprehensive dossier produced by the commissioners. At Edinburgh they also invited evidence from two distinguished rectors,[43] Carson, of the Edinburgh High School, and Williams, of the newly created Edinburgh Academy. Only in Aberdeen did they avail themselves again of a schoolmaster's testimony.[44] The reason for this state of affairs is pretty clear. Edinburgh, unlike all other Scottish universities, was under the direct control of Edinburgh Corporation; they made the appointments, inspected the institution, and were quite prepared to alter the academic curriculum. Needless to say this was a recipe for acrimony: on the one side the university regarded itself rightly as one of the leading seminaries in Europe; on the other the corporation, as paymasters and with clear statutory rights, saw it as their duty to control closely the workings of the establishment and its staff. So bitter did matters become that in 1826 the university took the corporation to the Court of Session, Scotland's highest civil court. This event was almost certainly the catalyst for Robert Peel to set up this commission. Edinburgh was the problem; then perhaps it was going to provide the basis for a solution. The first academic witness,[45] heard on 10 October, was George Dunbar, professor of Greek. He was called so early due to the ill health of the principal, the Very Reverend George Baird.[46] Lord Rosebery in the chair began proceedings by asking Dunbar the initial questions that became standard for all academic witnesses: confirming who they were, asking whether they had read the return made by the Senatus Academicus to the "List of Requisitions for Returns and Heads of Inquiry," i.e., the set of questions sent to all universities, and whether the professor had any suggestions for improvements or further comments to make. Dunbar had three complaints: there were not enough prizes for students, public examinations should be introduced, and the principal had visited his classroom only once in twenty years. When asked about how he taught, he claimed that in the junior Greek class some hundred sixty students were tested every week. The fact that the classes lasted a total of ten hours and the fact that this process would leave very little time for teaching may not have escaped the commissioners' notice. Dunbar was asked about the curriculum and choice of texts:

Question—Are there any regulations of the Senatus Academicus prescribing the course of study or any method of instruction in your class?

Answer—None that I know of.

Question—Are there any directions given to you by the Principal of any sort or kind at your induction?

Answer—None.

Question—Are you in every matter of that sort left as much to your own discretion as a private teacher would be?

Answer—Yes, entirely.[47]

This, as will be seen, was one of the more significant exchanges between Dunbar and the commissioners. He was asked too about Moor's *Greek Grammar*, a standard Scottish textbook reedited by him, that he used in his teaching:

Question—Is the Moor Grammar you use in Greek and English, or Greek and Latin?

Answer—In Latin and Greek.

Question—Do you think it would be any improvement to use a grammar that should be Greek and English, with a view to facilitate further the acquirement of the Greek tongue?

Answer—I consider the rules in Moor's Grammar so very simple, that any young man who comes to the university should be sufficiently acquainted with Latin to master them without difficulty.

But the commissioners would not let it rest:

Question—If the English rules were in verse, as in the Port-Royal grammar, would that be an improvement?

Answer—I do not think that would be an improvement.[48]

Dunbar also explained that he did not take a register, "the catalogue," but instead appointed a member of the class to be a censor and record absences. Finally he insisted that English or Irish students at Edinburgh were no more advanced than their Scottish peers: "my prime students are from the [Edinburgh] High School."[49]

Interestingly Dunbar was recalled as a witness by the commission on 10 May the following year, 1827, after the commissioners had made a visitation to the University of Glasgow. There Daniel Sandford, professor of Greek, had been interviewed. Dunbar was asked about the texts he used for his third, most advanced Greek class: 'They read *Oedipus Tyrannus* of Sophocles, part of the Oration of Demosthenes for [sic] the Crown." This was followed by a query about the cost of books for the junior Greek class: "Coll[ectanea] 6s—Gram[mar] 5s—Exercises 7s."[50] The commissioners recalled him for a third time later in the month. The questions now were much more pressing:

Question—Are the elements of Greek taught in your class?

Answer—Yes.

Question—One object today is to have your ideas as to the propriety of that plan—whether you think it better the elements should be taught in the first class, or, whether it should be required of the students coming to the university that they are previously acquainted with the elements?

Answer—It would certainly save me some trouble, if they were previously taught in some of the public schools; but I apprehend, the elements of Greek must continue to be taught in the university.[51]

Dunbar's argument, apart from obvious self-interest in the possible loss of fees from a hundred sixty students, was based on his view that there was not a supply of "sufficiently well-educated teachers" in the parish schools who could teach Greek. What Dunbar could not have known is that the return the commission had received from its survey of Scottish parochial schools showed that there were over 2,000 pupils studying Greek in the parochial schools. The commissioners then altered their line of attack by suggesting that six months of beginners' Greek could not possibly give "anything like a competent knowledge of Greek." "Even two sessions of six months could hardly produce an adequate knowledge." At this point Dunbar seems reduced to bluster: "In that time, if he has tolerable abilities and has paid attention, he may be able to read Xenophon, the Iliad and the Odyssey of Homer, perhaps Herodotus; but not the higher authors—and cannot therefore be thought to have a competent knowledge of Greek."[52]

The commission then delivered the final blow to Dunbar's position: if the young student had spent three years at school learning the elements of the language then the chance to produce good Scottish Greek scholars would be improved:

Question—Notwithstanding the acknowledged eminence of the Greek Professors in Scotland for the last fifty years is it not your opinion that the state of Greek Literature in Scotland is very low?

Answer—I must say that it is low, and I attribute that to the little or no encouragement given to Classical Literature. . . . I believe however that in Scotland in the present day Greek literature is known to a far greater extent than that period [Reformation Scotland].[53]

Dunbar also bristles when comparisons are made between the quality of his teaching at the university and at Edinburgh High School: "I go over more ground in six months than is done there in nine or ten."[54]

It seems fairly clear that the commissioners were less than satisfied with Dunbar's responses on this second occasion. It was perhaps his misfortune that he was the first academic witness called and that the commissioners were more than ready for him. It must also have been common knowledge to these Scots that Dunbar owed his appointment to Edinburgh, as assistant to Dalzel, professor of Greek, to the influence of Sir George Fettes, a former lord provost of Edinburgh.[55]

James Pillans, professor of humanity (Latin) at Edinburgh, was called before the commission on 4 December 1826 and was asked the standard introductory questions by the chairman, the lord president Hope. Pillans's answers defy belief:

Question—Have you seen the questions that were put by this Commission to the Senatus Academicus and the answers that were returned to them?

Answer—I have not yet had time to peruse them: a copy may have been sent to my house; but having been absent till within two days of the commencement of the College Session, I have not seen them.[56]

Question—In the return, the number of students who attended your class for the two years 1819–1820 and 1825–1826 is not mentioned, but left blank. Can you mention the reason for that?

Answer—I went abroad so immediately after the last course that I have not had time to make it out.[57]

It is difficult to know what to admire more: the insouciance of Pillans or the patience of the commission. He was then asked whether the relative youthfulness of his junior class was a problem. He attempted to turn this query to his advantage, by saying it was not an issue:

> I am tempted to mention, as proof of this that the junior class, at the moment I am speaking, is at work, writing an exercise I prescribed under the superintendence of a general censor who will collect the results and dismiss them without my reappearing again.[58]

He then proceeds to describe the way in which he has introduced the monitorial system, which he developed as rector of Edinburgh High School, into the university's humanity lecture room for the junior class:[59]

> I establish soon after the commencement of the session (as I did at the High School of Edinburgh) a system of monitors, or inspectors of exercises, taking care to select them from amongst the best scholars in the class. Who these are is ascertained by making all write an exercise in the classroom under my own eye. This is generally done in the first week of the session. That it may be a test of different stages of proficiency, the exercise prescribed consists of different parts beginning with the more easy, such as a sentence from Mair's Introduction, and advancing to more difficult translation from English into Latin. This first exercise I take into my own hands, mark the errors, and sum them up at the end; so that I am able in the course of two days, to make out a graduated list of students, according to the number of errors they have committed. By this means I am enabled very early in the session to select a sufficient number, to whom I entrust the charge of correcting and characterising the exercises of the rest.[60]

Pillans would mark these inspectors' efforts, discussing "all those offences against the rules of Latin syntax and grammar."[61] The benefit for the student of this system[62] is that work is marked promptly:

> Suppose it has been required to turn a passage of English into Latin, the ink of their version is hardly dry when the various inelegancies and faults of concord and government—are pointed out and corrected. The student is expected to note at the end of the passage these errors and to resubmit the next day a corrected copy.

All faults are noted by the monitors who make written reports to Pillans on all errors. The fair copies when produced, having passed a second inspection, are "expected to be carefully preserved and presented in a regular series, sewed or bound together, in order to secure a good certificate."

Pillans is then asked about prizes, which he views with some suspicion, as an essay set in January for submission in March could well be the work of many hands: "The most unequivocal test of talent is to have the exercise done in the classroom under the instruction of the Professor himself."[63] He is then asked about composition, that is, rendering an English translation back into Latin: this is a practice he does not adopt. This answer seems to surprise the commissioners, who believe it is "frequently practised in the English schools." Pillans, a former (private) tutor at Eton, demurs. Like Dunbar, Pillans does not call a "Catalogue," but unlike Dunbar he presents successful students in his class with a certificate:

> I have this session adopted a method of engraving the formula of a certificate on the back of the class ticket. The students were graded on three issues: "regularity of attendance, proficiency and propriety of behaviour."[64]

But Pillans seems unprepared for the next question, as to what happens if a certificate is lost:

> No, I have not hitherto kept any register for each individual case for the reason I have mentioned, that I issued these certificates in rather a hurried way at the close of the session when every student was anxious to get away, and wished to have his certificate immediately. If he applied to me afterwards, I gave him the certificate from general recollection, or from reference to my own notes.[65]

Pillans's ability to shoot himself in the foot seems to have been unimpaired throughout the lengthy cross-questioning. He was asked if Latin "cribs" presented a problem when marking students' work; he believed they did not:

> Fortunately the key in general use, and the only one I have seen, is full of the most egregious blunders; so that one has only to prescribe a sentence in which some of the blunders occur, and as error is infinite and truth is but one, I have a strong presumption that all those whose exercises agree in committing the error have had unlawful aid.[66]

But Pillans's major complaint against his students is not their use of an "unlawful aid" but their poor articulation:

> All my experience in teaching the youth of Scotland, goes to prove that there is no part of education in which they are so deficient, and so little susceptible of improvement, as in the power of pronouncing audibly, and intelligibly.[67] . . . The habits of pronunciation the students bring with them from all the different counties in Scotland are extremely bad, and so inveterate as to be almost unconquerable. The difference between the Scotch and English boys, in clear, articulate and pleasing declamation, is greater than in any other point connected with a liberal education.[68]

To remedy this "fault" Pillans started his senior humanity class thirty minutes early on Monday, 8:30 a.m., using the time to improve his students' elocution.[69] But he seemed to be fighting a losing battle, as he admitted that in the classroom he was forced to use "the Scotch way" of pronouncing Latin.[70]

The situation at St Andrews was very different from that at the capital. Playing no significant part in the intellectual excitement of the Scottish Enlightenment, Scotland's only collegiate campus seemed drifting to nowhere. This impression was perhaps confirmed when on the second day of hearings, 1 August, the seventy-three-year-old professor of humanity, the Reverend John Hunter,[71] was called. He had been in post for fifty-two years and in his opening statement said he was considering retirement.[72] The problem of the absence of any pension for elderly professors was not solved until the reforms of the 1890s.

In Aberdeen, the commissioners began with King's College. Their first interview was with the Principal, Very Rev. William Jack: his interview was short and troubled.[73] Jack admitted that he did not exercise all the duties of a principal that he had previously defined to the commissioners:

Question—Which of those duties, which you consider to belong to your situation, do you not now exercise?

Answer—I think the most important is that of admitter. The encroachments on the power of the admitter is perhaps the greatest defect in this University.

Question—To what offices do you admit?

Answer—The Principal admits the three Regents, the Chancellor of the University, the superior Officers.[74]

It then transpires that Jack had clashed with the senatus over the appointment to the chair of humanity in 1815, when two candidates had come forward, Drs. Dewar and Forbes, and because the senatus[75] was not unanimous Jack overruled their majority verdict. Yet again the case made its way to the Court of Session, where Jack was, it appears, overruled. Rather unwisely, given that the Lord Advocate and the Solicitor General, the two highest legal officers in the land, were sitting across the table from him, Jack was dismissive of Scotland's highest court. He was asked what was the legal verdict:

> An interim interdict; the court knew nothing of the matter. My feeling was to disregard the interdict. . . . No benefit was ever derived from going to a civil court with a College matter; my opinion is, that the superior authorities of the university have full power to decide every college question, and should not be interfered with.[76]

Moving on from his management techniques, he was then asked if he did any teaching, and when he replied in the negative it was pointed out that this was contrary to the charter of foundation. For Jack, it seems, appeals to tradition were highly selective. He then had to admit that all the records for the Visitation of 1619, the last inspection of the college in "modern times," had been lost. He continued by accepting that he never visited the classrooms of his university. All this produced what must be the *ne plus ultra* of all the commission's interchanges:

Question—What, in fact, do you do as Principal?

Answer—The duties of the Principal are increasing, numerous, and important.[77]

Finally he was asked, "Was it always the practice for the professor of humanity to teach chemistry?" Jack admitted this was because he had done it when professor of moral philosophy and the practice had continued. One can only wonder at Jack's reactions as he read the transcript of his evidence.

"HIGHLY INJURIOUS"
THE COMMISSIONERS GIVE THEIR VERDICT

If the Scottish universities were under any illusion as to just how radical the commissioners of 1826 intended to be, they were thoroughly disabused by their recommendations, issued to all the universities for comment in November 1828. The document was terse, comprehensive, and radical. In essence their proposals were twofold: a scheme of reform that would apply to all the universities and then a second section addressing particular local issues. The template, to be applied to all institutions, begins with this important preamble and with a decided opening salvo on the status quo:

> That it is the opinion of the commission, that it would in a high degree raise the standard of Classical Literature in Scotland, that the Elementary Greek classes in the different Universities be discontinued, and that no person be received into the first Greek class who has not been accurately instructed in Grammar, and had not attained such proficiency in the language as to read with facility the Historical parts of the New Testament and the first three books of the Anabasis. . . . That for ascertaining and securing such preparatory knowledge, there shall be, at the commencement of every Session a strict Examination, by not fewer than three persons properly qualified, not being Professors appointed for this purpose by the Senatus Academicus.[78]

More specifically there should be a national curriculum with the following features:

1. A four-year program with Latin and Greek part of the first-year program, two hours per subject each day. Subjects to continue in the second year again two hours per subject but no progression allowed until the first-year student has passed the second-year entrance examination. Greek is to continue into the third year, one hour per week.
2. All students receive a certificate on leaving a class at the end of session.
3. For the degree of B.A. students to be examined in "two decades of Livy or the orations of Cicero and the whole of Virgil or Horace or Juvenal—in Greek to be tested in Thucydides or Demosthenes or Aristotle's Ethics or Rhetoric—and in two tragedies of Sophocles." The examination to be either *viva voce* or in writing or both.
4. That professors within a specified time after appointment are to publish a syllabus or an outline of their programs of lectures.
5. Number of examiners for Arts degree is specified (six). No more than six candidates to be examined in one day.
6. The times when lectures take place are specified.
7. The fees are fixed at three guineas.[79]

The universities were then invited to respond to the provisional resolutions, which they did in no uncertain terms. All were aghast, but at different aspects. Edinburgh, which took six months to respond, still seemed to misread the situation and see the document merely as a basis for discussion rather than a determined program of reform. The Edinburgh faculty of arts felt that the abandonment of Greek would be

> highly injurious to the general education of the country . . . [so] till reform, therefore, begin in the right quarter, and be left to operate slowly and silently, the Faculty foresee nothing but mischief from the adoption of the measure proposed.[80]

But not even this thinly veiled rejection satisfied Dunbar, for he submitted a letter in which he reiterated the need for elementary Greek and warned that

> if the resolution should be attempted to be carried into effect, his income, derived almost wholly from the students attending his classes, would be seriously diminished and that he would, in consequence, look to them for an indemnification he would sustain. His commission entitles him to all the rights and privileges which his predecessors enjoyed, and these he would sincerely trust, will never be infringed by any arbitrary measures.[81]

While not quite as maladroit as Dunbar, the other classical professors echoed this view that elementary Greek must remain. Dunbar was not alone at Edinburgh, as the senatus regretted that the royal commission had not fulfilled its terms of reference in reviewing the constitution of the university:

> [T]he Senatus Academicus must express their disappointment and regret that nothing has been intimated to them of any design on the part of the Commissioners to direct their attention to the great and pressing inquiry concerning the constitution of the university.[82]

This observation received a very dusty answer from the royal commission: the university's comments are "erroneous and unfounded—irregular and uncalled for."[83]

THE BILL PRESENTED

After many years' delay, the 1836 bill for reforming Scotland's institutions bore very little resemblance to the recommendations made in the commissioners' report: the interest in the curriculum was replaced by a concern for management. The bill had nineteen clauses or "heads"; the most important change was suggested in the preamble:

> His Majesty shall appoint a Board of Visitors to the several universities and such Boards shall consist of not fewer than five or more than seven Members and shall subsist for a period of five years.

It then began to describe the composition and powers of these royal visitors:

> The several Principals of the Universities of St Andrew's [sic], Glasgow, Aberdeen and Edinburgh, for the time being shall be constituent members of the Board of Visitors.

But what was breathtaking was the powers that were to be granted to these royal visitors:

> The several Boards of Visitors shall constitute a Court of Review in the University in which such Boards are so appointed which Court shall have full power and authority to entertain and determine all questions in relation to the regulation and discipline of the University, the management and distribution of the Property and Funds—and generally all questions touching the affairs and interests of such Universities, of whatever kind or description.

This board was to act as the final court of appeal for any grievance:

> It shall be lawful and competent, for any Principal, Patron, or Professor in any of the said Universities, for any person having any right or interest in the affairs thereof, for any Graduate, student, Office-Bearer, or other person connected therewith to appeal to such Court of Review against any decision, deliverance or regulation made or pronounced by the Senatus Academicus or Rectorial Court, or by any other body, or person possessing or claiming to possess any jurisdiction, control or authority in regard to the regulation, discipline, property, and administration of, in, or concerning such University.

These boards also had the power

> to make such regulations, in relation to government, discipline and system of education . . . and to the management of and distribution of property and funds—as they shall think most conducive to the improvement in education in such Universities.

Furthermore each university was, within six months of the passage of this act, to submit

> such regulations, founded upon the reports . . . [of the] Commission
> of Visitation . . . [that] shall seem calculated to promote the poster-
> ity and success of such University as a place of education and the
> advancement of science and learning.

The powers also included being able to change the academic
hierarchy:

> It shall be lawful for such Boards of Visitors to make such regula-
> tion and it shall be lawful for such Boards regarding the abolition
> of Professorships within the Universities to which they shall be
> appointed.

These draconian powers admitted no right of appeal. They embraced
even the applicants for a chair:

> Every candidate for a Professorship shall transmit his recommen-
> dations and certificates to the Board of Visitors . . . and it shall be
> lawful for such Boards respectively, after consideration of such rec-
> ommendations and certificates, and such personal communication
> with the candidate as they think necessary, to report their opinion as
> to the candidate who ought to be preferred to his Majesty's Secretary
> of State for the Home Department if the patronage or nomination
> be vested in the Crown, or to the Senatus Academicus, or any other
> body or person—if the patronage or nomination be vested in the
> Professors, or in any such body or person.

The final major change proposed was that an investigation take place
investigating the possible merger of King's College and Marischal and
whether this would benefit "the advancement of science and learning."

All of Scotland's principal institutions: the country's universities, lawyers, and above all her presbyteries reacted with especial anger both to
the contents of the bill and the timing of its publication. The bill was laid
before parliament on 13 June 1836: after the parliamentary recess, but
more importantly after the annual meeting of the General Assembly of
the Church of Scotland. Lord Melbourne, the prime minister, intended to
allow only a week for the first and second reading of the bill. Parliament
was due to rise for the summer recess in late August and all of these factors suggested to many Scots that any debate within Scotland about the
bill was being deliberately denied.

A TIME OF PETITIONS

Once the bill was officially published, petitions rained down on Westminster. The first received was from the Lord Provost, magistrates, and

council of the city of Edinburgh, promptly followed by the chancellor and others of the University of St Andrews, and the Chamber of Commerce of Edinburgh, who wished

> to prevent said Bill which will have the effect of transferring the whole management and in great degree the patronage of the University of Edinburgh from a body chosen by the citizens to a small irresponsible Board of Visitors to be nominated by the Crown and the constitution of which and the members of which it is comprised nothing whatsoever is known from passing into law.[84]

To the synod of Glasgow and Ayr it represented "a measure injurious to the rights and dangerous to the usefulness of the University and to the Literature and Religion of Scotland."[85] The magistrates and inhabitants of the Royal Burgh of Inverary urged the lords "to stop its further progress till the inhabitants of Scotland have an opportunity of fully expressing their opinion upon a subject of such vast and vital importance."[86]

To the graduates of Marischal College the bill was "dangerous in principle and incapable of being converted into a safe and satisfactory measure of university reform."[87] The senatus of King's College warned that the proposed legislation would

> change and destroy the character of that education which has confessedly raised the country to a very high rank in an intellectual, moral and religious view.[88]

Rather foolishly, given Scottish sensitivities on this issue, during all this furor Lord Melbourne, the prime minister, insisted that the government would concede no rights to the Church of Scotland.[89] Only two petitions urged the passage of the bill, one from the Corporation of Aberdeen and the other from the dean of faculty and professors of Marischal College.[90] The death blow to the bill was delivered on 22 July, when a petition was received from the ministers and elders of the General Assembly of the Church of Scotland: they not only objected to the bill, but assured Melbourne that they would take the government through the Scottish courts. Such an act would threaten the very stability of the union: the bill was withdrawn. Scotland, for possibly the last time in the nineteenth century, had spoken with one public voice. Less than a decade later, in 1843, the Great Disruption[91] would split the established church and deny any opportunity for Scotland to speak through its Kirk, as a single, covenanted nation under God.

THE SCOTTISH BOOMERANG: THE DAVIE LEGACY[92]

George Davie was essentially a pejorist.[93] In 1961 he was lamenting the destruction of a European tradition within Scotland's universities: Anglocentric forces, he passionately argued, had altered the very nature of undergraduate studies, and by 1900 Scotland's universities looked south to Oxford and Cambridge rather than celebrating their links with Bologna, Paris, and Leiden. Yet it could be argued that most young Scots in the nineteenth century did not go to university but went to school, and it is here that the true battleground for the idea of the democratic intellect was fought, and here perhaps lost. In 1888 a national Leaving Certificate was introduced in Scotland, but only forty of Scotland's nine hundred schools were allowed to present candidates for this new examination: this action more than any other violated the idea of the "democratic intellect." The Scotch Education Department,[94] based in London, wanted only the "best" Scottish schools to enter this examination that was utterly new to Britain.

On the other hand, it could be argued that Davie's celebration of a certain kind of university education bore fruit a decade after his book appeared. In 1971 the Open University accepted its first undergraduates with no barrier at the point of entry, and these new students, in the arts faculty, took a first-year course that was generalist and included philosophy. Thirty years later this university has taught two million students and has more undergraduates studying Latin and Greek than any other British university. So perhaps the "democratic intellect" has prevailed after all.

In terms of the classics and Scotland, let the last word be with a man who was too ill to attend the investigations of the 1826 royal commission, George Jardine, professor of logic at Glasgow. His *Outlines of Philosophical Education* (1825), based on his many years of teaching at Glasgow, gives perhaps the best description of the Scottish approach to the classics:

> In all our colleges a considerable part of the undergraduate course is devoted to the study of Greek and Latin; but, in those of Scotland, the attention is not so exclusively confined to the learned languages, as in the universities in the south. We do not, in this part of the kingdom, attach to classical learning that high and almost exclusive degree of importance which is ascribed to it elsewhere; thinking it of greater consequence to the students, to receive instruction in the elements of science, both mental and physical, than to acquire even the most accurate knowledge of the ancient tongues; of which all that is valuable may, it is thought, be obtained without so great a sacrifice of time and labour.[95]

Chapter 2

Classics and Welsh Cultural Identity in the Nineteenth Century

ᴄ—Ceri Davies

I begin with a quotation:

> It seems to us that the prime place in education should be given to
> the classics; not for the sake of the Latin and Greek languages in
> themselves, but for the sake of the books which have been written in
> them. These books are worth reading and understanding on account
> of their merits, as they are the product of all the best thinkers who
> were ever in the world before the days of Christ, apart from the
> writers of the Old Testament; furthermore, they provide the best
> preparation for anyone who wishes to devote the rest of his life to
> reading the work of the greatest thinkers who were in the world
> after that time.

It will not come as a surprise to learn that these words are an expression of the educational views of a university-educated Christian minister
of the mid-Victorian era. They were first published in 1865. It is not,
however, strictly accurate to describe them as a quotation, because they
are a translation of words that first appeared in print, not in English, but
in Welsh:

Y mae yn ymddangos i ni mai yr un a ddylai gael y lle blaenaf mewn addysgiaeth yw y *classics*; nid er mwyn yr ieithoedd Lladin a Groeg ynddynt eu hunain, ond er mwyn y llyfrau a ysgrifenwyd ynddynt. Y mae y llyfrau hyn yn werth eu darllen a'u deall o herwydd eu teilyngdod, gan eu bod yn gynnyrchion yr holl feddylwyr mwyaf a fu yn y byd erioed cyn dyddiau Crist, oddieithr ysgrifenwyr yr Hen Destament: ac heblaw hyny, dyma y paratoad goreu i'r neb sydd yn meddwl rhoddi gweddill ei oes i ddarllen gwaith y meddylwyr mwyaf a fu yn y byd ar ol hyny.[1]

The author was the Reverend Lewis Edwards (1809–1887), a native of rural Cardiganshire. University-educated he certainly was, but as a non-conformist Edwards was debarred from entering Oxford or graduating from Cambridge: his degree was from the University of Edinburgh. And ordained minister though he was, the ecclesiastical communion to which he belonged was not the established Anglican Church but the Welsh Calvinistic Methodist Connexion.

Lewis Edwards is a man of immense importance in the religious and cultural history of Wales in the nineteenth century.[2] During his time at Edinburgh University (1833–1836), in addition to his theological training, he was much influenced by the professor of moral philosophy, John Wilson, better known as "Christopher North," editor of *Blackwood's Magazine.* (The example of Christopher North was to play an important part in inspiring Lewis Edwards to establish his own periodical in Wales.) Soon after returning to Wales he also set about founding, at Bala in Merionethshire, a school, which would later become a college, primarily for educating prospective ministers. These are the opening words of the "prospectus" of the new school, established in 1837 by Edwards and his brother-in-law, David Charles:

Messrs. L. Edwards and D. Charles announce their intention of giving instruction at Bala in the Classics, Mathematics, and other branches of a liberal education.[3]

Nearly twenty years later, when what had begun as a "private adventure school" had developed under Lewis Edwards's tutelage into a more elaborate establishment, this is the summary which he gives of the students' studies:

1. English.
2. History and Geography, Ancient and Modern; but more particularly Greece, Rome and England.
3. Mathematics.
4. Latin, including Latin Grammar and Composition.

5. Greek, including Greek d[itt]o.
6. Biblical criticism.⁴

Two things in particular strike one about that list of subjects. First, there is no mention at all of the Welsh language or of the literature and history of Wales, although nearly all of Lewis Edwards's wards were native Welsh speakers and much more at home in Welsh than in English. The second matter is the emphasis on Greek and Latin and on classical ancient history. That is totally in accord with Lewis Edwards's thinking about educational priorities. The views expressed in the 1865 passage, with which I began, serve to reassert a point of view emphasized by him in a much earlier essay, first published in 1849:

> Dealler o hyn allan nad oes neb yn meddu hawl i son am ei ddys-geidiaeth, os na fydd yn alluog i gyfieithu unrhyw lyfr Lladin neu Groeg *heb gymhorth gramadeg na geirlyfr*. Dyma y dosbarth isaf: dyma y cyntedd nesaf allan. Cyn y dichon iddo gael derbyniad i'r dosbarth arall, yn yr hwn y mae y dysgedigion penaf yn cartrefu, y mae yn rhaid iddo fedru ysgrifenu Lladin a Groeg yn gywir, *heb gymhorth gramadeg na geirlyfr*, a hyny yn rhwydd ac yn rhydd. Dyma i chwi waith, lanciau Cymry; a gwaith y mae yn rhaid i chwi ymaflyd ynddo o ddifrif, os ewyllysiwch fod yn ddynion dysgedig.⁵

> [Let it be understood henceforth that no-one has the right to speak about his learning, unless he is able to translate any Latin or Greek book *without the help of a grammar or a dictionary*. That is the lower class; that is the outer court. Before he may be received into the higher class, wherein dwell the greatest scholars, he must be able to write Latin and Greek correctly, *without the help of a grammar or a dictionary*, and that easily and fluently. Here is your task, young men of Wales, a task you must earnestly undertake, if you wish to be learned men.]

A task, indeed, in a country which had no university of its own and few classical grammar schools. Lewis Edwards's words appeared in an essay entitled "Ysgolion Ieithyddol i'r Cymry" ("Grammar Schools for the Welsh"), an essay whose express purpose was "to call attention to the need for more grammar schools in Wales, that is, schools to impart thorough linguistic learning in the Latin and Greek tongues."⁶

The time when this essay was written, the late 1840s, is a time of huge significance in the history of Welsh education. The year 1847, just two years before the appearance of "Ysgolion Ieithyddol i'r Cymry," is particularly remembered for the publication, in three parts, of the *Reports of the Commissioners of Inquiry into the State of Education in Wales*, the "Blue Books" as they are often called after the color of their covers.⁷

These tomes were the work of three young Englishmen, R. R. W. Lingen, J. C. Symons, and H. V. Johnson, who had been appointed in 1846 by Sir James Kay-Shuttleworth, secretary of the Privy Council Committee on Education, to inquire "into the state of Education in the Principality of Wales, and especially into the means afforded to the Labouring classes of acquiring a Knowledge of the English language." The commission was established, at least to some degree, as the result of a sense on the part of many successful Welshmen, not least William Williams, MP for Coventry (and a native of Llanpumpsaint in Carmarthenshire) that Wales had become the seed-bed of disturbance and anarchy.[8] The Welsh needed civilizing. There had been the Merthyr rising early in the 1830s, the Chartist attack on Newport in 1839, and then the so-called "Rebecca" riots in the Welsh countryside in the early 1840s. The root of the trouble, so Williams surmised when he proposed in the House of Commons that an inquiry be made into educational provision in Wales, was the Welsh people's ignorance of English. That ignorance stood in the way of their progress and made potential rebels of them.

The three commissioners were promptly appointed. Educated at either Oxford or Cambridge, aspiring lawyers by profession, Anglican in their churchmanship, they travelled to Wales to look into matters. In Builth Wells, for ten days in October 1846, they conferred together "to test, as well as organise, the mode of investigation to be pursued."[9] Fortified by meetings with the bishops of Hereford and St. David's they then went their separate ways into the different counties of Wales. The *Reports*, which they produced in a very short time, are prodigiously informative about the educational facilities available in Wales. The main concern is with elementary education, including the Sunday schools, and with the provision (or lack of it) for learning English. Accordingly, Wales's few grammar schools receive scant attention, and some are deliberately excluded: for example, H. V. Johnson reports that "the grammar schools at Bangor, Ruthin, and Beaumaris, . . . not being, as at present conducted, available for the poor, were beyond the purpose of this inquiry."[10] Others of the endowed grammar schools are included, but the report is frequently unflattering, as in the case of the seventeenth-century foundation endowed by Bishop Henry Rowland's legacy at Botwnnog on the Llŷn peninsula:

> The free grammar school at Bottwnog, county of Carnarvon, is considered to be one of the most important in North Wales. . . . It is richly endowed with rents, amounting to 200l. per annum, besides residences for the master and usher, with other emoluments. The endowment was "for the maintenance of a free grammar-school"; but at present only one scholar is taught Latin.[11]

On the other hand, a nonconformist academy set up by the Rev. Dr. William Davies in Ffrwd-y-fâl, near Llansawel in a remote corner of north Carmarthenshire, comes in for rare praise, from R. R. W. Lingen:

> Ffrwd Vale Academy. This is not a school for the labouring classes, nor yet altogether removed from their sphere. The extensive reputation which it enjoys in the upper part of Carmarthenshire, and the kindness with which a number of particulars respecting it were furnished to me by its promoter and master, induce and enable me to give an account of it in considerable detail. . . . The entire range of instruction proposed to be given comprises every part of a good classical (including Hebrew), mathematical, and general education. . . . At the time of my visit I found 34 pupils on the books, all of them except three upwards of ten years old. Of the upper division only one had been with the Doctor for any length of time. I heard him construe two passages which I gave him, in Homer and Virgil, into remarkably good English, and parse them soundly. I was surprised to hear that he had been only 2½ years in school, and that at the beginning of that period he knew very little English.[12]

A passage of this kind is unusual in the Blue Books, not only for the picture which it gives of education beyond the elementary stage, but also for the positive note which it strikes. Generally speaking, the *Reports* are negative in tone and demonstrate in a graphic way how low the standards of elementary education were in many parts of Wales. It is true that Lewis Edwards (whose school in Bala receives no mention in the *Reports*) and William Davies and others were already taking action to try to raise the level of provision. Furthermore, Edwards's call for the establishment of more Grammar Schools, with the emphasis on Greek and Latin—and, implicitly, on English as the medium of instruction—is part of his response to the challenge of the Blue Books. Lewis Edwards's essay of 1849 anticipates by over thirty years the proposal of Lord Aberdare's committee that the number and spread of secondary schools in Wales be enlarged, a proposal which was realized in the passing of the Welsh Intermediate Education Act of 1889 and the setting up of a network of county schools. These developments, together with which can also be included the establishment of the university colleges that were to form the University of Wales, are among the positive outcomes of the 1847 *Reports*. The Blue Books did not of themselves create the concern with education (in the English mode, and through the medium of the English language) as the means to self-improvement which was to play a dominant part in Welsh life in the second part of the nineteenth century, but they certainly contributed to it.[13]

That is the positive gloss on the 1847 *Reports of the Commissioners*. They went down, however, in Welsh history as a grotesque travesty of the nation, and were anathematized as an act of treachery: *Brad y Llyfrau Gleision*, "The Treason of the Blue Books."[14] This came about because the commissioners and their assistants went way beyond the brief originally envisaged (by William Williams and those who supported his call for the inquiry) and took upon themselves to comment on, among much else, the moral state of the Welsh people. Take, for example, these words of J. C. Symons, the commissioner responsible for investigating the counties of Brecon, Radnor, and Cardigan:

> The morals of the people are of a very low standard. In fact, immorality prevails rather from a want of a sense of moral obligation than from a forgetfulness or violation of recognised duties. I am confident that as regards mendacity there is frequently no real consciousness that it is sinful, so habitual is disregard for truth whenever interest prompts falsehood. The whole people are kept back by their immoralities and low tone of principle.[15]

And the reason for it all?

> The Welsh language is a vast drawback to Wales, and a manifold barrier to the moral progress and commercial prosperity of the people. It is not easy to over-estimate its evil effects. It is the language of the Cymri, and anterior to that of the ancient Britons. It dissevers the people from intercourse which would greatly advance their civilization, and bars the access of improving knowledge to their minds. As a proof of this, there is no Welsh literature worthy of the name.[16]

The author's ignorance matched his insolence. Cambridge-educated he may have been, but he appears to know nothing about Celtic philology (which had been researched and written about, in Latin and in English, from the seventeenth century onwards by scholars like John Davies and Edward Lhuyd), and his dismissal of a literary tradition which extended back to the sixth century is wonderful.

Even more wonderful was the sense of outrage which the *Reports* provoked in Wales. Much of the commissioners' evidence was provided by Anglican clergymen. One, the Rev. John Griffiths, vicar of Aberdare, is particularly notorious for his blanket condemnation of the morality of Welsh women.[17] Not surprisingly, nonconformist Wales responded with intense indignation. "It is difficult," wrote the late Sir Glanmor Williams, "to think of any other single factor which did so much to exacerbate Church/Chapel relations . . . as the publication of the Reports of 1847."[18] Many have seen in the responses to the Blue Books the beginnings of the tradition of radical politics in Wales.[19] There also came about, as part of the Welsh-speaking nonconformist reaction, the purposeful creation of an image of a high-minded, civilized country which the commissioners had been totally unable to appreciate or comprehend. That was the image of "pure, peaceful Wales" (*Cymru lân, Cymru lonydd*), ready to embrace a Benthamite programme of utilitarian self-improvement and unquestioningly dutiful towards the greater good of the British State. This theme has been particularly explored, in relation to the Welsh literature of the nineteenth century, by Welsh scholars like E. G. Millward and Hywel Teifi Edwards.[20]

My concern is much more limited. It is true that the *Reports* drew justified attention to the inadequate and patchy educational provision in many parts of Wales. It is also true that Welshmen like Lewis Edwards, who were committed to improving that provision, saw the acquisition of English and education on the English model as a pattern to follow. That is not, however, the whole story. In 1845, two years before the publication of the Blue Books, Lewis Edwards had established a Welsh-language periodical, *Y Traethodydd* (*The Essayist*). This he had done in cooperation with Roger Edwards and Thomas Gee, two other leaders of early nineteenth-century nonconformity in Wales. Lewis Edwards's exemplars were those periodicals which he had experienced at first hand in Scotland, *Blackwood's Magazine* and its rival *The Edinburgh Review*. *Y Traethodydd* was a vehicle for discussing theology and philosophy. It was also used to address educational and cultural issues, to present literary themes, and to open up all sorts of new subjects for its largely monoglot Welsh readers. In the graphic words of R. T. Jenkins, "*Bu'r Traethodydd yn athro i Gymru*" ("Y Traethodydd became a teacher for Wales").[21] In two essays in the journal Lewis Edwards gave his own—measured, but trenchant—reaction to the Blue Books.[22] The whole thrust of *Y Traethodydd* was a demonstration that the Welsh language need not, in the notorious words of R. R. W. Lingen, keep a Welshman "under the hatches."[23]

High on the list of themes and topics presented in *Y Traethodydd* are essays and articles on classical literature and philosophy, and on classical education.[24] Lewis Edwards was particularly aware of the interest in Greek culture in Victorian England. Accordingly, in an issue of the journal in 1852, he published his own Welsh verse translation, with an explanatory note, of Homer, *Iliad* 6.369–502 (the section on Hector, Andromache, and Astyanax).[25] Sixteen years later, in the volume of collected essays entitled *Traethodau Llenyddol*, Lewis Edwards republished that translation, together with the opening 311 lines of *Iliad* 1, and added an extended introduction to the works of Homer.[26] He writes of William Cowper, W. E. Gladstone, and Lord Derby as students and translators of Homer. It is clear that at least part of his aim was to demonstrate the possibilities of doing in Welsh what English translators of the classics had been doing since the days of Dryden and Pope.

In *Y Traethodydd*, other writers were encouraged to write on classical themes. For example, in 1857 John Morgan contributed a long article on the history of philosophy, especially Greek philosophy.[27] In 1868 a series of articles was published on Plato's *Republic*, written by Thomas Charles Edwards, Lewis Edwards's eldest son, and in 1877–1879 an even longer series on Aristotle's *Politics* by a well-known Calvinistic Methodist minister, Griffith Ellis.[28] It was also in the pages of *Y Traethodydd* in 1866 that there appeared the first translation into Welsh of an entire Greek tragedy. This was *Antigone*, translated by the Rev. Owen Jones, a native of Llanuwchllyn and by then a Calvinistic Methodist minister in Blaenau Ffestiniog.[29] Owen Jones had been taught at Bala, before proceeding to University College, London, where he graduated. His translation of *Antigone* is a fascinating work, both accurate and still highly readable. Owen Jones has also added several pages of introduction to Greek literature, tragedy in particular. He is aware that he is walking a tightrope as he attempts to justify the production of this pre-Christian work for his Welsh nonconformist readership. "It may surprise," he says, "some evangelical Welshmen to find that a pagan holds such correct ideas, not about what is expedient, but what is right."[30] He also believes that it would be valuable "for the monoglot Welshman to see, in Welsh guise, some examples of works by the Greek poets, so that he may have some idea of what is read by our young men in the Colleges and is regarded as among the world's greatest literary achievements."[31]

Much more could be said about the classical contributions to *Y Traethodydd*, and to other nineteenth-century Welsh periodicals like *Y Beirniad* and *Yr Haul*. In 1868 there appeared in *Y Traethodydd* the Latin text and a Welsh translation of Horace, *Odes* 3.9: *Donec gratus eram tibi*.[32] The translation is the work of another of Lewis Edwards's old students at Bala, R. Llugwy Owen. Llugwy Owen was working in a slate quarry at the age of fourteen, but eventually made his way to Bala, and then to the University of London, before becoming a minister at Acre-fair in northeast Wales. For a time he studied in Germany and gained a doctorate from the University of Tübingen. Later in his life, in 1899, he was to be the author of a volume unique in Welsh, a work of three hundred fifty tightly packed pages on the history of Greek philosophy.[33] Back in the 1860s, also on the pages of *Y Traethodydd*, there appeared two long articles on Virgil, with translations of two of the *Eclogues*, parts of *Georgics* 1, and from the first four books of the *Aeneid*.[34] This time the author was John Peter ("Ioan Pedr") an independent minister and a man of extraordinary learning, even if his curriculum could sometimes appear somewhat "miscellaneous."[35] He started life as a millwright's apprentice, but was driven by a thirst for learning that embraced both classical and later European literature, as well as geology and philology. Among his publications and other papers, in addition to Virgil, there are Welsh versions of works by Homer and Horace, Goethe and Schiller, Pascal and Rousseau, Dante and Petrarch. One could likewise refer to others whose translations from classical literature, or whose discussions of classical themes, were published in *Y Traethodydd* and other journals.[36] My point, very simply, is that providing Welsh readers with access to at least some aspects of the classical legacy was part of the drive behind Lewis Edwards and other contributors to *Y Traethodydd*.

In the remainder of this paper mention may be made of two other spheres of Welsh culture in the later nineteenth century, spheres in which a sense of the classical past played an important role. The first is the Eisteddfod movement.[37] I shall not discuss the provincial *eisteddfodau* of the early nineteenth century, except to say that by the middle of the century, in the aftermath of the Blue Books, there was a great thrust towards establishing a National Eisteddfod, the first of which was held in 1861. During the twentieth century the Eisteddfod increasingly came to be seen as a bastion of the Welsh language. Things were not nearly so clear-cut in the middle of the nineteenth century. Many, the educational reformer Sir Hugh Owen most notable among them, were keen for the Eisteddfod to develop English-language activities, in particular as a forum for discussing contemporary issues. Owen called this the "Social Science Section" of the Eisteddfod. In part, at least, this was an attempt to present to the world a favourably up-to-date image of Wales and to justify the Welsh people in the wake of the calumnies of 1847. To this end Hugh Owen saw the English language as the necessary medium, just as Lewis Edwards and his fellow-educationalists (for all their writing in Welsh) used English as the language of training for their wards.[38]

Here too there is another side to the story. For the Eisteddfod also provided the focus for literary activity in Welsh: the highest prize to which a poet could aspire was the crown or chair of the National Eisteddfod for poetry written in the Welsh language. It is significant that, from the 1880s onwards, competitions for translating classical literature into Welsh become a regular feature of the Eisteddfod. In 1889, for example, a prize was awarded for translating *Iliad* 22. The winner was R. Morris Lewis, from Brechfa in Carmarthenshire, a clerk in an office of the Inland Revenue in Swansea. Morris Lewis's translating of Homer did not stop with *Iliad* 22. He went on to translate other parts of the poem, a collection that was published as a volume after his death.[39]

The most notable classical product to emerge from the National Eisteddfod of the 1880s was a volume containing a Welsh translation (or, rather, two Welsh translations) of Euripides' *Alcestis*, together with the

Greek text. This was the result of a competition at the National Eisteddfod held in Aberdare in 1885 at which the third Marquess of Bute offered a prize of £50 for the best version of Euripides' tragedy. Eighteen competitors entered the lists, submitting their work (as is customary) under pseudonyms. The three adjudicators pronounced that the palm of victory was to be shared between the Rev. D. E. Edwardes (a graduate of the University of Glasgow, and rector of a parish in Pembrokeshire) and the Rev. David Rowlands ("Dewi Môn"), who taught at the Congregationalist College in Brecon. The Marquess of Bute, rather than dividing the prize money between both translators, awarded them £50 each. Furthermore, he paid for the publication of their work and of Euripides' text in one, finely produced volume. Accordingly there appeared in 1887, printed by the Oxford University Press on behalf of the National Eisteddfod Society, the most ambitious "classical" volume ever to emerge in a Welsh context: *Yr Alcestis gan Euripides. Chwareugerdd Roegaidd wedi ei throsi i'r Gymraeg.*[40] One can only speculate why precisely *Alcestis* was chosen. My guess is that Robert Browning's influence is there, and his long poem of 1871, *Balaustion's Adventure: including a transcript of Euripides.*[41] As far as the two translations are concerned, they smack of the diction and style of their day, although I would say that David Rowlands's version has stood the test of time better than that of D. E. Edwardes. The chief significance of the Eisteddfod competition and of the volume, from a cultural and sociological point of view, is that they gave Wales its own version of a Greek drama, in a dignified format, at a time when there was a zeal for everything Greek over the border in England. Such interest in classics in Victorian Wales by the Welsh and by a cultural establishment like the Eisteddfod shows that they wanted to be seen to be as good as their neighbors across Offa's Dyke.

The other cultural sphere to be mentioned is the wider educational sphere and the part that classics played in it. Mention has already been made of the Welsh Intermediate Education Act of 1889. In the network of "county" schools, set up in the wake of that act, Latin was a required subject. Greek, along with Welsh, was to be optional.[42] These schools played an inestimable role in Welsh life from the end of the nineteenth century onwards. So too did the trio of university colleges which were established in the Victorian era—Aberystwyth (1872), Cardiff (1883), and Bangor (1884), the three to be federated as the University of Wales in 1893. From the start, the teaching of classical languages and their literature featured prominently in the provision made by the three colleges. When Aberystwyth opened its doors in 1872, the staff numbered half a dozen, but there was a professor of Greek and a professor of Latin. The principal, Rev. Thomas Charles Edwards, Lewis Edwards's eldest son, doubled as professor of Greek. Likewise, from the beginning there were two professors in Cardiff and Bangor.

In the context of thinking about the cultural effects of this increased awareness of the classics in the university context, I conclude with two images, both based on Cardiff. At the end of the century, in 1899, a lively society called the Frogs Classical Society was established in Cardiff, centered upon (but not exclusive to) the University College. Among its many activities was the staging of performances of Greek plays—some in Greek, others in English translation—in Cardiff theaters. This practice reached its peak during Gilbert Norwood's tenure of the Greek chair in Cardiff from 1908 onwards. In 1926 Norwood left Wales for Toronto, but he was still in Cardiff when his influential book, *Greek Tragedy*, first appeared.[43] During his time in Cardiff some adventurous productions of Greek plays were staged: *Iphigeneia at Aulis* (1909) in the White Hall Room, and the *Acharnians* (1911) in the New Theatre. After Norwood's departure the tradition continued under Kathleen Freeman, one of Norwood's most eminent students and herself a lecturer in Cardiff from 1918 onwards. That is one image: the image of classical productions, in the same mould as what had been happening from the mid-Victorian period in Edinburgh and Oxford and Bradfield, and especially in Cambridge in its Greek play, with an attempt to recreate what were assumed to be the modes of the ancient Greek theater.

My second image is of another scholar who joined the University in Cardiff early in the twentieth century, W. J. Gruffydd. He was an early product of one of the new Welsh county schools, Caernarfon in his case, and went on to Oxford to study classics. In 1906 he became a lecturer in Welsh in Cardiff. He was a member of the Frogs Classical Society, and contributed to an English translation of *Iphigeneia at Aulis*, which was prepared by members of the society for the 1909 production.[44] W. J. Gruffydd is a towering figure in Welsh literary life in the first half of the twentieth century. He became an influential professor of Welsh at Cardiff, founded and edited *Y Llenor* (the most eminent literary journal in twentieth-century Wales), was elected member of parliament for the University of Wales, and much else. Toward the end of his life he produced, for broadcast by the BBC's Welsh Home Service, the 1950 translation of *Antigone*.[45] Gruffydd was also a writer who, as a young man, challenged many of the conventions of Welsh poetry, and was one of a group of poets around the turn of the century who heralded a major renaissance in Welsh literature. As a precocious nineteen-year old, in 1900 he published, together with R. Silyn Roberts, a volume of poetry called *Telynegion* ("Lyrics"), which drew on much of his classical learning.[46] The poem which best conveys what the classical world meant to the young W.

J. Gruffydd is the *pryddest* (a long ode, written in nontraditional meters), which he entered for the crown competition at the 1902 National Eisteddfod. His subject was *Trystan ac Esyllt* ("Tristan and Isolde"): that is, a romantic theme from the world of Arthurian and Celtic literature, used by Gruffydd as *enfant terrible* to attack the way in which (so he maintained) a puritanical Christianity had destroyed a world of earlier innocence. Particularly interesting, in the context of this paper, is that in the second part of his *pryddest*, entitled "Lacrimae Musarum." Gruffydd turns not to the world of Celtic mythology but to the gods of classical antiquity as symbols of that lost innocence:

> Mae'r goleu a'r gwirionedd wedi mynd.
> Ble mae'r holl dduwiau a'r duwiesau fu
> Yn crwydro'r goedwig las mewn dyddiau gwell?
> Ai ofer ydoedd Groeg? A gollodd Zeus
> Am byth ei folltau tân o flaen ein Crist?
> Lle gynt y dawnsiai'r gwiddan dan y coed
> A thorf o'i gylch yn nhemel lân y wig,
> - Ac aml nos, ac ust yr hwyr yn drwm
> Ar fron y ddaear, fe ddoi Pan ei hun,
> Ardderchog Ban, brif-deyrn yn llys y dail,
> I gyfarch gwell i'w mysg, ac hyd nes doi'r
> Rhosynog wawr i spio dros y bryniau
> 'Roedd siffrwd gan y ddawns, a'r pibau main
> Yn chwythu cainc llawenydd.[47]

[The light and the truth have gone. Where are all the gods and goddesses who roamed the green forest in better days? Was Greece in vain? Has Zeus lost for ever his thunderbolt before our Christ? Whereas before, the wizard used to dance under the trees, surrounded by a crowd in the holy temple of the wood,—and many a night, when the silence of the evening was heavy on the breast of earth, Pan himself would come, Glorious Pan, chief-ruler in the court of the leaves, into their midst to greet them, and until there came the rosy dawn to spy over the hills there was the rustling of the dance, and the slender pipes would blow a tune of joy.][48]

The poem's lament for the surrender of ancient religion to Christianity reflects the tradition of Schiller's *Die Götter Griechenlands* ("The Gods of Greece"). Shelley and Swinburne lurk not inconspicuously, and there are echoes too of Elizabeth Barrett Browning's "The Dead Pan." The essential point now, however, is that the ancient Greek world is part of the way in which this young Welsh-language poet, on the threshold of a new century, saw and expressed his vision. Both the classical education he had received and his Welsh literary perspective were equally important to him. This was the brave new world of Welsh literature in the twentieth century. It was also the beginning of a new and remarkably vigorous era in the history of Welsh and Celtic scholarship: many of its most notable protagonists were to be classically trained.

The thrust of this paper has been to demonstrate that the classical contribution to the mixed cultural scene in Wales in the second part of the nineteenth century was not an inconsiderable one. Attitudes adopted towards the classics reflected something of the tensions of a people trying to come to terms with the claims of two languages upon their allegiance. In many ways the classical was part of the English educational scene after which so many Welsh people hankered. That, however, is not the whole story. The Greek and Roman legacy also played its part in literary and cultural aspirations that found their expression through the Welsh language. It might have come as a surprise to the authors of the 1847 Blue Books to discover, some fifty years later, that speakers and readers of Welsh were not quite so dissevered as they had thought from the things which (to use J. C. Symons's expression) "would greatly advance their civilization."[49]

Chapter 3

Kathleen Freeman
An Apostle and Evangelist for Classical Greece

ᴘ—Eleanor Irwin

Kathleen Freeman was an unusual classicist in early twentieth-century Britain,[1] not only because she was a woman, but also because she was not interested simply in the undergraduate who came fresh from school with the ability to read Latin and Greek, but wanted to introduce the ancient Greek world to those who had not previously learned Greek.[2] To this end she translated Greek authors and interpreted ancient values, at first for university undergraduates, but later also for a reading public hungry for ideas. She was admired as an inspirational teacher but ignored (and even despised) for her lively translations and her interest in practical questions of topography and criminal investigation.[3]

The reference in the title of this chapter, "apostle and evangelist," attempts to capture her activities outside the university and her zeal in presenting the ancient Greek world. During the Second World War, while she still held her university post, she found new students and a new audience in the armed forces and in readers of the *Western Mail*. After the end of the war, she resigned from the university (though she was not yet fifty years old) and continued to write, now for ordinary people outside the university, not only providing the kind of help they needed to under-

49

stand but also inviting them to engage with ideas through acquaintance with ancient Greece. Her translations of the pre-Socratic philosophers and her study of the Greek city states continue to be consulted and still appear on university reading lists.

Freeman was convinced that the ancient Greeks had important lessons for modern society in addressing problems, whether in the administration of justice, resistance to tyranny, or the causes of crime; and she communicated these ideas with the enthusiasm of an evangelist. Through the Philosophical Society of England she helped to launch a scheme, albeit short-lived, for adult education and independent study, developing a reading list and serving for two or more years as Director of Studies. In all her writing—whether in newspaper columns, articles, translations, or studies of ancient society—she never ceased to believe that the Greeks were worth knowing.

Kathleen Freeman[4] graduated (B.A. 1918, M.A. 1922) from the University College of South Wales and Monmouthshire, now Cardiff University, and was awarded a D.Litt. in 1940 for *The Work and Life of Solon* and six articles.[5] She remained at Cardiff as a lecturer in Greek for twenty-seven years from 1919 to 1946. During these years she also published poetry, short stories, novels, and mystery stories in addition to her classical research and lecturing. In 1923 her earliest classical article, "The Dramatic Technique of the *Oedipus Coloneus*," appeared and in the following year (1924) three sonnets "Friendship" in *Adelphi*, and "Candour" and "Liberation" in *The Golden Hind*. Nineteen twenty-six was a year of unusual productivity with a book of short stories, *The Intruder and Other Stories*; a novel, *Martin Hanner, A Comedy*; and *The Work and Life of Solon*.[6]

Between 1928 and 1936 she experimented with different styles of fiction in four novels[7] and in 1936 invented a new persona, Mary Fitt, under whose pseudonym she was to write twenty-seven mystery novels and many short stories. From 1936 she separated the classicist (Kathleen Freeman) from the writer of fiction (Mary Fitt), a separation that she guarded with some mischievous pleasure until the 1950s.[8] The apparent exceptions to this division of output were *Gown and Shroud* (1947), a novel in which clay tablets in an unknown "Xanthian" language were at the heart of the mystery,[9] and three short stories based on court cases in the Attic orators (1950, 1951), all of which she published as Kathleen Freeman because of the specialized classical Greek knowledge displayed. As Mary Fitt she was elected to the Detection Club in 1950 and invited to become a member of the Society of Authors in March 1948, six months *after* she had joined as Kathleen Freeman.[10] Once the identity of Mary Fitt became known, the name was sometimes corrupted to Miss Fitt

(= misfit), with a hint of her eccentricity and her (unconventional) friend-ship with Dr. Liliane Clopet.

Of Mary Fitt, Freeman wrote enigmatically: "in my character as Author I was born some years later than Myself, in that part of the world which lies between classical Greece and Elizabethan England."[11] Classi-cal Greece is easily interpreted, but Elizabethan England is less obvious. Freeman's earliest literary publications were highly personal reflections on relationships in sonnet form.[12] Elizabethan England invites us to make a connection with Shakespeare's sonnets and in particular with the "Dark Lady" who caused the playwright such grief. One of the suggested identifications of this woman is Mary Fitton, whose name we may see modified as Mary Fitt.[13]

Also in 1936, the year in which Mary Fitt made her writing debut, Freeman published the first of eight articles on Greek poets and philoso-phers in *Greece and Rome*. In the spring of 1939 she entered into corre-spondence with the publisher J. M. Dent, hoping to publish these articles under the title *Aspects of Greek Life and Thought*, but her manuscript was declined on the grounds that the market for such a book was too limited. Even the offer of a grant in aid was not enough to change the publisher's mind.[14] When, after the war, she began to publish books on classical subjects, she avoided this criticism by writing for a wider audience.

Little is known of Freeman's life before university. She was born in Yardley, near Birmingham, England, on 22 June 1897 to Charles Henry Freeman and Catharine Mawdesley.[15] The family moved to Cardiff[16] where Kathleen attended Canton School for Girls.[17] Classical languages were not offered in the girls' school at the time though Canton School for Boys, which was housed in the same building, offered Latin.[18] We have no information about Freeman's first encounter with Greek. She was to write in her preface to *The Greek Way*: "one can learn to read easy Greek in a year or less" (p. vii).[19]

In parents and schooling she was unlike other women classicists of her time who generally came from privileged and educated families and attended independent prestigious schools or were tutored privately. To put her life in context, I have compared her with five women in the *Dictionary of British Classicists* who were born within ten years of Free-man: Dorothy Lamb (b. 1887), Winifred Lamb (b. 1894), Sylvia Benton and Jocelyn Toynbee (both b. 1897, the same year as Freeman), and A. M. Dale (b. 1901).[20] The fathers of these five women held positions that required a good education. Dorothy Lamb's father was a mathemat-ics don, Winifred Lamb's a landowner and liberal MP, Sylvia Benton's a judge of the Chief Court of India, Jocelyn Toynbee's the Secretary of the Charitable Organization Society, and A. M. Dale's a civil engineer. Even more tellingly, the mothers of two of these women—Winifred Lamb and Jocelyn Toynbee—had themselves been students at Cambridge, and Winifred Lamb's grandparents had been significant benefactors of Newnham. Four of these women read classics at Cambridge: Dorothy Lamb, Winifred Lamb, and Toynbee at Newnham, and Benton at Girton; Dale won a scholarship to Somerville College, Oxford.

Their studies at Oxford or Cambridge opened other doors, to the British School at Athens and work on archaeological digs and to positions at Oxford or Cambridge. Only Dale and Toynbee held positions in other universities. Toynbee began as tutor at St. Hugh's, Oxford (1921–1924), and was at University College, Reading for three years (1924–1927) before returning to Newnham (1927–1962). Dale, after ten years at Lady Margaret Hall (1929–1939) and war service at Bletchley, was appointed reader in Greek at Birkbeck College, University of London (1952–1959) and professor of Greek (1959–1963).[21]

Unlike the women classicists described above, Freeman did not belong to a financially privileged family and had not gone to one of the schools which prepared girls for the Oxbridge colleges. If she had private tutoring, she does not mention it or credit a tutor. Instructors could be an impediment; as she wrote in the preface to *The Greek Way*, "Better to study alone with a good textbook than to put oneself into the hands of a worshipper of grammar." There was, however, a tradition of education in the family. The 1881 census records that her paternal grandfather Charles (1828–1885) had been ordained in the Church of England and was teaching school in Birkenhead "without cure of souls." He died at the age of 57 when his son, Kathleen's father, was eighteen or nineteen.[22] At his death, Charles Henry apparently gave up any hope of further education and became a commercial traveller, in all likelihood to support his mother and two sisters.[23]

Freeman had one stroke of good fortune. At the University College of South Wales she studied Greek with Gilbert Norwood and was his junior colleague as lecturer in Greek until his departure for Canada in 1926 to become chair of Latin and classics at University College in Toronto. Norwood (1880–1954) had established his scholarly reputation with *The Riddle of the Bacchae* (1908), but he was also known for "a burning desire to open ancient literature . . . to a wider public."[24] He did not confine his writing to academic papers and books; he published short stories and opinion pieces and was a popular after-dinner speaker.

With Norwood's encouragement, Freeman published her study of Solon with a translation of his poems (1926), dedicating it to him. She kept in contact with him, sent him drafts of her articles for comment, contributed an article to his *Festschrift* (1952),[25] and remembered his formative influence in a letter of condolence to his widow Frances (1954): "To me the thought of Gilbert's death is a real sorrow, for as I am sure you know, I owed him very much especially for his inspired teaching."[26]

Norwood was succeeded as professor of Greek at Cardiff by H. J. W. Tillyard (1881–1968), a distinguished Byzantinist and graduate of Gonville and Caius College, Cambridge, who had been a student in the British School at Athens for several years. Like Norwood, he encouraged his colleague Freeman, specifically in her intention to publish her collection of *Greece and Rome* articles. In 1946 Tillyard retired and was succeeded by L. J. D. Richardson (1893–1979), who had been lecturer in Latin at Cardiff (1926–1946).[27] In October of that year, Freeman submitted her resignation; she was perhaps disappointed at not being appointed Tillyard's successor, and also aware of the dissimilarities between the successful candidate Richardson and herself, which ran deeper than the obvious gender difference. Richardson took a traditional philological approach to classical studies, whereas Freeman put her emphasis on the history of ideas.[28] Richardson was a graduate of Trinity College, Dublin, a far more prestigious institution than University College, Cardiff. He served as honorary secretary of the Classical Association of England and Wales for twenty-five years.[29] His publications included articles in *Hermathena*, *Classical Quarterly*, and *Classical Review* and an occasional contribution to *Greece and Rome*, as well as a Greek prose composition, "The Indian Mutiny of 1857, after Herodotus," for which he won the vice-chancellor's prize at Trinity College, Dublin in 1915. His articles dealt with esoteric subjects like "Agma, a Forgotten Greek Letter" (1941). Shortly after his appointment as professor of Greek he contributed an elaborate spoof "A Little Classics Is a Dangerous Thing" to *Greece and Rome* (14 [1947]: 41). It bristles with examples of bad Latin: incorrect plurals like *vade meca*, incorrect singulars like "every *strata* of society" and wrongheaded translations like "nothing but good has come to us from the dead," for *de mortuis nil nisi bonum*. He closes the essay with lines purported to be drawn from Ovid: *in medio tutissimus . . . Ibis* [with a capital I] and *omnia suspendens . . . Naso* [with a capital N]. It reinforced his emphasis on precision of language and, of course, required competence in Latin to detect the jokes.

Freeman's career at the university had been unexceptional. After one article in *Classical Review*, she chose to contribute to the newly established journal *Greece and Rome*. This journal, begun in 1931, proclaimed that articles were "intended to be accessible to non-specialists," with "all Greek and Latin quotations . . . translated." (Richardson's tongue-in-cheek essay mentioned above was obviously an exception to this rule). It was to be "the most suitable journal for undergraduates and for those with a general interest in the ancient world who wish to be kept informed of what scholars are currently thinking" while also "of interest to professional scholars."[30] By choosing to publish almost exclusively in *Greece and Rome*, Freeman was aligning herself with those who wrote for non-specialists. Her articles on Anaxagoras (1935), Epicurus, and Callias son of Hipponicus (both in 1938) anticipated her later work on the pre-Socratics, as her article on Thourioi (1941) preshadowed her book on the Greek city states. She showed her lighter side in her article on a children's game, the copper fly (1936), and "Vincent or the Donkey" (1945).

There is good evidence that her students in the University College of South Wales and Monmouthshire appreciated her.[31] Most of them would have been in the same position as she had been when she was admitted, with no Greek or very little. To help them she translated the fragments of the Pre-Socratic philosophers (with Greek confined to footnotes) many years before Kirk and Raven published their *Presocratic Philosophers* (1957) with Greek in the text and translations in the footnotes. Freeman lectured on these early philosophers with an awareness of her students' limited experience in Greek while avoiding the temptation to talk down to them.[32] Like Norwood before her[33] she made translations of Greek drama and directed student performances, including a performance of Sophocles, *Philoctetes* in November 1939 just after the outbreak of war. (The translation was not published till 1948.)[34]

At the outbreak of the Second World War, Kathleen Freeman had to all appearances a satisfying life as a university lecturer and success as a popular writer. Evidence of her financial success included a house, "Lark's Rise," on Druidstone Road in St. Mellons on the outskirts of Cardiff,.which she and her lifelong friend, physician Liliane Clopet, had built for themselves in the 1930s, incorporating a surgery for Clopet.[35] It would be rash to speculate about the nature of the friendship between Freeman and Clopet, though they may have provided a clue by the house name "Lark's Rise" if indeed it echoes Shakespeare's sonnet 29:[36]

> then my state,
> Like to the lark at break of day arising
> From sullen earth, sings hymns at heaven's gate;
> For thy sweet love remember'd such wealth brings
> That then I scorn to change my state with kings.

Another indication of Freeman's financial success is evident in her travel to most parts of Europe[37] and even further afield, "not only cruising past Stromboli on a summer night but also able to spend long summer days in the Arctic Circle."[38]

The Second World War proved to be a watershed for Freeman, providing her with new readers and new students. In 1940 she began to contribute columns to the *Western Mail*, a Cardiff-based newspaper, translating from Greek quotations about justice and tyranny which seemed to her appropriate to the conflict with the Nazi aggressors. She compiled these columns into a slim volume with the provocative title *It Has All Happened Before: What the Greeks Thought of their Nazis* (1941). She continued to apply her knowledge of ancient writers in *Voices of Freedom* (1943), which included selections translated from two ancient visitors to Britain, Pytheas the Massiliot and Julius Caesar.[39]

She also lectured "on Greece etc." (as she said in her *Who's Who* entry) for "the Ministry of Information and in the National Scheme of Education for His Majesty's Forces stationed in South Wales and Monmouthshire."[40] She had visited Greece in the 1930s and her familiarity with the Greek terrain, customs, and language[41] made her a valuable resource for soldiers about to be stationed in the Mediterranean. It is not difficult to imagine the satisfaction she felt in teaching such students for whom knowledge might mean the difference between surviving or dying. In these two very different experiences, her propaganda writings and her teaching of military personnel, Freeman encountered an audience unlike her undergraduate students.

Just after the end of the war she resigned from the university (1 October 1946). We have her statement of what she hoped to accomplish; for she wrote in her *Who's Who* entry that she resigned to "devote" herself "to writing and research."[42] Indeed, between 1946 and 1954, she published eight books on classical subjects. In the preface to the first of her postwar publications, *The Pre-Socratic Philosophers: A Companion*, she explains that the book was "the fruit of a number of years' experience of reading early Greek philosophy with university students." She commented mildly that "many have not the time to read all the material collected in Diels" and "some would be glad of some guidance at first." She wished the book "to be useful *also* to those without a knowledge of Greek" (emphasis mine) and so kept Greek quotations out of the text. The *Ancilla to the Pre-Socratic Philosophers* that followed was a slimmer volume containing the translations of the Greek fragments without the commentary. The *Companion* was dedicated to Liliane Clopet, with a Greek quotation from Hippocrates praising her friend's compassion and skill as a physician: *en gar parei philanthropie, paresti kai philotechnia* ("if the love of humanity is present, the love of skill is also present").[43]

Work on the Attic orators which had been prepared for her university classes also appeared in 1946 as the *Murder of Herodes and Other Trials from the Athenian Law Courts*. It was more than a translation of speeches; she commented on the system of justice and the conventions of the courts. It is an indication of her talent for vivid translation that Lysias's speech *In Eratosthenem* ("On the killing of Eratosthenes the seducer") which first appeared in Herodes, was included virtually unchanged in collections of short stories.[44] A few years later she wrote up three more Athenian court cases and published them in the *London Mystery Magazine* (1950, 1951) as "Murder in Athens" (Antiphon 6), "Mystery in Athens" (Andocides, *On the Mysteries*) and "Scandal in Athens" (Isaeus 6, *On the Estate of Philoctemon*), the last of which was later included in an anthology.[45] In these short stories she built on what the speeches provided by way of evidence to suggest motive and opportunity. She contributed an essay on the first of these court cases (Antiphon 6) to Gilbert Norwood's *Festschrift* (1952), thereby illustrating her equal comfort in writing short stories and academic papers.

The Greek Way: An Anthology, published in 1947, was a very different collection of translations from prose and poetry meant to show a light-hearted side to the Greeks: "an Aladdin's cave," to illustrate "the Greek genius for living as well as for thinking" (v). She dedicated *The Greek Way* (as she had the *Companion*) to L.M.C.C. (Liliane Clopet), gracefully modifying Theocritus's tribute to his physician friend Nicias in gender and case to read *iatroi ousei kai tais ennea de pephilemenei* ("for one who is a physician and dear to the Nine").[46]

In her preface to *The Greek Way* she advised her readers to learn Greek because "there is nothing which will give you so much entertainment in return for an initial effort." She compares the demands of Greek to doing difficult crossword puzzles or playing bridge, and protests that "Greek is not nearly as difficult as people maintain." Her deliberate attempt to demystify Greek and to encourage adults to embark on a study of the Greek language is a revealing insight into her attitude to classical studies.

Greek City States was published in 1950. She eschewed the usual focus of Greek historians on Athens and Sparta, and studied instead nine other city-states with whose topography and history she was very familiar.[47] She had an uncanny eye for settings, as is often seen in her mysteries, and she used that in bringing the city-states to life. She saw geography as a metaphor for conduct; in an address to the Philosophical Society of England in the same year (1950), she contrasted classical Athens, the city of imagination, with the heavy dullness of Byzantine Istanbul.

God, Man and State, published in 1952, had begun as two articles in *The Philosopher*: "The idea of God in the Pre-Socratic Philosophers" and "The Concept of Man in the Greek Philosophers." She expanded them and added essays on society, education, and law, as well as an epilogue drawing explicit lessons from the Greek experience for contemporary society. In her preface she cautioned:

> Greek thought is not uniform. On all subjects there were many different views, sometimes directly opposed. The object of study-

ing these is to seek, not a dogma, but a criterion; not to bow to an authoritative pronouncement, but to examine, weigh and come to one's own conclusion. (v)

Nineteen fifty-four saw the publication of *Paths of Justice*, a study of the Athenian legal system beginning with Solon, examining Athens "in its prime" through the Attic orators, and looking soberly at later corruption and decay. Much of the material in this book recalled her earlier books, *Solon* and *The Murder of Herodes*, as well as her wartime columns. For behind the study in *Paths* lay a concern that communism posed a threat to democracy and justice. She concluded the preface with Solon's dictum: "The people must fight to defend their laws as they would their fortifications."

Two other books appeared in 1954: a single-volume revision of the Quennells' three books on *Everyday Life in Ancient Greece* and the translation from Italian of Mario Untersteiner's *I sofisti*. These were her last books on the classical world. In 1954 she suffered a serious health crisis and was in bed and unable to work or meet her deadlines for seven weeks.[48] In spite of her medical condition (probably hypertension), she continued to write, though at a slower pace: a study of Jane Austen (*T'other Miss Austen*, 1956),[49] six mystery novels (the latest appearing in 1960 after her death), and *Doctor Underground* (1956) under the pseudonym Caroline Cory, a fictionalized account based, it is said, on Clopet's adventures during World War II in the French underground.[50] Before her illness, she had begun to write children's books, mostly adventure and mystery stories with fine touches of local color and spunky girl characters. She brought the total of these to a dozen, among which *Man of Justice: The Story of Solon* (1957) introduced her early hero to yet another audience.

A recurring theme in the prefaces to her classical work is her interest in "ordinary men and women," whom she envisaged as her readers. For their sakes she produced readable, lively translations, and provided notes to illumine unfamiliar practices. Her popularizing of the Attic orators in three short stories (1950–1952) was an attempt to catch the interest of non-classicists, as was *The Greek Way*, which held out through translations the delights of being able to read Greek. Almost every one of her mystery novels included some tantalizing classical tidbit—whether quotations from one of the Greek philosophers, a plot based on a myth,[51] or Greek as code.[52] She wore her learning lightly and used it to demonstrate the rewards of study.[53]

By far, however, Freeman's most significant activity in classics—apart from her books—was her involvement in the Philosophical Society of England, an organization that had been formed in 1913 but had almost disappeared for lack of members by the beginning of World War II. After the end of the war the society was reorganized and reenergized with a new mission. It set about to attract new members, offered lectures to the public, and created opportunities for its members to meet and discuss serious issues. Most daring of all, it introduced a curriculum of study and the possibility of earning recognition with a thesis presented to a committee. It had been possible previously to become a fellow of the society but this privilege could now be earned and was open to a wider group, many apparently clergy who lacked an academic degree.[54]

Freeman published a formidable, ten-page reading list in ancient and modern philosophy in *The Philosopher* (1949). She served as director of studies for the society and chaired the examining board to which aspiring fellows might submit a thesis. In 1951 she was elected chair of the council of the society. Two of her essays appeared in *The Philosopher* (1949, 1951) as did her luncheon address (1952) and an account of a dinner in honor of Gilbert Murray at which she praised him for his interest in "ordinary people" (1951). The honoring of Gilbert Murray may have been an attempt to coopt a well-known academic and public figure—he had been chairman of the League of Nations from 1923 to 1938—and to give credibility to the society. But Freeman's acquaintance with Murray predated this honor. He wrote the preface for *It Has All Happened Before* (1941), and Freeman had paid tribute to his Greek language teaching in *The Greek Way* (1947). For his part, he had been a fan of Mary Fitt long before she had been "outed" as Kathleen Freeman.[55]

Freeman and others in the society recognized native ability and reasonable ambition in those who had not been able to attend university and had no expectation of doing so. This was particularly true in the postwar period when returning veterans were trying to recover lost years and position themselves for advancement. The society gave permission for these people to place initials after their name: F.Ph.S. (Fellow of the Philosophical Society) or the more modest A.Ph.S. (Associate of the Philosophical Society). More offensive (even hubristic) was the wearing of a green and gold gown on "practical" occasions. Early in 1952 the society took what turned out to be the disastrous step of declaring that all holders of chairs and readerships in philosophy in British universities were entitled to become honorary fellows of the society. This could not be ignored.[56]

The Waynflete Professor of Metaphysical Philosophy at Oxford, Gilbert Ryle, was enraged by this offer. He wrote a letter to the *Spectator* (28 March 1952) claiming that the society was pretending to be a university and repudiating the proffered fellowship in these words: "To accept a 'Fellowship' would be to concede that the title was professionally reputable, and so to decoy innocents into buying bogus academic titles and hoods." The pejorative "buying" implies that fellows had done no work but merely paid a fee.

Shortly thereafter, a question was asked in the House of Commons by Tom Driberg M.P., seeking clarification of the status of the society (Hansard, 19 April 1952), a question to which the minster of education, Baroness Horsbrugh, made the noncommittal reply: "Unless this society applies to me for a grant, I am afraid that I have no business to inquire into it."

Though in the short run the society defended itself against the criticisms and answered Ryle's objections point by point (*Spectator*, 10 April 1952), in just over a year it caved in under the pressure. On 22 April 1953, an extraordinary general meeting of the society adopted amended regulations for the associateship and fellowship.[57]

In all the discussion, Freeman was not a direct target; in fact, Ryle may have acknowledged her qualifications in a backhanded compliment:

> [W]*ith one exception*, no officer and no member of the Council or its Examining Board is known by me to have any philosophical credentials whatsoever. Some of them have no university degrees. (emphasis mine)

The members of the examining board in 1951 were Dr. Kathleen Freeman, M.A., D. Litt.; Dona Eva Parnell Bailey de Sanchez, A.R.C.A., F.C.L.A.; Robert Poots, M.B., B.Ch.; Rev. James A. F. Czanne; Rev. Albert D. Belden, D.D.; Rev. Gomer Evans, M.A., B.D.[58] Freeman withdrew from the society after the failure of the grand idea and dropped the society's name from her *Who's Who* entry.

The tempest over the society was a struggle over gatekeeping, a contest of amateur versus professional. On the one side the university departments saw philosophy as an academic field and feared that they would lose their power to give credentials; on the other, people like Freeman considered themselves amateurs, "lovers of philosophy," and wanted to open opportunities for learning to anyone who wanted to learn.[59] There was also a concern that philosophy was being confused with theology because of the number of clergy active in the society.

Where did Freeman's interest in ordinary people come from? It must have come partly from her own very ordinary background and her gratitude for the opportunity of a university education. It certainly was encouraged by Gilbert Norwood, her instructor whom she took as her model. But, in addition, the Second World War gave her an introduction to ordinary people, those who read her columns in the *Western Mail,* and enlisted men who learned about Greece from her before setting out to war.

After the war and after her resignation from the university, she continued to use Greece to teach; "The lesson of ancient Greece," her *apologia* for education and individual freedoms, appeared in *World Affairs* (1948).[60] A slim volume, *Fighting Words from the Greeks for Today's Struggle*, was published in the United States during the Cold War (1952). In this she returned to the Greeks as examples of both good and bad and for ammunition against the threat of communism. She was fortunate in having an income from her writing and a supportive friend in Liliane Clopet, both factors which gave her the freedom to resign from the university. Whatever the reason for the resignation, it freed her to publish classical work, most of which had been developed when she was at the university. But now she could choose her audience and from the first of those post-war publications (on the pre-Socratics and the Attic orators) she made it clear that she wanted to make her writing accessible to those with little or no Greek. In *The Greek Way* she reached beyond a student audience to a more general and older one, though she did not want them to be satisfied with mere "classics in translation," but hoped to whet the appetite for learning Greek and reading the originals. Her books on the Greek city-states and on Greek ideas and her work in the Philosophical Society of England continued this trend of communicating with anyone who wanted to learn. Her ideal was of the true amateur who studied out of love.

Freeman died of congestive heart failure in 1959 at the age of sixty-one.[61] She had tried to open up the ancient Greek world to people outside the universities. She enjoyed popular success and influence through her books though she was at times overlooked or patronized by her academic colleagues. She was ahead of her time in her educational ideas, though, possibly in the Philosophical Society she got ahead of herself. She succeeded academically beyond what might have been expected of someone of her background and was a model and inspiration for others who longed to climb Parnassus.

Chapter 4

Greek, Latin, and the Indian Civil Service

ᴗ—Phiroze Vasunia

The whole question of the future of the East is full of interest, and is, perhaps, the greatest political question in the world.

—Benjamin Jowett[1]

. . . a corps of men specially selected, brought up in a rigour of bodily hardship to which no other modern people have subjected their ruling class, trained by cold baths, cricket, and the history of Greece and Rome.

—Philip Mason[2]

In his essay "Comparativism and References to Rome in British Imperial Attitudes to India," Javed Majeed shows how Greek and Latin figured prominently in the examinations for the Indian Civil Service, the prestigious administrative body that David Lloyd George called "the steel frame."[3] Greek and Latin were not just used to attract and shape a class of ruling "gentlemen," but were also part of a complex structure of attitude and practice designed "to preserve the ICS as a monopoly of European

61

officers."[4] Majeed's insightful essay sheds light on the role of the Indian Civil Service (ICS) examinations and on the function of classics in colonial contexts, although it is mainly about comparative approaches to the British and Roman empires. Much earlier, Robin Moore, J. M. Compton, and Clive Dewey also wrote about the examinations and the circumstances leading to their creation in the middle of the nineteenth century, and John Roach discussed them in the context of a larger Victorian interest in academic examinations.[5] Richard Symonds, briefly and more recently, touched upon them in his *Oxford and Empire*, as did Christopher Stray in *Classics Transformed*.[6] And there have been passing references in the scholarship here and there, and especially in ICS histories, to Lord Macaulay, Benjamin Jowett, and the rise of Greats. The time seems ripe to build on this work, to situate it more directly within the histories of empire and classics, and to explore details of the relationship that have remained obscure. My essay uses relatively neglected archival sources and critically develops this earlier material; it is offered as a contribution to our understanding of cultural reproduction, the politics of knowledge, and modes of colonial domination.

Throughout the nineteenth century, the Indian Civil Service consisted largely of men who were born and recruited in Britain. Even after 1855, when it was thrown open to competitive examinations, the number of Indians who served in the ICS remained extremely low.[7] By one count, the average number of recruits who attended Indian universities was never greater than four percent until about the end of the nineteenth century, and until the First World War the number of Indian servicemen still remained very low in comparison to their British counterparts. Despite the statements of many imperial policymakers in Britain, few real efforts were taken in the nineteenth century to increase substantially the number of native recruits, and the competitive examinations were not even held in India until 1922. Perhaps it is not surprising that the number of Indians in the ICS was kept low in the nineteenth century, given the role played by the bureaucracy in the maintenance of empire.

The place, however, taken by Greek and Latin in this system of imperial control requires some comment. I do not say that Greek and Latin in themselves kept Indians out of the ICS. For a range of ideological reasons, the British imperial administration in the nineteenth century could never accept a large Indian presence in the Civil Service. After an Indian candidate, Satyendranath Tagore, the elder brother of Rabindranath Tagore, passed the competitive examination in 1864, for instance, the reaction of the authorities was to lower the maximum weight given to Sanskrit and Arabic in the examination.[8] In this environment Indians were not likely to be encouraged to enter the ICS, and indeed many sections of the British government and press were explicitly against the opening of the service to Indian candidates.

At the same time, Victorian political and intellectual elites sought to manipulate admission to the Indian Civil Service and used it to further their own domestic agenda. As a consequence of their actions, Greek and Latin played a prominent part in the training and examination of recruits to the ICS, especially in the second half of the nineteenth century. It is true that Greek and Latin did have an important place in the training college at Haileybury during the early education of "writers" for the East India Company, well before Macaulay and Jowett introduced changes to the system in the 1850s. But the later achievements of Oxford Greats in the ICS open competition were made possible, in part, by deliberate manipulation on the part of figures within the university and government. Greek and Latin were instrumental to these efforts to create a class of imperialist "gentlemen," ideally drawn from Oxford or Cambridge, schooled in the highest traditions of the ancient universities, and endowed with good status and character.

This is a story not just of the hegemonic force of empire but also of its points of adaptability and fragility. The story of Greek and Latin in the nineteenth and early twentieth centuries belongs equally to the history of classics and to "the historical experience of overseas domination."[9] The cultural and political circumstances surrounding the uses of Greek and Latin in the Indian Civil Service can be recalled and mapped descriptively. They are interesting because they indicate that Greek and Latin were not just part of a Victorian national culture in Britain but also of the colonial experience in places such as India. The implication of metropolitan and colonial narratives in each other allows us to see that Greek and Latin served as vehicles for the management of such domestic categories as bourgeois civility and middle-class identity as well as for the regulation and maintenance of imperial power. In other words, Greek and Latin authorized and participated in imperial culture, and also intersected, in metropolitan and colonial contexts, with such issues as race, class, and gender.

THE EAST INDIA COMPANY'S TRAINING COLLEGE
AT HAILEYBURY

The desire to give civil servants an education in Greek and Latin, as well as recurring anxieties about the class and status of recruits, can be seen in the founding of Haileybury and in its subsequent history. Lord Wellesley, who came to Bengal as governor-general in May 1798, had been forced to compromise over his original scheme for the College of Fort William in Calcutta, the "University of the East" that was designed to be established in India on the Oxford and Cambridge model, when, in 1803, the East India Company decided not to offer European subjects as part of the curriculum.[10] A proposal, however, dated 29 January 1804, from a British official in China (the East India Company also accounted for a large part of the China trade until 1833) made the court of directors reconsider its response to Wellesley. The letter from Canton asked that writers not be sent to China until there had been "A Completion of Education and System of Occupation under the direction of the Honourable Court [that] might form them to be more capable Servants of the Company and give them a chance to become more distinguished members of Society than they could be, when quitting Europe at the very early age they frequently do."[11] This proposal was then taken up by the Committee of Correspondence, which produced an influential report under the guidance of Charles Grant on 26 October 1804.[12] The report proposed that the curriculum for the new college of the East India Company should contain provisions for vocational training, but also called for "an education comprehending . . . the usual course of classical learning." The future civil servants of the company would pass an important and formative period of their life undergoing such an education: "[I]t is the only period their destination will allow for the acquisition of European Literature and Science, and in a word, on the use which is made of it must depend, in a very material degree, their future Character and Services." This mandate for classical learning was further elaborated in terms of class and civility:

> Classical Learning which usually forms the basis of a liberal education may be reckoned as a thing of course in that rank of society to which Persons destined for the service will generally belong, and the advantage or rather the necessity of it will be evident upon the slightest survey of the many important functions they have to perform. Without some foundation of this kind of Learning, which is intermixed with every other cultivated among us, it will be difficult to raise any great superstructure of that liberal knowledge which is required in Men invested with Public Trusts.

Thus, the report evinces a hope that the students will become "good subjects," "enlightened Patriot," and "good servants for the Company," but also places classical learning at the heart of the system that will turn them into the equals of men educated at the best establishments in Britain. While the report strongly advocates the teaching of other subjects including oriental languages, not least because "France flourishes in Oriental learning," the importance given to Greek and Latin in this curriculum may be gleaned from the suggestion that the headmaster of the college himself teach classics in addition to "the principles and Duties of Religion and Morality."

Beginning in about 1806, then, candidates were nominated for admission to the East India Company's training college at Haileybury, outside of London. In this phase appointments to the civil service and to the college at Haileybury were controlled by the Court of Directors of the East India Company. These directors made appointments to Haileybury for a range of reasons—the official petitions include such reasons as friendship, kinship connections, business relationships, company service, political recommendation, and recommendation of the Board of Control. In short, this was a system of patronage, and it remained in the hands of about "fifty or sixty interconnected extended families" that were "centred essentially in London and drawn from banking and commercial families and landed groups in Scotland and the south-east of England."[13]

Candidates for Haileybury did have to sit for an entrance examination, which was given by a professor and a principal, and which assumed a knowledge of classics and theology. Initially, the examination was a formality, but by the 1830s, entering students had to demonstrate competence "in the Four Gospels of the Greek Testament"; translate "some portion of the works of one of the following": Homer, Herodotus, Xenophon, Thucydides, Sophocles, and Euripides, among Greek authors; and Terence, Cicero, Tacitus, Virgil, and Horace, among the Latin; and answer questions in "ancient history, geography, and philosophy."[14] In the late 1830s, about 75 percent of the candidates passed the entrance examination, and many of them were helped by external schools and crammers.[15] In slightly earlier times, men such as Warren Hastings (1732–1818), Sir John Shore (later Lord Teignmouth; 1751–1834), Lord Mountstuart Elphinstone (1779–1859), and Charles Metcalfe (1785–1846) had had their classical educations broken off in favor of more practical pursuits, often to the dismay of their schoolmasters, because of the perception among their family or patrons that a career in India called for other qualifications.[16] But now, while there was a system of patronage in place for Haileybury, students nonetheless had to demonstrate in their entrance examinations some level of competence with classical antiquity; and it was expected that the students nominated by the directors either would have acquired the skills from their earlier education or could be crammed into passing. It is pertinent to note that in this period about 14 percent of the entering students went to the elite public schools before coming to Haileybury.[17] More students at Haileybury came from the special crammers and grammar schools and the clergy than from public schools.

Classics had a significant but limited role in Haileybury life. The curriculum at Haileybury called for "a classical education, good command of English composition, European literature and science, political economy and Oriental learning."[18] The first principal of the college was the Rev. H. Samuel Henley, who had been a "sizar" at Queens College, Cambridge.

Before coming to Haileybury in 1805, he had also taught at the College of William and Mary in Williamsburg, Virginia, and then at Harrow, and had published works on classical subjects, including *Observations on the subject of the fourth Eclogue, the allegory in the third Georgic, and the primary design of the Aeneid of Virgil, with incidental remarks on some coins of the Jews* (1788) and an *Essay towards a new edition of the Elegies of Tibullus, with translation and notes* (1792).[19] The early professors of "classical and general literature"[20] came from Oxbridge backgrounds and included Edward Lewton (who taught from 1806 to 1830), from Oxford, and Joseph Hallet Batten (1806–1815), a graduate of Trinity College, Cambridge, who succeeded to the principalship on Henley's retirement. The others to teach classics at Haileybury were James Amiraux Jeremie (1830–1850) and William Edward Buckley (1850–1857). The college itself was housed in a building designed, by William Wilkins, in the Greek style, complete with Ionic porticoes.[21] In the nineteenth century this building had the largest quadrangle of any educational building in England outside of the Great Quad in Trinity College, Cambridge.

The students' facility with Greek and Roman material can be appreciated from the immense number of allusions, references, and translations that appear in the articles of *The Haileybury Observer* from 1839 onward.[22] In a poem composed in Latin elegiacs for the *Observer*, W. S. Seton-Karr, a former headboy of Rugby, recalled with regret that the Greek and Latin of his public school had been forced into an accommodation with the Oriental studies at the college.[23] This juxtaposition of European and Oriental learning was one to which the contributors frequently returned, and was satirized already in the introductory issue by Henry Lacon Anderson:

> I think it is hard, to leave Greek or Hindi,
> On a special invite from a *Pro* to drink Tea;
> And your bow having made, (most distressing of jokes)
> To find the Pro's letter,—*proh pudor!*—a hoax.[24]

Other noteworthy contributions to the *Observer* include one by Robert N. Cust, a former headboy of Eton, who wrote a prose work called "Pugna Amwellensis," which was ostensibly from the lost books of Livy and was composed in Latin intermingled with a kind of college slang.[25] A. J. Arbuthnot, under the pseudonym *Kriketophilo*, wrote a description of a cricket match in Homeric Greek with the title *Synagoge ton Kriketophoron*.[26] While still a student in the college, Monier Monier-Williams, who was subsequently a professor at Haileybury and later Boden Professor of Sanskrit at Oxford, contributed translations from the Greek to the *Observer*.[27] It is also pertinent to recall that Charles Merivale, who wrote one of the most influential histories of the Roman empire published in the nineteenth century, was a student at Haileybury. He said in his *Autobiography* that his studies there were "the stepping stones of the course" that had led him "to be through later life a student and a man of letters."[28]

In addition to classical Greek and Latin, instruction was also given in Sanskrit, Persian, Arabic, Hindustani, and Bengali, despite the limited teaching resources for these subjects in England.[29] At Haileybury, the curriculum emphasized the classical languages of Sanskrit, Persian, and Arabic over the vernacular languages, as if to match the English educational system and its privileging of Greek and Latin in the curriculum.[30] It should be stressed that Sanskrit and Persian were required of the students at Haileybury, and all students had to pass an examination in Sanskrit before they were given their appointments in India.[31] Sanskrit was the only language in which all students had to pass an examination, even though many officials noted that it was unlikely to be useful in the day to day tasks of the civil servant. Later, in 1813, by parliamentary law, students were also required to show proficiency in one or two so-called European departments in order to receive the passing certificate from Haileybury.[32]

Bernard Cohn is probably correct in suggesting that students gained little from their education at Haileybury and that they "learned a smattering of Oriental languages, of highly dubious value to them" and "nothing about India per se, except perhaps to pick up or confirm some prejudices."[33] It is certainly true that the Greek and Latin studied for the entrance examination and then further studied in the college would have given the students very little preparation for their lives as civil servants in India. The model of European classical culture encouraged the teaching of Sanskrit and Persian by distinguished faculty at Haileybury, at a time when these languages were taught nowhere else in Britain, but as Sir George Campbell, who served in Bengal, put it, Sanskrit would be "not more useful to an Indian magistrate than a knowledge of the tongue of the ancient Germans would be to a modern commissioner of police."[34]

Haileybury was never lacking in criticism from politicians, the public, and the company's Court of Proprietors during the roughly fifty years of its existence.[35] Thomas Robert Malthus, who taught at Haileybury from 1806 to 1834, and whose book, *An Essay on the Principle of Population*, was in its second edition by the time he assumed his position at the college, had on at least two occasions published statements in which he vigorously defended the institution and its curriculum. It is striking that, in the second statement (that of 1817) he points to the requirement that students need to pass examinations in Greek and Latin and arithmetic ("the usual school education of the higher classes of society") and to bring testimonials from their schoolmasters. Malthus's tactic is notable since he himself had insisted on the teaching of oriental languages at Haileybury. Yet it emerges from his remarks that he presents oriental languages as merely vocational or practical, whereas real improvement and pedagogy for him occurs only through the classical languages of Europe.[36] He remains silent about Sanskrit and Persian, which Haileybury also offered to its students, presumably because they did not have, or were perceived by his readers not to have, the same effects on the young mind as Greek and Latin.

It was Macaulay, in 1833, when the status of the East India Company (and therefore also of Haileybury) was being debated in parliament, who explicitly connected Greek and Latin to the class and status of civil servants. Already from this early date, he supported the introduction of open competitive examinations for the selection of Indian civil servants. While he was persuasive in other respects, however, this part of his support proved to be in vain in 1833, and open competition was deferred. As George Otto Trevelyan wrote in 1876, the directors of the East India Company "were not going to resign without a struggle the most valuable patronage which had existed in the world since the days when the Roman Senate sent proconsuls and propraetors to Syria, Sicily, and Egypt."[37] Nevertheless, Macaulay's speech of 1833 gives some context to his later actions in the early 1850s, when he was successful.[38]

Victor Kiernan once said that Macaulay "knew too little about the wisdom of the East, and spent too much of his time at Calcutta reading Greek poetry."[39] Given his passion for the languages from an early age, it is perhaps not surprising, even if the vehemence of his remarks is palpable, that Macaulay found the time to discourse at length on Greek and Latin in a speech ostensibly concerning the monopoly of the East India Company. In the speech of 1833, he makes significant rhetorical moves as he proceeds from discussing "young men above par—young men superior either in talents or in diligence to the mass"[40] to discussing examinations in Greek and Latin. There is a remarkable disjunction between evaluating the utility of any language, whether Greek or Cherokee, in producing superior men, and staking out a claim for the absolute value of the classical languages in testing aptitude. In his "Minute" on education, which appeared about two years after this speech, Macaulay explicitly subordinated the worth of Sanskrit and Persian literature in relation to the Greek and Latin and to European literature more generally.[41] As he finishes the speech of 1833, too, he speaks about the transformation of Indians into a breed of Europeans. Even if British rule in India comes to an end, he says, "it will be the proudest day in English history" because it will mean that Indians have "become instructed in European knowledge and have demanded 'European institutions.' "[42] He concludes: "But there are triumphs which are followed by no reverse. There is an empire exempt from all natural causes of decay. Those triumphs are the pacific triumphs of reason over barbarism; that empire is the imperishable empire of our arts and our morals, our literature and our laws."[43] No less salient than the claim for English trusteeship or the anxiety about imperial decay is Macaulay's triumphalist vision of European literature and the arts and its association with reason over barbarism. It is a vision that, in the pervasive context of empire, points to gentlemanly civility and European letters as the central elements of a regime that encompasses the Company's civil servants and their colonized subjects.

THE MID-CENTURY REFORM

What is striking about the historical record in the first half of the nine-teenth century is the unimportance of Oxford and Cambridge either as potential sources of candidates or as preferred institutional models. Classical Greek and Latin were part of ICS training, in this earlier period, but they were typically part of a wide-ranging curriculum that involved several academic subjects and disciplines. It was Macaulay and Jowett who moved the elite British universities to the center of training for ICS recruits, specifically by giving Greek and Latin a large weight in the com-petitive examinations. The impetus for reform of the ICS and for open competition came not from a desire to make the system more egalitarian or genuinely to open up the ranks to candidates from all backgrounds, but rather to increase the domination of Oxbridge in the examinations and to increase the number of "gentlemen imperialists" in the ICS.

Jowett, in particular, worked vigorously in the early 1850s to win sup-port for the proposed reforms to the ICS. At the time a fellow and tutor of Balliol College, he canvassed William Ewart Gladstone, as the member for Oxford, to support his vision of competitive examinations. In a letter dated 23 July [1853], Jowett wrote to Gladstone:

> The proposal is, in one word, to throw open the final examina-tion. The change is slight, but the advantages are very great—to the University almost incalculable. . . . I cannot conceive a greater boon which could be conferred on the University than a share in the Indian appointments. The inducement thus offered would open to us a new field of knowledge: it would give us another root striking into a new soil of society: it would provide what we have always wanted, a stimulus reaching beyond the Fellowships, for those not intending to take orders: it would give an answer to the dreary

question which a College Tutor so often hears asked by a B.A. even after obtaining a First Class & a Fellowship—"What line of life shall I choose, with no calling to take orders & no taste for the Bar & no Connexions who are able to put me forward in life?" . . . I will not trouble you to answer this letter, believing sincerely that, if you think its object desirable & at the present time practicable, you love Oxford too well not to do what you can for it.[44]

Always one to think about the worldly implications of scholarship, Jowett was clearly campaigning for his students at Oxford and wanted them to gain as large a number as possible of the appointments into the Indian Civil Service. His vision of the open examination was endorsed or supported not just by Gladstone, but also by other prominent figures such as Charles Trevelyan, who was Macaulay's brother-in-law; the Rev. Dr. Charles Vaughan, the headmaster of Harrow; Robert Lowe, then the secretary to the Board of Control; and Lord Aberdeen, the prime minister.[45] Not least among Jowett's supporters was Henry George Liddell, then the headmaster of Westminster but soon to be the dean of Christ Church, and also joint editor, with Robert Scott, of the Greek-English *Lexicon*, the first edition of which had appeared ten years earlier, in 1843.[46] On 14 December 1853, Jowett wrote again to Gladstone to point out that "the election by examination to the Civil Service in India & possibly at home" would place "Oxford in its true relation to the Church & the Country" and "have the greatest effect upon it."[47] Jowett, together with others such as Trevelyan, was explicitly arguing that students from the elite universities ought to have the lion's share of appointments to the Indian Civil Service, not just for the betterment of the nation but for the sake of the universities as well.

In November 1854, a committee consisting of Macaulay, Jowett, and others submitted a report to the Board of Control. As a consequence of the Macaulay committee's report, Haileybury ceased to admit new students after January 1856, and the college itself closed its doors in December 1857. The committee made a series of other recommendations for the examinations of candidates for the ICS, almost all of which were adopted by the government and implemented in the months following the report's submission.[48] Now, as Macaulay's committee argued, the examination would be "not less severe than those examinations by which the highest classical distinctions are awarded at Oxford and Cambridge."[49] As a result of the overall recommendations, examination papers were set in several subjects, with the most marks given to English, mathematics, and Greek and Roman subjects.[50] While no subjects were compulsory, the weight given to classical subjects in the open competition sent a clear signal to candidates who were preparing to take the examination.[51]

Table 1

Examination of Candidates for the Civil Service of India, 1855

Subjects	Marks
English composition	500
English literature and history	500
Language, literature, and history of Greece	750
Language, literature, and history of Rome	750
Language, literature, and history of France	375
Language, literature, and history of Italy	375
Language, literature, and history of Germany	375
Mathematics, pure and mixed	1,000
Natural Science	500
Moral Sciences	500
Sanskrit language and literature	375
Arabic language and literature	375

In the first few years of open competition, the system seemed to achieve its stated goal of attracting Oxbridge graduates; in the very first year, 70 percent of the successful candidates were from Oxbridge, and in the first five years about 60 percent of the successful candidates were Oxbridge-educated. But in the 1860s a decline occurred in the number of Oxbridge graduates who wanted to enter into the ICS. The decline was caused by various factors, but one of them was the lowering of the maximum age limit for admission to the open examination. The Macaulay committee had recommended the age limit of twenty-five, but it fell to twenty-three in 1859, to twenty-one in 1865, and to nineteen a few years later. This meant that Oxbridge graduates, who typically graduated when they were older than twenty-one, were at a disadvantage when it came to qualifying for the open examination. The low point for Oxbridge graduates occurred in the late 1870s when a mere 4 percent of the ICS recruits came from the two universities. However, although the number of students from Oxford and Cambridge who passed the open competition might not always have been high in this period, a significant percentage of successful candidates chose to spend their probationary years (i.e., the period of one or two years between the open competition and the final examination) at the two institutions, which, therefore, managed to exert an influence on them at a later stage of recruitment if not earlier. These attempts were taken by the universities since, apart from other considerations, the Indian appointments were prestigious, and success in the final examination was generally a given.[52]

Benjamin Jowett was also one of the key figures to reverse the decline of Oxbridge students in the open competition. As the result in part of efforts by Jowett, in Oxford, and Henry Sidgwick, in Cambridge, a dramatic turn around was achieved by the early 1890s when, once again, a high percentage, about 78 percent, of the successful candidates to the ICS examination were Oxbridge men.[53] For this increase in graduates from the elite universities, several factors were responsible, as we shall see below, but even in the revised syllabus for the open competition, classics retained its share of the total marks. It accounted for 20 percent of the total in 1860 and about 20 percent again in 1900, while the other languages, including Sanskrit and Arabic, were diminished in relation to their earlier importance. So it seems inevitable that, as late as "1938, the last normal year of British Rule before the Second World War and Independence, of the eight provincial Governors who were members of the I.C.S., six were Oxford men, all of whom had read Greats and taken their degrees between 1897 and 1910: of the remaining three Governors, who were appointed from outside the Service, two were Oxford men."[54]

THE OPEN COMPETITION

In mentioning the dominance of Oxford and Cambridge in relation to the ICS, I do not mean to deny that reform movements were attempting to make changes at the universities, nor do I wish to imply that there was no mobility among the social groups that sent students to the two universities.[55] English educational reform in the nineteenth century has been thoroughly documented, and there is no space to explore it further here. The high degree, however, to which the ICS examinations were contested can be appreciated from the correspondence and official documents of the second half of the nineteenth century. While the age limits and the popularity of crammers were a frequent source of complaint, the curriculum was also widely discussed inside and outside governmental circles. Anxieties, comments, and criticisms about the ICS examinations were expressed as early as 1855, when the changes were introduced.

By 1875 Lord Salisbury, the secretary of state for India and also the chancellor of Oxford, was conducting an official review (begun by his predecessor, the Duke of Argyll) of the selection and training of candidates. In the previous year, he had received a letter from Henry Liddell, now the dean of Christ Church and also chairman of the university's Committee of Council for Reporting on Indian Education, who said that Oxford was prepared to make "such alterations as might, on deliberation, be deemed expedient" to enable greater numbers of ICS recruits to pass through the university. This letter was followed by another, from George Phear, the vice-chancellor of Cambridge, who referred to Liddell's letter and, as if not to be outdone, pointed out that the ICS "would be greatly benefited if the successful candidates could enjoy the advantages of moral and mental training afforded by University residence" in Cambridge.[56]

"The secretary to the Civil Service Commissioners at this time was Theodore Walrond, an old Fellow of Balliol College, who lost no time in discussing the matter with Jowett."[57] Soon after, in a letter dated 27 December 1875, Jowett dispatched a lengthy missive to Salisbury in which he suggested six changes, among which were "limiting the number of subjects which a candidate is allowed to offer to four" and reducing the overall marks given to English subjects in the entrance examination. He disagreed with Liddell on the question of the age limit, and while Liddell suggested eighteen or nineteen as the maximum, Jowett said that it should be twenty-one or, better, twenty-two. In his letter Jowett brought up the subject of crammers [private tutors], and his suggestions were also intended to minimize the role played by cramming in the examinations.[58] In 1874, according to the Civil Service Commission, 84.2 percent of successful candidates had received preparation at crammers, as compared to 32.7 percent in 1865.[59] Many of these, however, had also been educated at public schools and universities, and the cramming seemed to follow or accompany the education received elsewhere.

In 1875 large numbers of civil servants and other officials in India wrote letters, as part of Salisbury's review, about their views on ICS recruitment and training procedures. Not all writers were sympathetic to Oxbridge's claim over the ICS, nor were all in agreement about the importance of classical subjects to the work of the ICS. Out of this vast archive, I select the views of four writers to indicate the range of positions it was possible to take on the subject. First, E. Mc. G. H. Fulton wrote from Karachi to say that even in his day "the proportion of marks given for classics was far too low compared with that given for other subjects" and that "the marks might be doubled" for Latin and Greek.[60] Second, W. Muir argued that, as with the education of English gentlemen, ICS men should also be obliged to know "Latin and Greek, mathematics, English literature and history." But he added that candidates from India should be allowed to substitute Sanskrit, Arabic, and Persian for Latin and Greek.[61] The viceroy, Northbrook, seemed more flexible than some of his subordinates. He did not believe that knowledge of Greek and Latin should be compulsory and, although "an Oxford man," he felt that ignorance of the classical languages should not automatically disqualify candidates from service in India.[62] And fourth, Nanabhai Haridas, an Indian judge of the High Court, wrote that Sanskrit and Arabic were of greater importance for ICS officers than Greek and Latin and that "the Indian classics require to be placed upon a proper footing in relation to their European sisters, as regards the maximum number of marks obtainable in them." The current marks, he said, "do not seem correctly to represent either their difficulty or their importance."[63] Significantly, Haridas does not consider the place of ancient languages on the examination but rather he advocates giving an equal status to both Indian and European classics.

The outcome of the review was not entirely favorable to those who championed the cause of Oxford Greats but it was favorable to Oxford in other ways. The weight given to Greek and Latin changed only slightly after Salisbury's review, and where the classical languages used to count for 750 marks each, now Greek counted for 600 marks and Latin for 800.[64] Sanskrit and Arabic remained at 500 marks each. Out of the overall total number of marks, Greek and Latin together nonetheless accounted for a fractionally higher proportion than under the old system, because of reductions in other subjects. (The English subjects now counted for 900 marks, against 1,500 earlier, and mathematics counted for 1,000 marks, against 1,250 earlier.) With Liddell, but against Jowett, who asked for the age limit to be returned to twenty-two (the limit was reduced to twenty-one in 1866), Salisbury also decided to lower the age limit to nineteen. This was potentially a blow to Oxbridge undergraduates, who would not be able to complete their degrees if they also wished to join the ICS, but it was a much bigger blow to native Indians, who typically needed more time to pass the examination if they were to come to Britain for further preparation.[65] Salisbury, however, also required the successful ICS candidates (i.e., the probationers) to spend at least two years at a university before proceeding to India. In effect, this alteration meant that large numbers of ICS men, each on an annual allowance of £150, passed their probationary years at Oxford, mainly, and Cambridge, to a lesser extent, before arriving in India. Needless to say, Salisbury's measures excited further comment, and were often seen as injurious to the non-elite universities. Lyon Playfair observed in parliament: "His Lordship naturally attached great importance to the distinguished University of which he was the head, and so the Chancellor of Oxford, moved by Oxford, reduced the age to 19 to suit Oxford."[66]

The new system was found to be unsatisfactory in more than one quarter. The educators at Oxford and Cambridge wanted their undergraduates to compete and flourish in the open examination and not just in the final/probationary examination. The presence of ICS probationers, many of whom came with the stigma of the crammers and had little or no university education, was scarcely any compensation for the colleges' inability to secure places in the open competition. Between 1878 and 1882, a scant 4 percent of the ICS recruits came from Oxford and Cambridge combined in the open competition. Between 1887 and 1891, Cambridge's share rose to 15 percent but Oxford was still at 5 percent—this was not quite what Jowett had aspired to.[67] The two-year probationary course was also not perceived to be on a par with the normal university degree in Classics or mathematics. Nevertheless, it should be admitted that Jowett was generally welcoming to the ICS probationers.[68] He appreciated the opportunity given to him by the probationary period to mould students into the future guardians of India. He remained concerned about the relative youth of the probationers and lamented that they were not able to receive a normal Oxford degree in the time they spent at the university. He made several recommendations to the India Office and the Civil Service Commissioners, advocated the teaching of subjects that would be of practical use to the ICS probationers, and at one time even suggested a lengthening of the probationary period so as to give them the opportunity to obtain a university degree.[69] In 1889 he cosigned a letter with Henry Liddell and James Bellamy, the vice-chancellor, in which they asked the secretary of state for India to keep the probationary period to two years and affirmed to him the university's continued interest in the probationers' education.[70]

Assuredly, Indians also exerted pressure on the government. The curriculum was not familiar to Indian candidates, and the age limit of nineteen prevented them from gaining the necessary education in India and England to stand a realistic chance in the open competition. This pressure increased steadily, and in the 1880s a commission was convened and asked to make recommendations to the government. *The Report of the Public Service Commission for 1886–1887*, chaired by Sir Charles Aitchison, guardedly noted the level of Indian discontent and attempted a response. The raising of the age limit to twenty-three was found to be acceptable. Despite demands made in India, and despite the apprehensions of three Indian members, however, the commission stated that it was "inexpedient to hold an examination in India for the Covenanted Civil Service simultaneously with the examination in London." Nor was the commission disposed "to make the examination of a less English and a more Oriental character and to adjust it on terms more favourable to Native candidates."[71] But two further requests were put to the commission on behalf of native candidates: to bring the level of marks assigned to Sanskrit and Arabic to the level of Greek and Latin, and to add Indian vernacular languages to the open competition, placing them on a par with modern European languages.[72] The second request was denied by the commission, again on the view that such a measure would lower "the distinctive English character of the }." Without any sense of contradiction, however, the request concerning Sanskrit and Arabic was endorsed, with the proviso that "the difficulty and searching character of the examination in those languages" be "materially enhanced."[73] The commission claimed that the examinations in Sanskrit and Arabic were too easy and that some candidates had obtained higher marks in these examinations than they would have at Indian universities. While the commission did not quite recommend that Sanskrit and Arabic be deemed equal to Greek and Latin in the examinations, it did nonetheless invite the civil service commissioners "to take into their consideration the question of the adequacy of the marks at present assigned at the open competitive examination to the Sanskrit and Arabic languages, and the suitability of the standard exacted."[74]

In 1892 Viscount Cross, the secretary of state for India (from August 1886 to August 1892), implemented some of the recommendations made by the Aitchison Commission.[75] The age limit was raised to twenty-tree. The possibility of simultaneous examinations in India and London was ruled out, as was the introduction of Indian vernacular languages to the open competition. No change was made to the marks given to Sanskrit and Arabic. The probationary period was reduced to one year. Moreover, the government did implement an important change in the open examinations. "[T]he formal structure of the examination—the papers set and the number of marks allocated to each—was modified to bring it into closer accord with the chief Oxbridge honours courses."[76] Greek and Latin were now allotted 750 marks each, against 600 and 800 respectively in the previous scheme. More importantly, Greek history and Roman history were introduced as separate subjects, and allotted 400 marks each.[77] Thus, classics now accounted for 2,300 marks in literary and historical subjects alone. To this total, one could add the 400 marks for logic and mental philosophy (ancient and modern) and the 400 marks for moral philosophy (ancient and modern), if not also the 500 marks for Roman law, given that philosophy was an important part of Greats in Oxford.[78] Possibly as a concession to Cambridge, a new subject called "Advanced Mathematics" was also part of the list, and allotted 900 marks, so that mathematical subjects now counted for 1,800 marks.

Table 2
Open Competition for the Civil Service of India, 1893

Subjects	Marks
English Composition	500
Sanskrit Language and Literature	500
Arabic Language and Literature	500
Greek Language and Literature	750
Latin Language and Literature	750
English Language and Literature (including special period named by the Commissioners)	500
French Language and Literature	500
German Language and Literature	500
Mathematics (pure and applied)	900
Advanced Mathematical subjects (pure and applied)	900
Natural Science; i.e., any number not exceeding three of the following subjects:—	
Elementary Chemistry and Elementary Physics (N.B.—This subject may not be taken up by those who offer either Higher Chemistry or Higher Physics.)	600
Higher Chemistry	600
Higher Physics	600
Geology	600
Botany	600
Zoology	600
Animal Physiology	600
Greek History (Ancient, including Constitution)	400
Roman History (Ancient, including Constitution)	400
English History	500

(Natural Science subjects bracketed together: 1,800)

Table 2 *(cont.)*

General Modern History (period to be selected by Candidates from list in the syllabus issued by the Commissioners, one period to include at least Indian History)	500
Logic and Mental Philosophy (Ancient and Modern)	400
Moral Philosophy (Ancient and Modern)	400
Political Economy and Economic History	500
Political Science (including Analytical Jurisprudence, the Early History of Institutions, and Theory of Legislation)	500
Roman Law	500
English Law, viz.:—Law of Contract.—Criminal Law—Law of Evidence and Law of the Constitution	500

The impact of these changes was dramatic and immediate. In 1887 to 1891, 5 percent of Oxford undergraduates entered via the open competition; for 1892 to 1896, the figure rises to 52 percent. In the same periods, the equivalent figures for Cambridge are 15 percent and 25 percent. Oxbridge graduates together accounted for about 77 percent of ICS recruits in the years following the new examination requirements, as opposed to 20 percent in the years immediately prior.[79] By one count, about two thirds of the successful candidates offered Latin and Greek, and of the rest, more than half offered mathematics (mathematics and classics were usually not offered by the same candidate).[80] The benefits of the new system for Oxford and Cambridge, and especially for Oxford Greats, were clear.

Thanks to the labors of James Leigh Strachan-Davidson, the classical scholar who was a fellow and later master of Balliol, the ICS tilt toward classics became more pronounced in the next round of major changes, which occurred in 1906. First, the maximum number of marks that a candidate could obtain in the open competition was fixed, and the limit was set at 6,000. Second, the age limit was raised to twenty-four, which meant that an Oxford undergraduate could complete his degree in Greats and then take the ICS examination. And third, the marks given to classics subjects were raised further. In 1911, yet another round of changes took place in the open competition, and the marks for classics increased still further. With the maximum number of marks in the open competition still fixed at 6,000, Greek now counted for an astonishing 1,100 marks if the candidate selected optional verse and prose composition, Latin for 1,100 marks with the same options, Greek history for 500, and Roman history for 500. So, the total for classics reached 3,200 marks, without taking into consideration the marks for moral and metaphysical philosophy (600), logic and psychology (600), and Roman law (500), which remained unchanged. At the same time, the marks for Sanskrit and Arabic were raised slightly, now to 800 each. With such encouragement from the civil service commissioners, the Oxford undergraduate who chose to read Greats knew that the door was held wide open for him if he wanted a career in India.

Table 3
Open Competition for the Civil Service of India, 1911

Subjects	Marks
English Composition	500
Sanskrit Language and Literature	600
Arabic	600
Greek, not less than two sub-divisions, of which one must be Translation:—	
Translation	400
Prose Composition	200
Verse Composition	200
Literature, &c.	300
Latin, not less than two sub-divisions, of which one must be Translation:—	
Translation	400
Prose Composition	200
Verse Composition	200
Literature, &c.	300
English Language and Literature	600
Italian Translation, Composition, and Conversation	400

Table 3 *(cont.)*

Italian, History of the Language and Literature	200
French Translation, Composition, and Conversation	400
French, History of the Language and Literature	200
German Translation, Composition, and Conversation	400
German, History of the Language and Literature	200
Lower Mathematics	1,200
Higher Mathematics	1,200
Natural Science; i.e., any number not exceeding *four* of the following, or three if both Lower and Higher Mathematics be also taken:—	
Chemistry	600
Physics	600
Geology	600
Botany	600
Zoology	600
Animal Physiology	600
Geography	600
Greek History (Ancient, including Constitution)	600
Roman History (Ancient, including Constitution)	500
English History, either or both sections may be taken—	
I. to A.D. 1485–	500
II. A.D. 1485 to 1848	400
General Modern History	400
Logic and Psychology	500
Moral and Metaphysical Philosophy	600
Political Economy and Economic History	600
Political Science	600
Roman Law	500
English Law	500

OXFORD, GREATS, AND THE ICS

The stunning success of Oxford candidates in the ICS open competition lasted into the First World War. In the years from 1892 to 1914, 619 or 49 percent of recruits came from Oxford, 377 or 30 percent came from Cambridge, and 14 percent came from the Irish or Scottish universities. Most of the Oxford recruits had read Greats, and most of the Cambridge recruits mathematics. Only 5.4 percent of the officers who entered the ICS in this period were Indian.[81] Of the Oxford colleges, Balliol's influence was taken as a matter of course, largely because of the impact of Jowett and, after him, of Strachan-Davidson. In the period from 1874/1875 to 1913/1914, 27.1 percent of Balliol matriculates worked in the British Empire outside the U.K., and of these 50 percent worked in the "Indian Services," and an even larger proportion, 58.4 percent, worked in India in some capacity or another.[82] Perhaps less well known is the success of smaller colleges such as Corpus Christi in the open competition. For instance, the college's annual noted that, in 1895, "6 Corpus men had been chosen in the previous examination and that 4 of them had been listed among the top 12 candidates; a remarkable achievement for such a small college."[83] Of students from Corpus who matriculated in the years from 1880 to 1914 and worked in the British Empire outside the U.K., 37.9 percent were known to have worked in the "Indian Services," while more generally 52.1 percent were occupied with some kind of work or other in India.[84] According to Richard Symonds, "most" of the Corpus students "read for Honours degrees in Classics."[85] Their attachment to Oxford and classics was intensely nostalgic and anything but simple. J. J. Cotton, who came from a family with Indian connections, wrote,

> O Corpus, proconsular Corpus
>   Thine Empire is over the sea.
> Though others in Lit. Hum. may dwarf us
>   Thou holdest the wide East in fee.[86]

Malcolm Hailey, who came third in the open competition and was among the most admired of British ICS administrators, wrote some 1,200 pages of letters to P. S. Allen, the president of Corpus, during his first seventeen years in India. In 1901 he wrote to Allen:

> Oxford means more to me than Oxford itself. I want to get back again to the parting of the ways and the world before me again and the confidence (which one had then) that one would do what one liked with the world, a dull thing, to play with as one chose.[87]

In their attachment to Oxford, Hailey's letters are representative of the sentiments expressed, officially and informally, by the university's alumni in India.

How did Oxford's traditional closeness to the centers of power affect the selection and training of ICS candidates? "It would not be fair," Symonds writes, "to suppose that the Civil Service Commissioners in designing the entry examinations for the Indian and Home Civil Services, were deliberately favouring Oxford."[88] But the evidence tends to support the opposite view. Sir Arthur Godley, the permanent under-secretary for India; William St. John Brodrick, the secretary of state for India; and William John Courthope, the chief civil service commissioner, were Oxford men. In a speech to the Congress of Universities of the Empire in 1912, even Sir Stanley Leathes, the first civil service commissioner from 1910 to 1927, and a fellow of Trinity College, Cambridge, "concluded that the nearest approach to the ideal education for administrators in the Empire was in classics and history, which were subjects studied by a much higher proportion of undergraduates at Oxford than at Cambridge."[89]

The India Office records and the *Oxford Magazine* throw considerable light on the relationship between Oxford and the ICS. For instance, the India Office files contain a cutting from the *Oxford Magazine* for 26 October 1892 that was sent by Godley. Godley had distinguished himself in "Mods" at Balliol, but had been too sick to enter for Literae Humaniores; he was the brother of A. D. Godley, the classical scholar and fellow of Magdalen College. The article, which is titled "The Recent Examination for the Civil Service of India," considers the outcome of the ICS open competition, and concludes: "The result must be considered on the whole satisfactory. . . . We will remark at present that a more continuous attention to Greek and Latin scholarship seems to be called for than is usual among senior Oxford undergraduates."[90] In fact, the *Oxford Magazine* had begun to print articles every year on the open competition, and the India Office files contain several of the articles. On 30 October 1893, Godley now sent to Lord Kimberley, the secretary of state for India, an article on the ICS examination from the *Oxford Magazine* of 25 October 1893. The article was accompanied by a note from Godley: "Lord Kimberley. Please look at the marked pages on pp. 23 & 24. The result of this (the second) examination under the new system may be considered satisfactory."[91]

If we turn to the article in the *Oxford Magazine*, we find that out of fifty-six selected candidates in that year, forty-five are described as "University men," of whom twenty-eight come from Oxford, nine from Cambridge, four each from the Scottish and Irish universities; also mentioned, apparently outside this class, is a solitary candidate from Bombay (presumably not reckoned a university man). "As regards the Oxonians, 18 were in for Greats this year."[92] Further, the author is at pains to note that cramming in London was unnecessary for this examination, and that what really contributed to success was the "Oxford experience"—a phrase that is marked by hand in the India Office file.[93] "To ask whether our education, substantially effective as it is, may not be improved by the flowers of Powis square," the author continues, "is to raise a question which those who toiled in that garden through July, rather than a person who made holiday, should answer.[94] But it must have been hot in London, and we will not dissect the Oxford marks too closely."[95] Then comes another passage that evidently roused interest in the India Office since it, too, has been marked by hand in the file:

> Altogether the change in the system seems to have been successful. The I.C.S. is carrying off this year one quarter of the first class in Lit. Hum., several third-year men who might aspire to the same honor, as well as a proportion of the very best men who have (somehow) got into lower classes. Hereafter, when the examination has become more familiar, and the advantage of a pension (payable in gold) of £1000 more fully appreciated, even more 'Varsity men will compete. It is better to rule a province than to starve in a form room."[96]

Given that last judgment, it must have taken a strong editorial wit to follow this article with an unsigned essay about "The Master at Breakfast," in which the reader learns that Jowett "also quoted with great gusto *Od.* xi. 489–91, *bouloimen k'eparouros eon* . . . and gave us Macaulay's version of the lines: 'I had rather live in a garret in Lincoln's Inn than be Viceroy of all India.'"[97] Without going further into the meaning of Jowett's purported words, let us register, for the moment, both the excitement in Oxford about the success of classics undergraduates in the ICS open competition and the manifest approval shown by government officers of these results.

The India Office files are rife with correspondence and papers that show the lurking presence of Oxford and, less prominently, Cambridge. In 1893, for instance, Strachan-Davidson wrote to Godley to ask if he was giving away an extra place in the ICS and, if so, to consider the case of one of his students who took a second in Mods but failed in the ICS.[98] For 1904, the files contain a table comparing the number of recruits from Oxford and Cambridge for 1902 to 1904 and the remark "Allotment of Candidates successful at the Exam. of 1904."[99] According to the notes in another file, copies of which were being sent to India, that was the year when Oxford had forty-three successful candidates in the civil service examinations in general, and Cambridge had twenty-two.[100] On the occasions when decisions were implemented that were unfavorable to Oxford or Greats, the India Office would hear complaints from educators at the university: "Balliol will have only one European candidate likely to sit for Competitive Examination for the Indian Civil Service in August 1921" was in one note sent by the Indian civil service delegacy to the India Office, after the war, at a time when the number of Indians in the ICS began to increase.[101] Another complaint, from Reginald Coupland, the Beit Professor of Colonial History, was about the hardships faced by Greats students under the postwar regulations for the open competition, and it generated a flurry of correspondence going all the way up to the viceroy and indeed to a question put to the secretary of the treasury by Sir Geoffrey Butler in the House of Commons on 3 June 1924, even though it was noted in several responses that in fact Oxford had fared better than Cambridge in the new scheme.[102]

Moreover, it was Strachan-Davidson at Balliol who worked hard to bring about the changes of 1906 and 1911, which immensely benefited his own Greats students more than any others. He for one had been monitoring developments in the open competition as early as 1888, even while his colleague Jowett was still alive.[103] When his biographer J. W. Mackail wrote to the India Office for personal reminiscences, Sir Arthur Hirtzel replied, with a graceful delicacy: "the tradition is well remembered by several who were private secretaries to the Secretary of State or the permanent Under Secretary, of the great interest which was always taken by Mr. Strachan-Davidson in the supply, as servants of India, of those who had the advantage of the best education which Oxford University could give."[104] As Hirtzel goes on to note, the India Office supposed that it was none other than Strachan-Davidson who wrote the articles that appeared each year in the *Oxford Magazine* on the results of the open competition, and indeed the advance proofs of some of these articles appear in his papers. Strachan-Davidson seems to have followed the workings of the Civil Service Commission closely, and the copies of many ICS documents and letters can also be found, with his markings, among his papers.[105] He thought of Arthur Godley as an ally, and once asked Ingram Bywater not to let certain information reach Cambridge ears since he had obtained it confidentially from his friend at the India Office.[106]

Few cases show more clearly the web of connections that drew together Oxford Greats and the ICS than a proposal put forward in May 1898 by Bywater, the Regius Professor of Greek; Henry F. Pelham, the Camden Professor of Ancient History; and J. A. Stewart, White's Professor of Moral Philosophy, to create a single classical school combining the schools of Honor Moderations and Literae Humaniores into a course of study that would be completed in three rather than four years. No doubt with one eye on the three-year classics degree in Cambridge, the signatories to the proposal were trying to ensure that the Greats student could complete his degree and appear for the open competition examination without violating the existing age limit. In other words, they were attempting to change Greats to suit the ICS examination. Against Bywater and others, however, Strachan-Davidson argued for the age limit in the ICS open competition to be increased rather than for a shortening of the four-year Oxford course. He wrote to Godley that "a great system of education will be condemned to extinction, not on its own merits but because it will not be compatible with the I.C.S. competition."[107] A satirical leaflet, probably written by Strachan-Davidson himself, or at the least with his support, pokes fun at the proposal to create a single classical school and a three-year degree. According to the satire, the classics course should be reduced to just one year. The satire notes, "As the Classics are now so thoroughly taught and learnt in all Schools, it is assumed that all Honour students will be competent translators: it is proposed therefore that all translations, whether prepared or unprepared, be abolished." And it concludes: "Equal value to be given to ignorance and obscurity in every branch of the Examination."[108] Strachan-Davidson prevailed, and the degree course was left largely unchanged.

"The imperial mission of Oxford and of Balliol took its most imposing shape in relation to India."[109] To judge by his papers, Strachan-Davidson seems to have been fairly obsessed with the Indian Civil Service and the role of classics in it for the thirty years leading to his death in 1916. Unlike Jowett, he was not overly sympathetic to Indians or to any Indian cause. "I should say," he remarked in his evidence before the Islington Commission, "comparing Indian history with Greek history it is such a small thing." He added, "The questions at issue in Greek and Roman history seem to me infinitely bigger than anything that you get in the East as a matter of education."[110] For him, there could be no better preparation for the Indian Civil Service than the education imparted in Greats. Among his papers are a wealth of letters and memoranda that are especially revealing concerning the behind-the-scenes negotiations that took place prior to official changes in the open competition. His correspondents —and the targets of his suasion—included Godley, Courthope, Leathes, and Viscount Goschen (the chancellor of the university and a former cabinet minister), among others. "To some future historian of higher education in England, and of the English government of India," Mackail wrote, "they will no doubt be valuable sources, less for any actual results to which they led than as throwing light on the relations (so important an element in civilization) of organized national education with the direct service of the Empire."[111]

The papers suggest that it was Strachan-Davidson who, through a good deal of arm-twisting on all sides, managed to persuade the government to fix the maximum number of marks at 6,000 and raise the age limit to twenty-four in 1906. In 1903, moreover, Strachan-Davidson had lobbied to increase the marks allotted to philosophy, which was a vital part of Greats, but had run into opposition from classical scholars at Cambridge such as Richard Jebb, who sought to raise the marks given to composition in Greek and Latin verse.[112] Nevertheless, Strachan-Davidson persuaded the faculty of Literae Humaniores, the faculty of modern history, and the Hebdomadal Council in Oxford to authorize negotiations with the civil service commissioners "so as to give increased weight to the Philosophic in comparison with other and easier subjects."[113] He also convinced present and former professors of philosophy in St Andrews, Glasgow, Aberdeen, and Edinburgh to apply similar pressure to the civil service commissioners.[114] At a universities conference on 18 November 1903, representatives from Oxford, Cambridge, and elsewhere attempted to reach a compromise, but were unable to do so. In the end, the marks for philosophy were raised, though not by as much as he had hoped, and the fortunes of Greats undergraduates were secured for a few more years.[115] Strachan-Davidson's legacy endured for some years, despite his death and the war. From 1921 to 1941, which is often characterized as the period of the university's decline in terms of ICS appointments, Oxford accounted for 170 successful candidates, Cambridge for 158, and other universities for 77.[116]

INDIANS AND THE OPEN COMPETITION

The total number of Indians who succeeded at the open competition from 1855 to 1913 was eighty-four. M. A. Rahim puts this figure in perspective:

> During 1855–1913, the number of Indians who had entered the service through the competitive examination held in London, averaged merely three and [a] half . . . a year out of an average of fifty-three vacancies, or under seven per cent. The maximum number of Europeans successful at the London examination in a single year was eighty-one as against six of the Indians. On an average, ten Indians as against one hundred and seventy-nine Europeans took the London examination annually, the rate of Indian entry being 1.4 per cent. No Indians had appeared at the competitive examination for nine irregular years between 1855 and 1878.[117]

While Greats undergraduates were enjoying high success in the open competition before the First World War, Indian students were still unable to break through the barriers of the examination in any significant manner. Greek and Latin were not solely responsible for the Indians' lack of success in the competition, but they were certainly important contributing factors to the relatively low numbers in which natives gained positions in the ICS.

Table 4

Number of Europeans and Indians recruited in the ICS open competition, 1904–1913

(Source: *India Office Lists* and Potter 1986, 84)

Year	European	Indian
1904	52	1
1905	47	3
1906	58	3
1907	54	4
1908	49	3
1909	50	1
1910	59	1
1911	50	3
1912	40	7
1913	42	1
Totals	501	27

Nothing so direct as a formal or legal restriction lowered the number of Indians allowed to take or pass the competitive examination. But there were strong disincentives. Until the introduction of simultaneous examinations in India and Britain in 1922, the London location remained a problem for most Indians. It took time and money to travel to London. If preparation in Britain was necessary, as it almost invariably was given the syllabus for the examination, the student would need to draw on additional resources and perhaps on family connections. It was also a religious violation in several Hindu communities to journey over the sea, so the Hindu applicant who went to London by boat risked facing sanctions on his return to India. Against all these problems, however, the rewards of an ICS career were manifestly impressive. Quite apart from the power and prestige, the salary itself was high. By 1935 salaries had become so lucrative that the secretary to the government in Delhi earned per month Rs. 4,000, an amount that towers over the monthly incomes at the time of the prime minister of Japan (Rs. 622), the president of Poland (Rs. 1,560), a cabinet member in the United States (Rs. 3,412), or the secretary to the treasury in the U.K. (Rs. 3,333). The governor of the United Provinces (Rs. 10,000) earned almost twice as much as a cabinet minister in the U.K. (Rs. 5,555).[118] When Behramji M. Malabari, in *The Indian Eye on English Life*, refers to a career in the Indian services as "a prize in life," therefore, and says that it "has brilliant examples to fire the imagination of a spirited youth," he is implying that the appeal is not just for British but also for Indian families.[119] Aurobindo Ghose, who learned French, Greek, and Latin at St. Paul's School and Cambridge, was an exception in so far as he "was indifferent to the prospect of becoming one of the few natives privileged to enter this exclusive imperial bureaucracy."[120] He neglected to appear for the riding test in the 1890s even though he had passed the open competition.

Undoubtedly, imperial attitudes and policies were at work as well, though these could not always be voiced openly. Several Europeans were unwilling to accept the authority of Indian judges and supervisors, as the tumult over the Ilbert Bill demonstrated in 1883. Later, Curzon showed racial anxiety in dealing with the issue of ICS natives. Godley had already mentioned Curzon's attitude about native ICS candidates to George Hamilton, the secretary of state for India, when Curzon wrote from the viceroy's camp to Hamilton in a letter dated 23 April 1900:

> Some day I must address you about the extreme danger of the system under which every year an increasing number of the 900 and odd higher posts that were meant, and ought to have been exclusively and specifically reserved, for Europeans, are being filched away by the superior wits of the Native in the English examinations. I believe it to be the greatest peril with which our administration is confronted. MacDonnell says it is all due to Lord Dufferin, who might have insisted upon the racial qualification without exciting a murmur, whereas now there would probably be a storm.[121]

Curzon's fear was not that the natives were gaining admission outside of the examination system but that they were proving to be too successful at it. The actual levels of native recruitment make Curzon's anxieties seem overblown, but the viceroy's sentiments illustrate how reluctant government officials were to open up the ICS to Indians. In fact, the India Office was constantly monitoring the influx of Europeans and Indians and offering written judgement on the comparative numbers of the two groups.[122]

While the government sought to restrict the numbers of Indians in the ICS, many Indians and many Britons agitated for more native positions and better examination conditions. Much of this activity was linked to the movement for Indian independence and the demands for wider Indian representation in government. But even Indian officers inside the ICS and other officials objected to what they perceived as the unfairness of the syllabus. A strong refrain running through the testimony given by Indians before the Islington Commission in 1913 was the high number of marks given to Greek and Latin. If Greek and Latin were going to be weighed highly, the officials noted, then Sanskrit and Arabic should count for the same number of marks. Again and again, the officers recommended that Sanskrit and Arabic should be marked equally with the European classical languages.[123] As Dewan Tek Chand, an ICS deputy commissioner observed, on 9 April 1913, in Lahore, "Sanskrit and Arabic should be given exactly the same importance as Latin and Greek. At present not only Englishmen do not take up the Indian Classics, but even Indians eschew them and find them 'non-paying.' Some Indians take up Latin and even Greek in preference to Sanskrit and Arabic." Chand's point seemed to be that Indian students were not going to be able to compete with British public school boys in Greek and Latin. He added, "Indian History should be recognized as a separate subject to compensate the Indian candidates for their inability to take up Roman and Greek History for want of knowledge of Latin and Greek. If this is not allowed, then Roman and Greek History should be taken out of the syllabus."[124] In Patna, on 27 March 1913, Khan Bahadur Saiyid Fakhr-ud-din, a member of the Bihar and Orissa Legislative Council, went further and said, "I would recommend that Greek, Latin, French and German be eliminated."[125] Other officials objected to the use of Greek and Latin quotations in the non-classical parts of the examination.[126] To be sure, some Indians did not call for an outright dismissal of Greek and Roman subjects, but advocated a balance between the two. Saying that he wished to see the classical languages of both India and Europe in the examination, Sir Pherozeshah Mehta remarked that he had "a great veneration for the culture which can be imparted by a study of Latin and Greek."[127]

What was the Indian aspirant to do in the face of so many obstacles? He could turn to a guidebook for advice. In 1890 A. C. Dutt ("Late Scholar, Christ's College, Cambridge") offered advice to candidates for the ICS examination. He recommends Clifton, if the candidate is looking to join a public school, and does not rule out going to a crammer. As for subjects, he recommends mathematics, English literature, Sanskrit, and Arabic, which can all be learned in India, and French, German, and

Italian, which can be acquired in England. He quickly remarks that, since there is a choice of subjects in the open competition, the Indian student "need not wrestle with the Greek or Latin tenses, which are his most formidable opponents in other examinations in England."[128]

> To candidates from India intending to appear in Latin or Greek, we would give Punch's advice to those about to get married—"Don't." The standard is extremely high. Four or five passages are taken out of the works of authors like Vergil, Tacitus, Plautus, Aristotle, and Homer; which the candidate is expected to translate into English. Unlike the examinations of the Indian Universities, there are no books assigned, from which the passages are taken. A second paper is set, containing two passages from standard English writers to be translated into Latin or Greek prose or verse as the case may be. Thus the candidate who makes a respectable score in classics, must be a good classical scholar. Sanskrit and Arabic do not present very great difficulty to an Indian student who has studied them in India. It is very difficult, however, to obtain efficient instruction in them in England.[129]

For Dutt, the standards for passing in Greek and Latin, but not French, German, and Italian, are set too high. His point seems to be that the Indian student can learn the modern languages sufficiently well for the purpose of the examination but should not even attempt to compete with the British student in Greek and Latin. The Greek and Latin taught in the public schools and the British universities were too far ahead of anything that students could obtain in India. Unlike the case with the modern languages, no amount of cramming or prior preparation would enable natives to overcome the superior training of the British candidates in these fields.[130] But English literature was advisable, since it was widely taught in Indian universities and was practically instituted as an academic discipline in India even before it was taught in the British academy.[131] As Dutt's remarks also indicate, the expense involved in acquiring the requisite education for the open competition was considerable, and not all sectors of society were able to compete realistically for positions in the ICS, whether or not they wished to join it. Between 1892 and 1914, according to the government's classification, 13.1 percent of Indian recruits came from the landed classes and 73.7 percent from the educated middle classes (a group that included civil servants, lawyers, medical professionals, and teachers).[132] This same educated middle class was chiefly responsible for the founding of the Indian National Congress in 1885 and played a prominent role in subsequent nationalist struggles. When, in response to numerous demands from this group, the simultaneous examination was held in India for the first time, in 1922, it was notable for the fact that it offered fifty subjects and that Greek and Latin were not among them.[133]

CONCLUSION

Empire presents a constant and determining context to the role played by Greek and Latin in the history of the Indian Civil Service. It would be possible, given enough time, to show that Greek and Latin served as sites for continuous and highly charged negotiations of imperial power. For instance, the contested issue of the admission of Indians to the civil service, together with the reluctance to hold examinations in India and the relative subordination of vernacular Indian languages, point to anxieties about race and situate Greek and Latin directly in a relationship to racial discourses of colonialism.[134] While Haileybury was entirely closed to Indians, the competitive examinations were notionally open to all subjects in the empire. But that was the theory. In practice, when one of Macaulay's gentlemen passed the examination, the marks for Sanskrit were cut, while Greek and Latin maintained their immense share of the total, and in fact continued to count for ever higher marks until the First World War. The contradictions of the system were as manifest as they were deep. The British civil servants were conceptualized as gentlemen, as were the Indians, but it was widely assumed in the official correspondence that only the former would opt for Greek and Latin in their examinations while the natives would rather pursue other subjects. The empire operated on a racialized notion of civility, then, as official anxieties over the classification of mixed-race (Eurasian) candidates also illustrate. Greek and Latin sustained a mechanism that was notionally liberal and open but was in practice configured along racial axes. The native and the European may have belonged to one administrative elite, and they may have been contemporaries at Oxford or Cambridge, but the Indian appears as "a reformed, recognizable Other," to quote Homi Bhabha, "as a subject of a difference that is almost the same, but not quite." Or, as Bhabha glosses further this formulation, "almost the same but not quite white."[135]

The racialized notion of civility brings into sharp relief as well the question of class ideology, which is inseparable from race in colonial scenarios. Even as they came from different backgrounds and different schools, the British civil servants were conscious of their own class and status vis-à-vis one another, notwithstanding the *esprit de corps* that their memoirs often mention. It was clear to them that the public schools offered the most thorough training in Greek and Latin to their students, and that these students went on to the most prestigious universities, scored the highest marks in the examinations, and obtained the most desirable postings. Moreover, the anxieties, feelings, and imbalances felt by the civil servants were paralleled in another register by the state apparatus. Since the official petitions for Haileybury and the applications for the ICS asked candidates to state their fathers' occupations, the state machinery could all the more easily form an opinion about the social standing of recruits. The official memoranda and correspondence register a range of judgements about the social and familial background of the recruits, and it seems as if almost every year a vast machinery (letters, charts, diagrams, telegrams, proposals and counterproposals, measures and counter-measures) was mobilized around this very issue. But because empire meant the circulation of individuals over distant regions of the globe, the issue of class also cut through racial and national divides. Thus, class often mapped on to social origin, but also on to national origin since civil servants came from Ireland, Scotland, and Wales as well from England and from various groups in India. The prejudice against men from Scottish and Irish universities and against men who had opted for crammers was remarkable.[136] The official files are rife with correspondence from representatives of universities in Britain and Ireland and from the heads of crammers, all of them maneuvering and strategizing with and against each other so as to claim a larger share of appointments to the civil service. Some of the material points to affinity across racial lines, as on the occasion when a kinship developed between a European and an Indian subordinate who exchanged Latin tags with each other, but such affinity was complicated by the real limits placed on natives' ability to rise to the top of an intensely hierarchical civil service.[137] Numerous class alliances, fissures, and tensions were formed, then, within and across racial and national axes.[138]

Mrinalini Sinha has argued that class prejudice and bias in the Indian Civil Service was "also mediated by a racial politics that contrasted the 'manliness' of the British civil servant with the 'effeminacy' of the native civil servant."[139] As she notes, "[t]he mode of masculinity in the colonial administration was that of the 'gentlemanly administrator,' who came ideally from the good public schools and read Classics at Oxford or Cambridge."[140] In a memorandum dated 12 July 1875, C. A. Galton, of the Madras Civil Service, raised the question of manliness, and said that the ICS probationers were more likely to cultivate it in an Oxbridge environment rather than in London. "Nor do I regard as undeserving of consideration the facilities afforded at the Universities for manly exercises. Competition-wallahs have been reproached with effeminacy, as well as with deficiency, in the characteristics of a gentleman, and a taste for field sports and athletic exercises is more likely to be engendered by a residence at Oxford and Cambridge than in London."[141] At about this time in the official correspondence, the natives' masculinity could also be called into question. So a widespread stereotype developed of the clever but effeminate Bengali, that is, the Bengali who did extremely well at examinations but was also "weak-kneed, effeminate, effete."[142] The addition of a horse-riding test to the requirements for the ICS, however, would pose a further challenge to the feminized native, and was perhaps intended to be so by the colonial government, which insisted upon it as an important element of the entrance examination. What this means is that Greek and Latin were key features of an evolving definition of gentlemanly masculinity, in the context of a civil service that was marked by homosocial interaction and that accepted only single unmarried men as candidates for admission through most of its history. There were multiple lines along which imperial power was exercised, therefore, and to understand the workings of imperialism and colonialism is to appreciate the importance of hierarchies (whether based on gender, class, race, or nationality) across groups as well as within them.

In examining these complicated and intertwined relationships, I affirm that the implications of the ICS material for our understanding of empire and of Greek and Latin have yet to be spelled out, and may be connected to issues to which I have only alluded. But plainly there was an important relationship between classics and civil service education, long before Macaulay's Committee, and the later success of Oxford Greats in the ICS competition was achieved by concerted and wilful action on the part of powerful figures in the academy and in government. Our examples illustrate the contradictions inscribed at the heart of the imperial system in which the examinations remained genuinely open only in so far as they stimulated Oxbridge graduates to assume positions of power in a colonial setting. The Greek and Latin requirements should be situated within a complex and evolving context in which official fantasies coincided with the official desire to keep the Indian Civil Service largely free of Indians themselves.

I am grateful to the President and Fellows of Corpus Christi College, Oxford, for the invitation to spend a term in Oxford, and to the University of North Carolina at Chapel Hill for granting me leave from my teaching duties. Drafts of this paper were presented to audiences at Birmingham (the Open University conference on "Classics in Post-Colonial Worlds"), Cambridge (the Philological Society), Durham, Exeter, London (School of Oriental and African Studies), Reading, Stanford, as well as Hay-on-Wye (the UWICAH conference on "Classics in Nineteenth- and Twentieth-Century Britain"). I am grateful to the audience on each occasion for helpful comments and criticism. My heartfelt thanks go as well to Lord Butler, Giovanna Ceserani, Heather Ellis, Barbara Goff, Edith Hall, Stephen Harrison, Miriam Leonard, Fiona Macintosh, Javed Majeed, Helen Morales, Ian Moyer, Peter O'Neill, Julian Reid, Subir Sinha, Christopher Stray, Richard Symonds, and Tim Whitmarsh. An earlier version of this essay appeared in the *Cambridge Classical Journal: Proceedings of the Cambridge Philological Society*, vol. 51 (2005), pp. 35–71. I am grateful to the editors for giving permission to reprint the essay.

Part II

THE IMPACT OF BRITISH CLASSICS IN THE UNITED STATES

Chapter 5

Politics and Scholarship
Basil Lanneau Gildersleeve and
Nineteenth-Century British Classics

⌒—*Ward Briggs*

Basil Lanneau Gildersleeve (1831–1924) considered himself a patriot. It was a particular kind of patriotism: "I was Charlestonian first, Carolinian next, and then a southerner. . . . As against the North, we were southerners, as against England, we were national enough" (Briggs 1998, 35). My essay considers the impact of British classics on Gildersleeve as a scholar and academic statesman. But I also wish to show the deeper political background to his judgments of his British colleagues, for Gildersleeve's highest value was always placed upon the political goal of loyalty to his region and nation rather than upon accuracy or depth of scholarship. As I have described his views of English scholarship elsewhere, I shall necessarily repeat some of Gildersleeve's words here (Briggs 2002).

This sense of loyalty vitally informed his responses to the ancient as well as the modern worlds. Such political engagement as Gildersleeve's is, if not unknown, at least largely undocumented in other classical scholars of his place and time. Fortunately, however, this magisterial figure left us an abundance of autobiographical writings, over seventy editorials written during the Civil War, and nearly forty years of his quarterly column "Brief Mention" in the pages of the *American Journal of Philology*.[1] Diaries from his youth also detail his responses to political events. From such resources we can observe a great intellect as he observes the events of his time to a level of intimacy that reveals a deeply patriotic soul, loyal to his city in the nullification crisis,[2] to his region in the Civil War, and to his nation in the establishment on the world stage of American classical scholarship.

His complicated relationship with Britain begins with his forebears. In a late sonnet to his distant ancestor Pierre La Noue (born 1647), Gildersleeve credits the English and French traits:

> What if my Saxon strain has made me sturdy?
> Has given this mortal frame its fibre tough?
> Thy blood has taught my muse to sing and dance, . . .
> The music of my life I owe to France.
>
> (Mowbray and Norwood 1985, 31)

Both the English and French sides had examples of independence, sacrifice, and heroism against the British, from the era of the Mayflower through the Revolution and the War of 1812; examples that remained vivid in Gildersleeve's mind throughout his long life.

His American bloodlines reach back nearly to the European settling of the country. The founder of the Gildersleeve line in America was Richard Gildersleeve (1601–1681), a Puritan who emigrated from his native Suffolk to Massachusetts in 1635 rather than deal with Archbishop Laud. He was a founder of at least five colonies in Connecticut and New York, including Wethersfield and New Haven. Basil Gildersleeve's grandfather, Finch Gildersleeve (1751–1812), left the weaver's trade in 1775 and signed the Association supporting the Continental Congress. He joined the Continental Army in New York, served under Aaron Burr (1756–1836), and survived the horrible winter at Valley Forge. The young nation rewarded his heroism with a tract of 1,200 acres near Scipio in upstate New York. When Gildersleeve said of his own war service, "I believe I did not disgrace my Revolutionary ancestors," he was referring chiefly to Finch (Briggs 1987, 283).[3]

British cruelty appears in Basil Gildersleeve's maternal line. His mother's father, Bazile Lanneau (1746–1833) was one of the Acadians who were expelled by the British in 1755 from their Canadian homes and sent to America. Most of the Acadians fled to Quebec or Louisiana (like Longfellow's Evangeline), but Lanneau, his family, and six hundred others were put aboard a ship bound for South Carolina, where Catholicism was outlawed. The ship languished in Charleston harbor for two weeks. Bazile lost his mother and sister while the British temporized, leaving him an orphan in a strange city at the age of nine. Lanneau became a prosperous tanner whose home was confiscated by the British during the occupation of Charleston in 1782. After the Revolution he served three terms in the South Carolina General Assembly. In the War of 1812, his home was again confiscated by the British, "from some of whom he received insults and indignities, which he could never forget."[4] Basil recalled, "My own grandfather fostered my patriotism by telling stories about the insolence of the British during their occupation of Charleston" (Briggs 1998, 37).

In Gildersleeve's youth there were plenty of veterans of 1812 and many from the Revolution to celebrate each June the biggest holiday of the year, "Palmetto Day," commemorating the British surrender of Fort Sullivan in 1776. There were still some old loyalist families who sent their sons to Oxbridge, but "There was no such thing as Anglomania then, except perhaps in a limited circle in which the ancestral connection with England was kept up" (Briggs 1998, 37).

Thanks to the departure of the British in 1815 and the imposition of the Monroe Doctrine, the decade preceding Gildersleeve's birth was free from fear of European invasion. Though it is known as "The Era of Good Feelings," it was in fact an era of regionalism and sectional mistrust which came to a head when the Congress in 1828 imposed a 50 percent tariff upon imported goods, which hit South Carolinians and particularly Charlestonians so hard that the ensuing controversy was often called "Carolina fever." "We export to import," said John C. Calhoun (1782–1850) who, in the year of Gildersleeve's birth, claimed the right of a state to nullify any unjust law (particularly any punitive tariff) of the federal government. A year later he resigned the vice-presidency to return to the U.S. Senate to fight for his state's rights. Thus Gildersleeve's earliest memories include his home and city singled out for persecution by an act of Northern aggression:

> Nullification, the forerunner of disunion, rose from a question of tariff. The echoes had not died out when I woke to conscious life. I knew that I was the son of a nullifier, and the nephew of a Union man. It was whispered that our beloved family physician found it prudent to withdraw from the public gaze for a while, and that my uncle's windows were broken by the palmettos of a nullification procession; and I can remember from my boyhood days how unreconciled citizens of Charleston shook their fists at the revenue cutter and its "foreign flag." Such an early experience enables one to understand our [Civil] [W]ar better. (Briggs 1998, 395)

With nullification, the North replaced Britain as the South's worst enemy, and Britain remained one of the South's best trading partners.

The "Silver Age" of classical studies in America was coming to a close and the debate over the state of classical studies in America was less an educational than a political one (Reinhold 1976, 181–213). The classics had served the Founding Fathers well, but now the new nation argued whether to seek independence from British dependence on classics. Could the traditional classics-based curriculum be truly American? There were calls for a national literature by Joel Barlow (1754–1812), a national university by Benjamin Rush (1745–1813), and a new type of American scholar by Ralph Waldo Emerson (1803–1882), all of which were directed away from studies that were considered elitist, irrelevant, and useless. To many it was patriotic to eschew the classics. But classics had a remarkable resiliency in the schools and continued to live on despite assaults.

In the home of the Reverend Benjamin Gildersleeve (1791–1875) there was no such debate about the value of ancient literature. With his father as teacher until he was twelve, Gildersleeve devoured the classics of antiquity. "It was, as I remember it, a very tumultuous affair, that earliest education of mine. I could read when I was between three and four years of age, and signalized the completion of my fifth year by reading the Bible from cover to cover" (Briggs 1998, 39). He also read Plautus, Terence, and the first books of Ovid's *Metamorphoses*. In 1843 he translated Plato's *Crito* "to show myself worthy of the gift" and then "I translated the so-called Anacreon into English rhyme, untroubled by questions of higher criticism and pagan morality" (Gildersleeve 1909, 14), and apparently British sympathy. All this, before he was thirteen. By fifteen he had read "all Caesar's Gallic War, all Vergil, all Horace, a number of Cicero's Orations, the Laelius and the Cato, Sallust, Juvenal, parts of Tacitus. These I recall distinctly, as also Cicero's *De Oratore*" (Briggs 1998, 68).

There being virtually no American literature, the boy read what was at home, his father's favorite poet, John Milton, then what was considered too "immoral" for the home of a divine: Shakespeare (Briggs 1998, 41) and the novels of Sir Walter Scott, so popular among Southerners at the time that Mark Twain blamed the Civil War on "the Sir Walter disease":[5]

> [S]ome of my happiest hours have been spent among the scenes conjured up by the Wizard of the North, as he was then called, though I had to hold myself in readiness to tuck the volume under the sofa pillow whenever I heard a certain heavy step. In his old age my father became a novel-reader himself, but I never confessed my sin to him. (Briggs 1998, 41)

In any case it was by reading English novels that Gildersleeve conceived the notion of becoming a creative writer before he and his family left Charleston. He said, "I only drifted into classical philology. I am a *littérateur manqué*" (Miller 1930, 372).

His earliest views reflected the Anglophilia of his native city. 'Brought up in old-fashioned ways and in an old-fashioned environment, which might almost be called "colonial," I had been taught or at all events had conceived a profound admiration of English scholarship, especially in its lighter manifestations' (Miller, 365). In 1844 English scholarship was the gold standard, at least in the Gildersleeve household.

After one year at the College of Charleston, Gildersleeve moved with his family at the age of thirteen to Richmond where his father had been called to edit a larger religious newspaper. Not so dependent on the export trade and not feeling as beleaguered by the nullification issue as South Carolina, Virginia, which thought of itself as the mother of the republic by virtue of having produced six of the then eleven presidents, maintained a determinedly federal outlook that tempered the young man's ardent regionalism.

Basil longed to go to the University of Virginia, but it was "under the ban of the Presbyterians" as "more or less hostile to religion" (Bruce 1921, 3:133). A friend of his father had assumed the presidency of Jefferson College in western Pennsylvania and thence Basil was sent. There away from his family for the first time, rooming alone, and unchallenged by his schoolwork, he made books his friends and read some seventy-five in his time at Jefferson, including over thirty novels, mostly Dickens, Tupper, Hood, and Smollett, with some continental writers like Eugene Sue and Mme. de Staël.[6] By April he had found himself "morally much under the influence of Carlyle" thanks to reading *Sartor Resartus*, but before long he began to read Goethe, "the most important of all the teachers I ever had," "the guide of my youth" (Briggs 1998, 45).

His judgment of Britain was aimed not at the great scholars but at the way those men were treated by a system that did not know how to treat genius. In February 1847 he found in an old copy of Joseph Dennie's (1768–1812) Philadelphia-based *Port-folio* (1801–1812) some scholarly spoofs by the great Cambridge Hellenist Richard Porson (1759–1808). He purchased one of his first works of classical scholarship, a four-volume edition of Porson's Euripides (Leipzig: Tauchnitz, 1810–1811). Then he remembered Pope's treatment of Bentley in the *Dunciad*:[7]

> It is sad to look at the full-length caricature of Bentley, which Pope has drawn, with such malicious distortion, in his *Dunciad*, and to reflect upon the uniform fate of all those great men who have been sent to that ungrateful people. In seeking and acquiring a teaching class that "gives little offence" they have received their 'just punishment': their ideal teacher is Dr. Richard Busby (1606–95), the headmaster of Westminster School, known more for his severe discipline than his scholarship, of whom Oliver Goldsmith wrote,

Yet he was kind; or, if severe in aught,
The love he bore to learning was in fault. (Miller 1930, 367)

Slowly his Charlestonian admiration of the British had begun to wane.

As I grew up, I found that the authors of all the great dictionar-
ies, the great grammars, the great works of reference bore German
names and, when at the age of sixteen I began in earnest the study of
German, there was an end of any deference to English scholarship.
(Miller 1930, 365)

The second formative event of Gildersleeve's youth occurred after
the move to Richmond. The Mexican War (1845–1848), America's
first foreign war, was conducted by a military that was predominantly
Southern, led by Virginian general Zachary Taylor (1784–1850). One
of America's most impressive military campaigns, it was also the first to
be photographed and covered by newspaper correspondents, so young
enthusiasts across the nation received daily reports from the front lines
of smashing victories. The teenaged Gildersleeve recorded in his diary a
thrilling account of the battle of Resaca de la Palma (Gildersleeve 1847,
9 May). While many have traced Southern participation to the desire to
expand slavery into the new territories acquired by Mexico's defeat, Gildersleeve's generation took great pride in the achievements of Southerners
in winning this national victory.[8]

When his "Teutonomania" began in earnest at Princeton (1848–1850),
Gildersleeve noticed that the humanists were British-trained while the
scientists were largely trained in Germany. From this he concluded
that the English were essentially amateurs and Germans were serious
investigators. Graduating fourth in his class, Gildersleeve gave for his
Belles Lettres Oration, "A Comparative View of English and German
Literature." By now he was, as he said, "daft on the subject of German"
(Briggs 1998, 62).

There was of course never any question of his going to England for
postgraduate work after Princeton. Britons in Charleston and Richmond
tended to be schoolmasters, not professors. Germany offered exciting
discoveries, majestic professors who were publishing great works, col-
legial fellow students, and most of all, a Ph.D., something no university
in Britain could offer.[9] But chiefly, Gildersleeve still bore the family
grudge against the British. In the following quotation one can see how
the wounds inflicted by the British on his family bled into his view of
British scholarship:

[I]n the fifties an American Anglomaniac was a rarity and the German attitude towards English scholars gave no offense to the patriotic American neophyte, for I was brought up on the memories of

my revolutionary ancestors. I bore a deep-seated hereditary grudge against those whose forbears were responsible for the expulsion of the Acadians, the sufferings of Valley Forge, the burning of Norwalk, the insolent behaviour of British officers during the occupation of Charleston, and I was quite ready to be impressed by the judgments of my German masters. (Miller 1930, 366)

In his three years of postgraduate study at Berlin, Göttingen, and Bonn (1850–1853), there is little mention of Britain or the British in his diaries. He met no Englishmen in Germany, and though he traveled extensively, he never set foot in the British Isles. He found it easy to share his professors' dismissive attitude toward British scholarship:

> I learned to imitate my [German] masters, who all, or nearly all, were supercilious in their bearing toward English classicists. Every now and then, they said, England gives birth to some great genius, such as Bentley, such as in a lesser degree Porson. . . . Few of the German classical scholars of my day even pretended to know English and I have had to act as interpreter of English announcements of important discoveries, such as Babington's Hyperides.
> (Miller 1930, 366)

When he returned to Richmond and no prospects, he found that the events of 1848 had deposited a number of Germans in his home city, where he could now enjoy *Lagerbier* and attend a *Turnverein* (Briggs 1987, 13). Flush with a Ph.D. with honors from Göttingen, he published his maiden essay, "The Necessity of the Classics," which praises German research and sets classical study in the center of American cultural life. (Gildersleeve 1854). Gildersleeve does not spare the English system, with its concentration at all levels on verse composition rather than accurate philology.

> Classical education in England has been, for long years, one huge polypus of verse-making, an exercise which, however useful, still stands, in a pedagogical point of view, far behind the exercise of writing prose, not so much on account of the disproportion in numbers between those who possess the faculty divine and those who do not, as because vapidity and inanity cannot conceal themselves so well on the plain ground of the pedestris oratio, as in the flight of an anser inter olores, nor loose syntax and careless constructions shelter themselves behind the convenient plea of poetic license.
> (Gildersleeve 1854, 13)

Citing errors in metrical quantities by men from William Paley to William Pitt, he characterized the English as "The most earless nation on earth, which cannot show a single composer of real eminence—prides itself upon an accuracy for which there is no parallel save that of a deaf musician" (Gildersleeve 1854, 12).

Gildersleeve had little confidence in reformers like Matthew Arnold and John Stuart Blackie.[10] In "The Limits of Culture" (1867) he wrote:

> Nor can we feel astonishment or resentment when reformers declaim against the fearful waste of time in the classical schools of England, in which the prime of boyhood is spent over the composition of execrable Greek and Latin verses, to the exclusion of other valuable matter even in the domain of the classics themselves. In order that one boy may improve a knack at versification, five hundred are sent out without a decent knowledge of Latin prose composition so that the foreign sneer—that is to say, "You cannot expect better Latin from an Englishman"—is, at least, comprehensible. (23)

In 1856 he was appointed to the chair of Greek at the University of Virginia, the institution his father, like many Virginians, considered godless. Moreover, Thomas Jefferson, attempting to create a radically different American university, composed his first faculty entirely of foreigners, mostly English, including the classicist George Long (1800–1879), and the brilliant Jewish mathematician James Sylvester (1814–1897). Most of the British had left the frontier college town within the decade and been replaced with Virginians like the classicist Gessner Harrison (1807–1862), Long's protégé. Soon the University had its first Ph.D. and others with European rather than English training, such as Dr. Maximilian Schele De Vere (1820–1898) in modern languages.

Though most of the faculty found a way to serve the Confederate cause in the Civil War, only two faculty members actually enlisted in the line, the two classicists. Lewis Minor Coleman, professor of Latin, was killed at Fredericksburg in December of 1862, and Gildersleeve was shot in the leg carrying orders for General John B. Gordon near Weyer's Cave in the Shenandoah Valley of Virginia in September 1864. Gildersleeve served in the summers after teaching all the Greek and Latin during the four years of war. For nearly two years (1863–1864) he contributed fire-breathing editorials to the most widely read paper in the South (and parts of the North), the *Richmond Examiner* (Briggs 1998, 115–339).

Like most Southerners he expected support from the British (as well as the French), including Gladstone, then Chancellor of the Exchequer, but Britain would not recognize the Confederacy, did not break the Union blockade, and declared that Britons in America could not be impressed into service on either side (see further Berwanger 1994). The 1862 treaty forged by Lincoln's secretary of state, William Seward (1801–1872) and the U.S. minister to Great Britain, Charles Francis Adams (1807–1886), with Lord Lyons in 1862, suppressing the African slave trade and guaranteeing English neutrality in the war, was considered a betrayal of the South, flushing away any vestiges of Anglophilia: "The [Civil] war changed the attitude of the South toward England" (Briggs 1998, 38). After the Emancipation Proclamation of 1863 altered the pretext of war from one of Southern sovereignty to human slavery, no European nation could support the South.

When Seward attempted to enlist the British on the side of the North in 1864, Gildersleeve wrote of the Yankees:

> they have made such free use of the British lion. If the chestnuts are not too hot, his leonine majesty will rake them out of the coals for the Ape of Illinois [Abraham Lincoln] and for Seward, his showman, and if they are too hot and the awakened dupe utters an angry roar, the Yankee menagerie-keepers have but to stroke his bristling mane or, if the worst comes to the worst, to retire in pretended fright from the scene of the action. (Briggs 1998, 270)

Following the war, he remained a staunch regionalist and this regionalism informed his scholarship. The majestic style of Pindar may have been part of the Theban poet's appeal for Gildersleeve, but no small part was played by Pindar's "experience of the losing side." In 1885 his New York publishers tried to have him remove the following paragraph from the introduction to his edition of Pindar's Olympian and Pythian Odes, but Gildersleeve refused; he was not being provocative, he was stating the lesson from Pindar that was nearest his own experience:

> The man whose love for his country knows no local root, is a man whose love for his country is a poor abstraction; and it is no discredit to Pindar that he went honestly with his state in the struggle. It was no treason to Medize before there was a Greece, and the Greece that came out of the Persian War was a very different thing from the cantons that ranged themselves on this side and that of a quarrel which, we may be sure, bore another aspect to those who stood aloof from it than it wears in the eyes of moderns, who have all learned to be Hellenic patriots. A little experience of the losing side might aid historical vision. (Gildersleeve 1885, xii)

Of Pindar Gildersleeve said, "If he had not been a true Theban, he would not have been a true Greek." His familiar essays, dating from thirty years after the war, "The Creed of the Old South" and "A Southerner in the Peloponnesian War," show how thoroughly his understanding of the modern world was bound up with his understanding of the ancient. This extended to events, as he compared Sphacteria to the battle for Morris Island, South Carolina, or Plataea to Vicksburg, but it was indicative of the deeper affinities he continually found between the era he studied and that in which he lived (Briggs 1998, 399).

The idealistic view of Germany began to pale after the Franco-Prussian War of 1870. Gildersleeve wrote in 1878, "Since the late war with France it is no secret that the land of scholars has lost much of its attraction in the eyes of scholars, because it has become so strong, so despotic. 'Brutal' is a hard word, but the type of German materialism is the most brutal of all" (Miller 1930, 330).

Thus we have seen that Gildersleeve, eternally associated with the Old South and its creed, had in fact truly national bloodlines, a Northern (and English) hero of the Revolution on his father's side, and a Southern (and French) victim of 1812 on his mother's. He had fought heroically and written passionately for his region before, during, and after the war. With the call to be the first academic appointment at the new Johns Hopkins University in 1876, he fulfilled a partly political role. It was important to Baltimore, a city known for its Southern sympathies, that the South with its proud humanistic tradition be represented in this new kind of national graduate university. Johns Hopkins in his will had even provided special scholarships for Southern boys. From this position Gildersleeve wrote and lectured frequently on the rising role of the learned professions in America.[11] He also became famous for two often reprinted political pieces, "The Creed of the Old South," and "A Southerner in the Peloponnesian War" (Gildersleeve 1892, 1897).

Of course Gildersleeve was also responsible for defining and helping to professionalize American classical study from this new American university founded on the German model (Hawkins 1960). In 1879 he set forth his program, comparing the German seminary he was recreating in America to "the tutorial grind of England" (Gildersleeve 1879, 126). He depicted the particular qualities that distinguished American from European stereotypes and made them especially suited to deal with the ancients:

> An audacious, inventive, ready-witted people, Americans often comprehend the audacious, inventive, ready-witted Greek à demi-mot, while the German professor phrases, and the English "don" rubs his eyes, and the French savant appreciates the wrong half.
> (Gildersleeve 1879, 122)

His encounters with the "dim dons" of his description during his maiden voyage to Britain in 1880, seeking a Latinist for the Johns Hopkins University, have been elaborated elsewhere (Briggs 2002, 118–20). His letters back to Hopkins president Daniel C. Gilman (1831–1908) are masterpieces of description, but they rely not so much on evaluation of scholarship and specialty as on physical performance, following the model of the just-quoted stereotype (Briggs 1987, 89–123). Arthur Woollgar Verrall (1851–1912), of Trinity College, Cambridge, "would be a laughing-stock on account of his peculiar mode of speech" (100), while Jebb is

> an excessively nervous man and all the time he is lecturing tries to make a double spiral twist out of his legs and casts from side to side an agonized stare at his auditors. His voice is high-pitched, fashionable English style, though not so disagreeable as most readers of that persuasion make it. And his utterance is broken every few minutes by a distressing hysteric cough. When he translates poetry, he lets his voice fall into the lower ranges, which are not unpleasant, only you wonder which is his own voice. Of course the language is elegance itself and the literary judgment in the main sound.
>
> (Briggs 1987, 102)

Of Robinson Ellis (1834–1913), professor of Latin at University College, London, he said, "A more awkward, ungainly, unworldly, blundering man it is impossible to conceive" (Briggs 1987, 103).

Even the Reverend Walter William Skeat (1835–1912), Anglo-Saxonist at Cambridge, and the unemployed Henry Sweet (1845–1912), the model for Shaw's Henry Higgins, fit the vaudeville mold: "Skeat had the aspect of a tired and discouraged teacher of a girl's school and has no literary faculty that I can learn. . . . Sweet, though a very young-looking man of his years, seems to be largely employed in the study of his spectacles, has no vivacity—no go" (Briggs 1987, 99). As at Princeton, he found that "[t]he scientific men are much more alert—more like ourselves" (99).

In Gildersleeve's view, the Scottish system hardly strained the teacher: at Glasgow, "For five months work Jebb receives some £1200. [Professor of Latin George Gilbert] Ramsay [1839–1921] very much more" (Briggs 1987, 94). In fact, though, whether Gildersleeve realized it or not, the Scottish system was not the English: Jebb and Ramsay had lecture classes of over 100 students of widely varying age and educational experience; very different from Oxford tutorials.[12] At Edinburgh William Young Sellar (1825–1890) though "very clever" is "supremely lazy at least—works only as the fit seizes him—and is utterly ignorant of the course of study on the continent" (94). The dullness is highlighted by the exception: Lewis Campbell (1830–1908), professor of Greek at St Andrews, was "not a very strong man," but he "is bright and enthusiastic and his speaking face is a pleasant contrast to the wooden visages one encounters on every hand" (103). There are the learned but frequently the not so learned: In Dublin he found that the Hellenist John Pentland Mahaffy (1839–1919) "knows everything," while the two Latinists, Louis Claude

Purser (1854–1932) and Arthur Palmer (1841–1897), "know little or nothing" (Briggs 1987, 91–92). The model of everything wrong with the system was Benjamin Jowett (1817–1893), Regius Professor of Greek at Oxford, "a laughing stock among Greek scholars for his inaccuracy, his strength lying simply in the elegance of his style" (Briggs 1987, 103).

Nevertheless, they are productive: "What surprises me is that men whom [Peter Guthrie] Tait [1831-1901], [professor of mathematics at Queen's College, Belfast] represents as given up to cards and chess and all manner of extraneous studies and amusements should still accomplish so much more in the way of authorship than our own American professors, who stick more closely to their work" (Briggs 1987, 94).

But learning without personality holds no appeal for Gildersleeve and the issue lies with the system:

> While the boys here [at Cambridge] are very charming and straight-forward, the continuance of schoolboy life, if I may say so, into maturer years breeds a certain ineptness for dealing with our prob-lems and the best scholar in the world who has not diversified his life more than some of the specimens I meet here, would be singu-larly unfit for organizing a new department. (Briggs 1987, 100)

"The peculiar constitution of the English universities is almost necessarily fatal to the development of those qualities which we want in a classic," he wrote Gilman (Briggs 1987, 99). Though the Scots have more "fire" than the average Englishman, "Scotland is not very promising soil for the rearing of the kind of men we want. The best are themselves exotics or natives largely grafted on" (Briggs 1987, 96).

The model of everything that was right about the system was Gild-ersleeve's favorite at Oxford, Ingram Bywater (1840–1914), later Regius Professor of Greek: "if there were a man in Latin at all like him, he would be worth all the compassing of sea and land which I have undertaken" (Briggs 1987, 102–3).

The verve and vigor, however, Gilman and Gildersleeve were looking for were not to be found and the dons knew it: "Bywater said he thought we should find better and broader men in America. . . . Nettleship declares there isn't a suitable man except [tutor at Exeter College, Oxford, Henry Francis] Pelham [1846–1907], and Pelham is rich[,] besides hav-ing switched off to the historical side" (Briggs 1987, 107). Gildersleeve concluded from London, "There is no more hope of a professor of Latin in England than there is in America and the complaints of utter deadness are as rife here as they are there" (Briggs 1987, 109).

Despite the oddities of their lecture styles, Jebb, Campbell, and Ellis, along with W. M. Lindsay (1858–1937) and A. E. Housman (1859–1936), contributed to Gildersleeve's *American Journal of Philology*, launched later in 1880.[13] The support of these eminent scholars did much not only to enhance the quality of the young journal but to gain it the international recognition that Gildersleeve had hoped for. Whatever disappointments Gildersleeve's "long compassing of land and sea" may have brought to the Johns Hopkins, it signaled a turn away from Gildersleeve's resentment and deprecation of the British and their scholarship. His relations with his British contributors were long and cordial, reaching fruition in 1905 when he received a D.Litt. from Cambridge on 14 June, and from Oxford on 28 June.

By the second year of World War I, at the age of eighty-five, Gildersleeve's views had oscillated back in favor of British scholarship, now accusing the Germans of the failures of literary acumen as he had faulted the British for errors of quantity (Miller 1930, 364–76). To what extent was this due to the political alliance of the United States with Britain against the imperial Germans, now demonstrating the brutality of German materialism in ways Gildersleeve had not dreamed of in 1878? Or was it the British contributors? "Of late years personal intercourse with English people on their own soil and generous recognition and cooperation on the part of English scholars, have made the 'Old Home' a place of pleasant sojourn for me" (Briggs 1998, 38).

By 1916 the reformed Cambridge Tripos of 1879 and the Oxford revisions of 1880 had broadened the scope of subjects in classical study at the great institutions, removing the heavy emphasis on composition that Gildersleeve had so despised (Stray 1999). The young generation of Gilbert Murray (1866–1957) and Jane Harrison (1850–1928) were incorporating anthropology and comparative religion into their studies of classical myth and ritual. Murray in particular, unlike Sellar, knew German work, and was in contact with the great Ulrich von Wilamowitz-Moellendorff (1848–1931). Murray himself had also written an article in the *Quarterly Review* on the distinction between German and English scholarship in which Gildersleeve, who praised the article, was himself praised. That Wilamowitz said, according to Gildersleeve, "the only hope for the future of Greek scholarship is in England" at last united Germany, England, and America in a way politics could not touch (Miller 1930, 369).

How to summarize Gildersleeve's politics? Again he provides the best description by analogy. When he describes his admired Aristophanes, he might well be describing the lifelong loyalty to his own region and nation and the ferocity with which he defended it.

> Aristophanes, it seems, was not a partyman. He was swayed by feelings rather than by programmes. He was a man of instinct rather than a man of ratiocination. He was a lover of the country

and the country deme, where life was easier and saner. . . . He had a pronounced aversion to sterile ambition, to hard and malignant egotism, to all intellectual curiosities, whether legitimate or not. The Athens, where all this was realized, was his Athens and he loved her passionately. Those whom he accused of corrupting her and ruining her, he hated as if they were his personal enemies; and in his advocacy of good understanding, harmony and mutual confidence, there were no bounds to the bitterness, vehemence, injustice, with which he followed up the men, who according to him fomented discord and hatred among the citizens. (Miller 1930, 130–1)

That he for a period wielded his pen like a claymore as ferociously against the British as he had against the North in the Civil War is less important than the fact that as so often in his long life (Gildersleeve 1901, 45–50), his views ultimately oscillated back to his comfortable boyhood admiration of the British originality, adaptability, and humanity that were his own ancestral birthright.

Chapter 6

Grace Harriet Macurdy

The Role of British Classics in the Self-Fashioning of an American Woman Scholar

ᴑ—*Barbara F. McManus*

Grace Harriet Macurdy (1866–1946)[1] came of age at a crucial moment, a time when women in America were just beginning to find opportunities for professional academic careers as classical scholars. The only well-trodden paths before her had been laid out by men, and there was pressure to stay on these paths as quietly and unobtrusively as possible, since American men were worried that female colleagues would hold back their own efforts to keep up with the British and German classicists confidently striding ahead of them. Instead of conforming to this pattern, Macurdy forged a new path, one that enabled her to win recognition as a classical scholar who also spoke authoritatively as a woman and who ultimately focused her research on the lives of ancient women. This essay explores how Macurdy fashioned herself as a new kind of woman scholar by exploiting opportunities offered in the American classical community while drawing inspiration and support from British classicists.

In the summer of 1908, Grace Macurdy became the first woman to teach in the academic program of Columbia University. When she wrote to Gilbert Murray about this landmark achievement, she characteristically couched her own accomplishment in terms of praise for his work, telling him that she had used his *Rise of the Greek Epic* in her class:

111

My students in that class were mostly men and of a very good sort, graduated from college and teaching in New York or thereabout. I was the only "lady-professor", as the janitor called me and had some fears about a new kind of work. But . . . every thing went well and in both years my students thanked me again and again for their acquaintance with your work.

(25 September 1909: GM 157.7–10)[2]

In his response, Murray linked her with what he saw as a similar situation in his own country: "It is very interesting that you have been lecturing to a class chiefly of men. Miss Harrison has sometimes done that over here, but very few other women scholars. It is all good for the cause" (6 October 1909: VC Autograph File; photocopy at GM 157.207).[3]

The situation of these two women classicists, each a pioneer in her own country, was not really so similar, however, though Murray was correct in claiming that both were "good for the cause." A key difference lay in their professional status, for Macurdy had earned a doctoral degree from a major university, had a recognized professional position carrying the academic rank of Associate Professor (albeit in a women's college), and was teaching credit-bearing courses to mostly male students at Columbia University (albeit in the summer program). Harrison, in contrast, did not have professional academic credentials, was never a member of the university at which she taught, and never lectured to men as part of their regular academic program.[4]

Part of this dissimilarity was due to the different way that higher education for women had developed in the United States and England, although the process began at approximately the same time in both countries. First, most women's colleges in America were founded as independent institutions, separate from colleges and universities for men. England had a very different model; there colleges for women began as residences informally attached to the large male universities. The male members of these universities had to vote on offering educational privileges to women, and they did so for the most part very grudgingly. Thus the opening up of full educational opportunities for women occurred much more slowly in Britain than in the United States.

Secondly, American women's colleges were founded with the goal of offering women a liberal arts education equal to that provided by colleges for men; since a significant percentage of their faculty were women, the very existence of these colleges prompted American universities to begin admitting women to their graduate programs and gave women opportunities for academic positions after they had earned doctoral degrees. In contrast, the British system was initially based upon the concept that women's education was essentially nonprofessional.[5] An anecdote from the centenary of the University of London, the earliest English university to admit women to degrees (Eschbach 1993, 122–23; Harte 1986, 126–27), shows how little the British academic establishment understood the American system as late as 1936. London had invited colleges, universities, and learned societies from around the world to send delegates to the centenary celebrations; these were listed on the official program by country. Under the heading United States, one finds a list of institutions whose order is presumably determined by prestige: first universities, then liberal arts colleges, then several institutes of technology. Instead of including Bryn Mawr, Smith, Vassar, and Wellesley among the liberal arts colleges, where they belonged, the program lists them under a separate, italicized heading, *Women's Colleges*, making the United States the only country to have two separate headings for institutions of higher education (UL, CT 7/2/2).[6]

Even more revealing is some behind-the-scenes correspondence. After the festivities were over, Bertha Putnam, a delegate for a learned society who happened to be a professor at Mount Holyoke College, wrote Sir Edwin Deller, Principal of the University of London, to ask why Mount Holyoke had not been invited to send a delegate to the centenary when Bryn Mawr, Smith, Vassar, and Wellesley had. Was this, she wondered, an aspersion on the quality of Mount Holyoke degrees (3 July 1936: UL, CF 1/36/718)? A memo from Deller to his assistant asks, "I take it that the omission (& it was omitted) of Holyoke from the Centenary Celebration was 'pure inadvertence'?" The assistant's reply was "Yes—coupled with the grossest ignorance" (6 July 1936: UL, CF 1/36/718).

To appreciate Grace Macurdy's story fully, it is necessary to understand this background, along with what I have termed "the double legacy" of women classicists in the United States (McManus 1997, 31–35). The positive side of this legacy stems from the early foundation and flourishing of women's colleges in the United States, for late nineteenth- and early twentieth-century American women had educational and professional opportunities in classics available nowhere else in the world. The negative side of the legacy was created by the number of women who took advantage of these opportunities to become professional academic classicists, embarrassing many male classicists in the United States and making it more difficult for these men to combat their sense of inferiority toward German and British classicists, who were still effectively excluding women from the profession. Consequently, American women who wanted to take full advantage of the professional opportunities in classics had to enact a complex gender performance that masculinized their scholarship and disembodied them as women.

As noted above, Grace Macurdy did not conform to this pattern. Her story is that of a true pioneer, a person without viable role models who gradually fashioned herself as a respected classical scholar without downplaying or suppressing her gender in her scholarship or her life. In other words, Macurdy sought to become "a woman and a scholar" in such a way that neither side of the equation would diminish the other. She was greatly helped in this effort by her close contact with British classicists, from whom she received more recognition than from her own compatriots. The American recognition accorded her younger colleague Lily Ross Taylor made Taylor's style of "honorary male" scholarship[7] the model for subsequent American women in the profession until the advent of modern feminism in the late 1960s, when women classicists began adopting a model in some ways analogous to that created by Macurdy.

It is clear from the whole tenor of Grace Macurdy's adult life that her overriding purpose was to be—and to be acknowledged as—an excellent scholar in her chosen field of Greek. The lack of documentation for her early life makes it difficult to trace the genesis of this drive, but a comment in a letter to Gilbert Murray suggests that her mother had a role in it:

> My mother had a large family, nine of us, and high ideals of education for her means. I educated the two youngest brothers as a sort of sacred task, because my mother felt that her children must have college training, if possible. (4 February 1911: GM 157.15–18)

Macurdy came from a family that was far from affluent; her father was a carpenter who never owned his own home or business, and the family frequently moved from one rented lodging to another in Watertown, Massachusetts. Her older brother and sisters were not educated beyond high school, and Macurdy herself attended the local public (state-funded) schools. Macurdy had none of the social, educational, and financial advantages typical of girls who attended college at that time; only her exceptional talent and drive enabled her to secure admission to the recently opened Society for the Collegiate Instruction of Women in Cambridge, popularly called the "Harvard Annex," to commute there for four years by horse-drawn trolley, and to graduate with highest honors in classics in 1888.

After teaching for five years at the Cambridge School for Girls and taking postgraduate courses at the Annex, Macurdy became an instructor in the Greek department at Vassar College at the age of twenty-seven. During her first years at the college, Macurdy emphasized her role as a scholar, to the amusement and sometimes exasperation of her students. As one student, Adelaide Claflin, wrote to her mother, "Miss Macurdy expects every body to be able, like herself, to have at her tongue's end every thing she ever heard or read" (1 February 1894: VC Student Letters). A year later this same student described her efforts to persuade

Macurdy to accompany some students to a performance of Buffalo Bill's Wild West Show:

> She listened with a great deal of contempt at first. She has never even been to a circus in her life, her taste running chiefly to Latin and Greek plays and Boston lectures. But she really became interested in Buffalo Bill's career, and said she really believed she would like to go. I think she was most induced by the fact that Buffalo Bill is the brother of Mrs. Irvine, the President of Wellesley College. . . . Miss Macurdy amuses us so much sometimes—I used to read jokes about Boston people in the newspapers, and thought them all very much exaggerated, of course. But Miss Macurdy certainly goes far ahead of anything I ever read about Boston intellectuality.
> (19 May 1895: VC Student Letters)[8]

Macurdy's "Boston intellectuality" was rewarded with a scholarship from the Woman's Education Association of Boston that enabled her to study at the University of Berlin in the 1899–1900 session with the noted German philologists Ulrich von Wilamowitz-Moellendorff (see Fowler 1990; Calder 1994) and Hermann Diels (see Schütrumpf 1990), and to travel in Italy and Greece. On her return she resumed her teaching position at Vassar and enrolled in the graduate program at Columbia University, from which in 1903 she received a Ph.D. in Greek (the only other woman among the eighteen doctoral candidates was a geologist). In accordance with Columbia requirements, she had her dissertation privately published; its subject, *The Chronology of the Extant Plays of Euripides*, reveals the influence of her work with Wilamowitz (Macurdy 1905). At the beginning of 1906, she sent a copy of this publication to Gilbert Murray. Murray's response to this unsolicited gift was at first rather stiff, but soon their letters took on a warmer tone. For example, in response to a letter from Macurdy praising his translation of the *Trojan Women*, Murray wrote:

> Your letter, which happened to come at a time when I was depressed & rather disgusted with my work, gave me the greatest pleasure & encouragement. Besides caring for the poetry and the meaning of the plays, you are a real scholar and an understander of Euripides, which makes it that much the more valuable to me that you should like my work. (15 August 1907: VC Taylor 8/33)

Macurdy sorely needed this praise, since she had found out in January 1907 that her department head, Abby Leach, was seeking her dismissal from Vassar. In fact, Macurdy later submitted this letter, along with another from Murray, as evidence of her scholarly reputation to the committee of Vassar trustees that would decide her fate. Thus the early stages of Macurdy's friendship with Murray, a man and a Briton, played out against a backdrop of vicious enmity from a woman and a compatriot, Abby Leach, who waged a relentless campaign to oust Macurdy from Vassar and in effect destroy her career.

This epic struggle is copiously documented through hundreds of letters in a large box in the Vassar archives simply titled "The Leach-Macurdy Conflict."[9] In 1907 Leach began sending out feelers for a faculty member to replace Macurdy and started to restrict the Greek courses that she would allow Macurdy to teach. In January 1908, Leach formally proposed to the Vassar president, James Monroe Taylor, that Associate Professor Macurdy be dismissed at the end of the semester, giving as her reasons that the work she needed was largely "supplementary" and more suited to a younger, "adaptable" person, and that she had discovered errors in the Greek prose work of a student that had not been corrected by Macurdy. Her final reason was quite revealing:

> I think it was a mistake, although I advised it, to try to do work for her degree at Columbia and carry her teaching at the same time and I think that she let her work here suffer. Since taking her degree, she has not the same interest in certain sides of the work and makes use of a method that is calculated to impress students but not to train them. (17 January 1908: VC Taylor 8/33)

Leach wanted an acolyte, not a colleague who would equal and indeed surpass her own distinction as a classicist.

In the middle of the semester, before the trustees had had any opportunity to act on her request, Leach very publicly took the class in freshman Greek away from Macurdy and reassigned it to the new instructor in the department; she also continued to write letters to Taylor criticizing Macurdy's teaching and scholarship. However, when the trustees committee met they unanimously reappointed Macurdy and directed Leach to give her a fair share of the work of the department. Soon after this occurred, Taylor received a letter from two graduate students in the Greek seminar taught by Leach, Sarah Morris and Ruth Andrus; it is worth quoting at length to demonstrate how far Leach was willing to go in her campaign against Macurdy:

> An incident has recently occurred of which, it seemed to us, you should know. . . . Tuesday, February eighteenth, we met in the evening for our Greek Seminar in Miss Leach's room. She then expressed her feeling towards Miss Macurdy, to us as a class, giving as her reason the statement that five years ago she thought one of Miss Macurdy's prose papers poorly done, and from that time on Miss Macurdy's work had pulled down the department. . . . In connection with her criticism of Miss Macurdy's work, Miss Leach

warned us against an exaggerated idea of Miss Macurdy's mental
ability, taking up minor details of her Doctor's thesis and showing
them untenable to prove her point.

(22 February 1908: VC Taylor 8/33)

For the next several years Leach continued to take courses away
from Macurdy and to steer students away from the courses that she did
allow Macurdy to teach; then she would again propose that Macurdy
be dismissed, now giving the reason that Macurdy did not have enough
courses or students. Leach also wrote to alumnae asking them to criticize
Macurdy and even wrote derogatory letters about Macurdy to the president of Columbia University and to several Greek professors there who
had taught her. When a new Vassar president, Henry Noble MacCracken,
took office in 1915, Abby Leach presented all her "evidence" to him and
again requested that Macurdy be dismissed. Instead, the following year
MacCracken himself proposed that Macurdy be promoted to a permanent position with the rank of full professor, which the trustees granted.
However, Leach's campaign did not cease until her death from cancer in
December, 1918. In 1919 Macurdy was appointed chair of the Greek
department, a position she held until her retirement in 1937, when she
eloquently expressed her gratitude to MacCracken:

> Those years under your presidency have been my happy and fruitful
> years. I cannot be thankful enough that you came to Vassar College
> when you did. It meant for me liberation of my work and of my
> spirit. (26 October 1936: VC MacCracken 43/46)

Unfortunately, a physical impediment coincided with this "liberation,"
since Macurdy found out in 1919, at the age of fifty-three, that she was
losing her hearing. A few years later she was almost totally deaf, but she
did not let this handicap interfere with her "happy and fruitful years." She
learned to lip-read fluently and used every available mechanical device to
enhance what little hearing she had, from ear trumpets to bulky acousti-
cons and eventually smaller bone-conduction hearing aids.

From the story I have just told it should be obvious why Grace
Macurdy never took Abby Leach as a role model. But there were other
reasons as well. Up to this time Leach was the only American woman
who had achieved any distinction in classics (see Zwart 1971; Briggs
1996–1997; Halporn 1999), but the distinction was not the type sought
by Macurdy. Leach had impressed the Harvard professors William Watson Goodwin (see Briggs 1999; Reinhold and Briggs 1994; Gulick 1931a)
and James Bradstreet Greenough (see Reinhold 1994; Gulick 1931b) by
her very considerable talents as a linguist, so much so that her achievements were used to promote the foundation of the Harvard Annex. Her

work on educational issues led to positions as the first female president of the American Philological Association (1899–1900) and president of the Association of Collegiate Alumnae (1899–1901). However, despite her undoubted linguistic skills and knowledge, her mind was narrow and rigid, and she had little depth of insight into ancient literature, which is amply illustrated by the following simplistic misinterpretation of Sophocles in a letter she wrote to Gilbert Murray:

> I am inclined to agree with you in dating the Electra of Sophocles later than that of Euripides but think you hardly do justice to Sophocles. God's in the heaven, all's right with the world is the doctrine of his serene spirit. (25 February 1907: GM 12.79–82)

Although she lectured frequently on educational topics, she published only two articles in scholarly journals, one of which was her presidential address to the APA. Even some of her students were able to see through the veneer; as one, Margaret Shipp, put it:

> Miss Leach may know a lot and be very famous, but she is absolutely the most uninteresting instructor I ever came across. . . . She is about as flexible as a wooden post, [and] she says the most squelching things with a 'smile that won't come off.' She is invaluable to the college however as a figurehead to introduce lectures etc, for she is remarkably handsome and fine looking, and her clothes are perfect. (25 October 1903: VC Student Letters)[10]

It is no coincidence that her campaign against Macurdy came to a head after she learned that Macurdy was to begin teaching in the summer program at Columbia; having once been a "first woman," she apparently could not deal with a younger colleague's achievement of that status.

So Macurdy first turned to Gilbert Murray as a mentor and even as a kind of model. Her letters are full of praise for his work, and statements like the following show how closely she linked her work and thought to his:

> It is true of me, as it is of many others, that what you have written has unlocked thought on one subject after another. I feel intensely . . . that what you have written expresses my own best—not that I would have thought of it unprompted, but when I read it in your words I recognize it as what belongs to me.
> (3 November 1917: GM 157.129–31)

But she also knew that she could never pattern herself after him. Jane Ellen Harrison, on the other hand, was not so Olympian a figure as Murray; she was, moreover, a woman, the only Anglophone woman who had achieved some standing as a classical scholar by the turn of the century. Hence Macurdy turned toward Harrison as a possible role model. This move is very apparent when one looks at the focus of her early scholarship. Her first seven articles in scholarly journals from 1907 to 1911 are straightforwardly philological, but by 1912 she was concentrating almost exclusively on etymology of names, mythic and religious origins, and ethnology. Her researches led her not only into the depths of the library of the British Museum, but also on adventurous treks through Greece and the Balkans. She began corresponding with Harrison, sending her some articles for suggestions and advice, and the two women met a number of times during Macurdy's travels. Harrison went out of her way to introduce Macurdy's work to a British audience in *The Year's Work in Classical Studies*, discussing five of Macurdy's articles:

> We welcome from America a new worker of high originality. Prof. Grace Macurdy won her spurs by an article on Paean and Paeonia. The path she then cleared has broadened to a veritable highway. . . . Vassar College is much to be congratulated on its professor, the new *Chorizousa*. (1915b, 75–76)[11]

Macurdy's first book, *Troy and Paeonia* (1925), is the culmination of this phase of her work. She asked Harrison, Murray, and J. A. K. Thomson, all of whom had read parts of the book in manuscript, to write letters to Columbia University Press recommending publication: "I am only a gleaner after you all, but I do wish to get the book done and out" (8 December 1923: GM 157.138–39). However, she chose to dedicate the book to Harrison alone, and the dedicatory inscription prefigures Macurdy's concept of the woman scholar as an individual who does not have to suppress her personal qualities in order to be accepted as an intellectual: "I dedicate this work to Jane Ellen Harrison, one of the greatest of living scholars, the splendor of whose intellect is equalled by the candor and generosity of her spirit" (Macurdy 1925, v). Harrison's response, written less than three years before her death, indicates her delight with the book and the tribute:

> At last the long looked for book has come! How can I tell you the intense pleasure you have given me. I feel it a great great honour to have such a book dedicated to me. I sat up late last night to read it right thru & was filled with fresh wonder at the vigour and originality of yr mind. . . . Dear Miss Macurdy you have given me one of the greatest pleasures in my life & I thank you from my heart. (30 December 1925: VC Biography File, Macurdy 2)

Troy and Paeonia received generally positive reviews, except from critics hostile to the Cambridge ritualists such as Alexander Shewan, whose nasty piece in the *Classical Review* (1927) provoked a feisty response from Macurdy (1927). Campbell Bonner's mixed review in *Classical Philology* explicitly links Macurdy with Harrison:

> In general the reader will find more of profit in the chapters which deal with ethnological relations, folk-customs, and place-names than in the interpretations of myth and religion. In the former field the author has added to our knowledge; in the latter her methods are too much like those of her admired fellow-worker, Miss Harrison, to gain the assent of cautious readers. (Bonner 1927, 438)

Another similarity with Harrison lay in Macurdy's somewhat eccentric style of dress, for Macurdy favored big hats, jewelry, and feminine clothes made of attractive, expensive fabrics that bore little relation to current fashion. One of her students, Evalyn Clark, described her clothing as "*sui generis*. It was not exactly what you'd find anybody else wearing at that time, but she didn't care. . . . It was very much in the Oxford tradition; I mean you dressed as you felt like, and that was it."[12] Macurdy kept her hair very long and wore it piled on top of her head; it was always escaping from her hairpins and wisping around her face. Another former student, Barbara Neville Parker, described her first impression of Macurdy in class:

> Her white hair was flying all around; she had a kind of loose attractive dress on and a beautiful blue chain of stones around her neck which exactly matched her eyes (not that she had planned this, for she never thought about herself as far as we could see). Then she started to talk about Greek art. Well, all I can say is that I spent more time on my long paper for Miss Macurdy than on all my other papers put together. Whatever scholarship I have done since, I believe stems from the enthusiasm which I got direct from Miss Macurdy. (3 February 1958: VC Biography File, Macurdy 3)[13]

Because of her regal bearing but slightly disheveled appearance, her Vassar students fondly referred to her as "the Drunken Duchess." Her large hats and abundant hair once saved her from injury when she was hit by a wastebasket full of burning paper that a panicked student had tossed out of a second-story window. Her hat was destroyed and her hair scorched, but she suffered no further damage. As Vassar's president Mac-Cracken tells the story, "When I asked our classicist what she thought at the time, she said: 'I just said to myself, the revolution has come. Be calm. Sophrosunë!' Classical training has its merits" (MacCracken 1950, 101). Despite such similarities, Harrison's model ultimately proved insufficient for Macurdy, primarily because Macurdy did want to be accepted as a "sound scholar." As a woman in turn-of-the-century Britain, Harrison was perforce confined to the margins of classical scholarship, so she chose to play up her femininity, selecting unorthodox subjects, exploring emotional dimensions of her topic, speculating and theorizing, writing personally and passionately. In America, however, Macurdy had professional academic standing and thus at least the possibility of acceptance into the scholarly fraternity. At heart she was a careful and exact philologist, not comfortable with an emotional style or a highly theoretical approach. But neither was she willing to suppress the fact that she was a woman and a feminist, a word she herself used in a number of letters. Unlike Harrison, Macurdy lived happily in a close-knit community of women for most of her adult life and had a strong circle of women friends, including colleagues and former students; she was also an active supporter of women's suffrage. Despite her close friendship with Gilbert Murray and J. A. K. Thomson, one cannot imagine Macurdy ever claiming, as Harrison did in her essay "Scientiae Sacra Fames," that she required "the mind of a man with its great power of insulation" to help her bring her ideas to fruition (Harrison 1915a, 130–31).

Like most academic women of her era, Macurdy remained single all her life, but she nevertheless experienced a kind of motherhood and also a sort of marriage. When her widowed sister died in 1918, Macurdy took over the responsibility of raising her orphaned children—a daughter of twenty-two, a son of eighteen, and a son of twelve. Her niece and youngest nephew, Bradford Skinner, came to live with her at Vassar, and her older nephew spent his summers and holidays from college with her as well. Macurdy always referred to them as "my children" and once wryly commented to President MacCracken that "she had prayed for a family when she was a girl, and the Lord had certainly responded!" (H. N. Mac-Cracken to B. Skinner, 12 January 1951, private collection). Bradford himself told an amusing story of meeting a Vassar alumna at a cocktail party who informed him that when he arrived on campus to live with Macurdy the Vassar students promptly dubbed him "the Duchess's Indiscretion" (B. Skinner to H. N. MacCracken, 8 January 1951, private collection).

What I am calling "a sort of marriage" is the close relationship that developed between Macurdy and J. A. K. Thomson, a British classicist who was thirteen years younger than she.[14] She had begun corresponding with Thomson in 1912 at the instigation of Gilbert Murray, who was taking Thomson under his wing at the time. Macurdy and Thomson met in 1919, when Thomson was lecturing at Harvard for a year. Thomson later wrote Murray, "I must say the atmosphere of classical study in America is far from stimulating. Really I think the most living person I met there was Miss Macurdy of Vassar. She may be a little mad about the Paeonian Apollo, but it is the right sort of madness" (26 August 1921: GM

172.21–22). Their friendship solidified when Thomson taught at Bryn Mawr from 1921 to 1922.

Macurdy was due for a 1922–1923 sabbatical year in England, and she worked very hard to secure a position for Thomson as her sabbatical replacement, going so far as to propose to President MacCracken that she would make an anonymous gift of $600 (nearly 20 percent of her own salary) so that Vassar could offer Thomson a salary of $2,000 instead of the usual $1,400 for an instructor. Despite the fact that this would put quite a strain on her own tight finances, she was very excited about the prospect of secretly helping Thomson in this way, but she was also aware of the oddity of this gesture. As she wrote MacCracken, "Mr. Thomson is such a fine young scholar and so fine in character and spirit that I would very much like to do this. . . . May I ask that no one except yourself and me should hear of this? My friends would think it quixotic and perhaps wrong in principle" (2 February 1922 and 6 February 1922: VC Mac-Cracken 27/34). Since she would be in England and Europe for the year, she was obviously not trying to keep Thomson near her; her excitement stemmed not only from the prospect of helping a friend, but also from the fact that she would be acting as a patron for Thomson, thus validating herself as an established scholar and putting herself in a position analogous to that of Gilbert Murray.

When the plan fell through for other reasons, Macurdy recommended Thomson for positions at New York University and Swarthmore and worked behind the scenes with Murray to help Thomson secure the chair of classics at King's College London. As she wrote to Murray, "I am very anxious indeed that our friend should have a position worthy of his talents. His sensitiveness is against his pushing, but he would fill any such post with honor and his great gifts would gradually be recognized" (17 December 1922: GM 172.53–56). Once Thomson was settled in London, Macurdy spent every summer from 1924 through 1938 and both of her sabbatical years in England, always renting a flat right next to Thomson's, and they frequently traveled together to Italy, Greece, other parts of Europe, Scotland, and Wales.

Although both Macurdy and Thomson carefully saved their letters from Gilbert Murray, they (or their executors) did not preserve their numerous letters to each other. Fortunately there are many other forms of evidence that have allowed me to reconstruct aspects of their relationship. At first glance it appears similar to Jane Ellen Harrison's relationship with Francis Cornford because of the age disparity and the fact that the attraction was based on both parties' intense commitment to their shared subject and deep respect for each other's intellect and scholarship. For example, in a recommendation of Thomson for a position at New York University, Macurdy wrote, "I regard him as the best and finest Greek scholar in England or America of the generation just younger than that of Gilbert Murray" (14 April 1922: GM 172.35). Similarly, Thomson's letter to Columbia University Press recommending publication of *Troy and Paeonia* states, "Professor Macurdy's studies in [the Homeric Question] and kindred subjects have long seemed to me easily the most original and suggestive, in many ways also the most learned, that have come from an American scholar during [the last ten] years" (December 1923: GM 175.252–53).

Macurdy's relationship with Thomson, however, differs in several significant ways from that of Harrison and Cornford. There are absolutely no signs of flirtatiousness, jealousy, or possessiveness in Macurdy's attitude toward Thomson. Moreover, the Macurdy-Thomson relationship was satisfyingly mutual and continued until her death in 1946. I myself doubt whether the relationship was sexual, though I have no hard evidence to substantiate or disprove this belief, but Macurdy and Thomson were certainly a "couple."

Evalyn Clark, a former student and subsequently a colleague of Macurdy, told me that it was widely known at Vassar that Macurdy was very attached to Thomson and that they frequently traveled together:

> I don't think anybody was thinking of scandals looking at her.
> . . . Well in the first place because she had sort of a disarming approach—nobody would ever think that this was being sort of illicit or anything. They were perfectly frank and open. She had a kind of a charm about her and an innocence, an air of innocence. (interview by author, 6 December 1997, Poughkeepsie, N.Y.)

When Margaret Floy Washburn, professor of psychology at Vassar, made her first transatlantic crossing in 1928 on a Cunard ship, she wrote Macurdy, "The ship's food is vile beyond words. . . . This is because the food is English. Your affection for J.A.K.T. must indeed be great. I understand now why you always come back so sylph-like in form" (10 April 1928: VC Autograph File). This joke between friends testifies to the easy acceptance of Macurdy's rather unorthodox behavior. As in her style of dress, Macurdy did as she pleased, and those around her accepted it.

All evidence points to an egalitarian relationship based on deep mutual affection and steady companionship. Writing to her future husband Bert Hodge Hill, Macurdy's former student and friend Ida Thallon closely linked the two, "Miss Macurdy and JAK Thomson are leaving for Athens in less than a week. Be good to them. They are rare spirits" (22 July 1924: ASCSA Carl William Blegen 16/3).[15] When Macurdy was in London, she and Thomson always entertained friends together, and if one was invited to any event, the other would always be included in the invitation. They jointly collected Greek artifacts, which were displayed in his flat, and even when she was in America Macurdy would invite friends traveling to London to visit Thomson: "J.A.K.T. would love to have you for dinner etc. and then you might like to look at our treasures of vases, of which his apartment is full. . . . And he will probably give you a detective story or two!" (19 January 1937: ASCSA Bert Hodge Hill 4/2) Besides their passion for all things Greek, Macurdy and Thomson shared a fascination with detective stories of the more intellectual sort. As Macurdy wrote her friend Ida, "I like my victims and my murderers to be gentlemen and scholars. These Crime Kate and Lefty Louie Crime Club stories I cannot read. . . . Well, I must buzz off, as Lord Peter Wimsey, the detective, would say" (13 April 1929: ASCSA Ida Thallon Hill 2/5). Even when World War II (and later her increasing age) prevented Macurdy from sailing to England, their relationship continued through letters. Macurdy fretted about Thomson's safety during the blitzes and sent him razor blades and other supplies still available in America. In 1942 Thomson wrote to Lady Mary Murray to thank her for a gift commemorating his relationship with Macurdy, "I have just returned from Bath and found here the charming picture of Miss Macurdy, which you have sent me as a Christmas card. I have a photograph of her, but not this one" (12 December 1942: GM 544.78).

The mutuality and equality of her relationship with Thomson, who accepted her as a Greek scholar on a par with men, finally enabled Macurdy to find her own style of scholarship and speak confidently as a woman. For Macurdy, this meant turning to ancient women as a topic. No female classical scholar had ever done this before, and the few male scholars who had written about women had done so in a highly ideological way (see McManus 1997, 5–14). Refusing to treat women in isolation from mainstream history, Macurdy chose to focus on ancient monarchies, an area of traditional history in which a few women did play significant roles. In the 1930s, she published books on *Hellenistic Queens* (1932) and *Vassal-Queens* (1937). In these books and related articles, Macurdy pioneered not only a new topic, but also new methods, anticipating many of the features that would come to characterize the feminist approach to the study of women in antiquity developed in the 1970s—focus on specific groups of women in the context of socioeconomic class, culture, and time period instead of an undifferentiated, abstract "Woman"; attention to the differences and biases of various types of ancient sources; and use of evidence from many areas besides literary texts, including inscriptions, papyri, coins, and sculpture.

Another similarity to more modern studies can be seen in the straightforward declaration of purpose with which she opens *Hellenistic Queens*:

> Since the statement is so generally made with regard to the queens of these royal houses that in them a woman is the equal of a man, it has seemed to me desirable to attempt to arrive at a clear idea of what is meant by this equality and to discover whether it prevailed alike in all three dynasties. . . . I have also discussed the question of the character of these queens, who are generally reputed to have been wicked. This reputation rests, as does the statement that they possessed power equal to that of the men, on the acts of a few of the many who were queens in the Hellenistic centuries. Of these few it may be said that if they were in nature and character the counterparts of the men, they should be judged by the same standard. If the women are to be compared to tigresses (a favorite simile for them) we must admit that the Macedonian blood produced tigerish men.
>
> (Macurdy 1932, ix–x)

In these books Macurdy uses a traditionally objective, scholarly tone based on voluminous research and citation; although she never explicitly mentions her own sex, it is clear that she is speaking as a woman scholar who is seeking to cut through prejudices and stereotypes about women which have marred earlier studies and prevented a judicious evaluation of the evidence. For example, she is sharply critical of John Pentland Mahaffy's (1895) analysis of the motives of Cleopatra VII: "His views about the psychology of female love . . . must surely have been gathered from an extensive reading of melodrama rather than from an experience of the facts of life," but she is equally contemptuous of Arthur Weigall's (1914) attempt to present Cleopatra "as a 'sympathetic' heroine: 'a dainty little queen with her fat baby at her breast'" (Macurdy 1932, 221).

Reviewers recognized the uniqueness of Macurdy's approach and emphasized her role as a woman scholar. William W. Tarn wrote of *Hellenistic Queens*, "It is interesting to have a woman's judgment on this remarkable series of women" (Tarn 1932, 167); he later favorably reviewed *Vassal-Queens*, commenting that "[Macurdy] is really vindicating woman's place in the then world" (Tarn 1938, 77–78). Although one reviewer complained of "a certain amount of special pleading" in *Hellenistic Queens* (Bellinger 1933, 359), most agreed with the viewpoint expressed in *Classical Philology*:

> Professor Macurdy has avoided every form of sensationalism and instead has presented a scholarly and decidedly welcome study of Hellenistic queens in which she evaluates without prejudice their personality, influence, and importance. (Larsen 1932, 315)

Macurdy had begun studying ancient queens as soon as she completed work on *Troy and Paeonia*, and it is clear that Thomson accepted this scholarly focus and perhaps even encouraged it. In fact, he invited her to participate in a series of public lectures he was organizing at King's College in the spring of 1925. Macurdy's gender and her topic, "Great Macedonian Women," were both unusual for such a university-sponsored public lecture at the time. She was not sure, however, how Gilbert Murray would respond to this new turn in her work. When she wrote him about *Hellenistic Queens*, her excessive name dropping signals her unease and seems designed to pave the way for a favorable response:

> I have sent you a copy of my book on Hellenistic Queens with some misgivings, as I do not know that you will [be] interested in my study of these ladies. . . . I have had some pleasant letters about it from Rostovtzeff and other scholars in America and England. They seem to think, as Ferguson wrote me, it was high time that some one should present such a dossier. . . . Tarn agrees with me about Cleopatra VII, on whom and Antony he has been working for two years for the CAH in its next volume.
>
> (26 March 1932: GM 157.151)[16]

Murray politely reassured her of his interest, but subsequent statements in her letters indicate that Macurdy was never confident that he fully understood or appreciated this turn in her scholarship. By this time, however, Macurdy no longer needed his approbation, and she forged ahead with her pioneering studies of women.

With the advent of World War II, Macurdy turned much of her energy to raising money for British War Relief; she was so successful in this effort that she was awarded the King's Medal for Service in the Cause of Freedom in 1946. Her last book, *The Quality of Mercy in Greek Literature*, published in 1940, temporarily moved away from the topic of women to focus on the development of "the humane virtues" in Hellenic thought. In fact, she was turning back to an earlier idea, for many years previously she and Thomson had planned to collaborate on a book on the history of pity in ancient literature. Her choice to return to this topic was greatly influenced by her horror at the inhumanities being perpetrated in Europe in the late 1930s.

This book is similar to much of Murray's and Thomson's writing, and it is not surprising that she chose to dedicate it to these two men. As she wrote to Murray, "I hope that it has something of the spirit of you both and all your books have been my constant companions for so many years and I have used them so constantly in class and out that I cannot conceive of my intellectual life without them" (16 December 1939: GM 157:173–74). However, even in this book Macurdy's interest in women flashes to the surface in many places, as when she dismisses claims that Euripides was a misogynist: "Women were one of the poet's 'causes'; he was interested in their psychology, not from malice, but because he realized that they, as well as men, had minds, and were potent for good or evil" (1940, 137).

She continued to write articles whose subjects reflected her interest in women (for example, Macurdy 1942 and 1944b). One of the final articles she published, "Had the Danaid Trilogy a Social Problem?" (1944a), exhibits the strong voice she had developed as both scholar and woman. In this article she spiritedly contradicts interpretations of Aeschylus' play *The Suppliant Women* by eminent male scholars (including Gilbert Murray himself) on the basis of her knowledge of Athenian law and custom and also on her perceptions as a woman. Rejecting the claim that the Danaids are portrayed as "unfeminine" women "actuated by a natural frigidity and hatred of men," she argues that the problem of the trilogy is essentially dramatic, not social:

> [The Danaids] are Aristotelian heroines "like ourselves" . . . [who] express the single terrified state of mind of girls who have undergone the horrid experience of being attacked by men whom they hate. This state of mind is neither unwomanly nor abnormal— rather, indeed, both womanly and normal.
>
> Moreover, it is not possible to divide Greek women sharply between the "Kinder, Kirche, and Küche" type and the "unfeminine" type. The Danaids, doubtless, in the end made as good wives and mothers as any other ladies of the heroic age.
>
> (Macurdy 1944a, 98–99)

When Macurdy retired in 1937, the *Vassar Alumnae Magazine* published four tributes from other scholars ("Tribute" 1937). Testifying to the importance of British classics in her life and career, two of these tributes were from Great Britain (written by Murray and Thomson), and the other two were from Vassar. Gilbert Murray's tribute is very positive, but it does not emphasize her uniqueness as a woman: "Miss Macurdy . . . is in the fullest sense of the word a true 'scholar,' of a kind which is rare in America and by no means common in Europe." Significantly, Murray begins his tribute with a very odd statement: "Soon after my own retirement from the Chair of Greek in Oxford I hear that a much younger scholar, Miss Grace Macurdy, is about to retire from the Chair at Vassar" ("Tribute" 1937, 9). Since Macurdy was born in exactly the same year as Murray, the "much younger scholar" is clearly a slip on his part, one that perhaps suggests that he was still thinking of her as a protégée rather than as an equal. On the other hand, the tribute by J. A. K. Thomson, which he described in a letter to Murray as "a more or less impartial appreciation of her work in scholarship" (29 March 1937: GM 173.190–91), recognizes the importance of Macurdy's status as a *woman* scholar and also hints at the role played by British classics in her achievement of this status:

I think that on this side of the ocean it is the general impression that Miss Macurdy was the first American woman to meet the Greek scholars of Europe and America on something like equal terms. She has reached that position by a combination, too rarely found, of exact linguistic knowledge with learning and historical imagination. The ancient world is alive for her, and whatever she writes is full of her personality. ("Tribute" 1937, 9)

Chapter 7

J. A. K. Thomson and Classical Reception Studies
American Influences and "Classical Influences"

〜Barbara F. McManus

The field of classical reception studies identifies itself as "a fairly new area of prominence in anglophone scholarship" (Hardwick and Stray 2007b, 2). Its recent growth has certainly been noteworthy, with the 2004 foundation of the Classical Reception Studies Network in the United Kingdom and a burgeoning series of books produced primarily by British scholars (Hardwick 2003; Martindale and Taylor 2004b; Martindale and Thomas 2006; Hardwick and Stray 2007a). In an article on "Reception Studies: Future Prospects," James Porter asks, "Is it too soon for the renewed field of reception studies to turn reflexively upon itself and to examine its own traditions from a critical and metatheoretical perspective?" (Porter 2007, 473). This essay aims to provide some background for such an examination of reception studies by looking at a British pioneer in this field, J. A. K. Thomson, whose work has been almost completely overlooked by modern classicists.

Research in the later reception of classical antiquity owes its new prominence and legitimation as a modern field of inquiry chiefly to the work of classicists in the United Kingdom, with American classicists increasingly following the lead of their British colleagues. The genesis of J. A. K. Thomson's work in reception studies, however, can be found at least partly in the United States, providing an excellent illustration of the principle that influences rarely operate in only one direction. Thus an exploration of Thomson's place in the history of reception studies will also illuminate a little-known two-way relationship between British and American classics in the first half of the twentieth century.

AMERICAN INFLUENCES

On 19 September 1919, a 40-year-old Scottish classicist stepped off the gangplank of the *S.S. Denis* onto American soil. James Alexander Kerr Thomson[1] had come to the United States to take up a one-year position as visiting lecturer at Harvard University, hoping that this would lead to some kind of permanent academic employment, since he had been eking out a living through part-time university teaching, secondary teaching, and examining in Scotland and England. Although America was to offer him another temporary position, as a sabbatical replacement at Bryn Mawr College in 1921–1922, his future was in London as professor of classical literature and chair of the classics department at King's College, a post he obtained in 1923 through the help of his mentor and friend Gilbert Murray (for a detailed study of Murray and Thomson, see McManus 2007). Nevertheless, his two years in the United States, teaching at an all-male university and at a liberal arts college for women, gave him a first-hand perspective on American education, which was greatly augmented by his life-long friendship and shared summers with Grace Harriet Macurdy, professor of Greek at Vassar College (see McManus, this volume).

During his years in the United States, Thomson had many opportunities for personal observation of the American classical community; besides teaching at Harvard and Bryn Mawr, he presented a paper at the 1919 annual meeting of the American Philological Association in Pittsburgh and made a lecture tour that included Vassar and what he described in letters to Murray as "the perfectly enormous Universities of Michigan and Illinois," examples of "those great State-owned machines run on strictly business principles" (25 May 1920; 15 January 1923: GM 171.232–33; 172.71–72).[2] His impression was not generally favorable. When Harvard asked him to contribute an article to *Harvard Studies in Classical Philology* (Thomson 1920), he wrote Murray that he was not perfectly satisfied with his piece, but "it would be difficult to be more depressing than some of the Studies. It is strange that American scholarship, even when very good, should tend to be so dull" (15 July 1919: GM 171.226–27).

Many years later he expressed much the same opinion to Sir Stanley Unwin when asked whether Allen & Unwin should commission a translation of Burckhardt's *Griechische Kulturgeschichte*: "Have you any means of discovering whether there is an American translation on foot? American classical scholars, not being as a rule very original, go in much more than English for translations from German" (30 November 1953: AUC 615/20).[3] On the basis of his own experience with Harvard University Press, he commiserated with Murray when the latter was having difficulties with publication of his Norton lectures (Murray 1927): "'Organization' is all very well for mass production, but it takes an exasperating amount of time and adjustments to get the engine started. If America goes on being standardized, it will end as a beehive" (27 March 1927: GM 172.189–90).

Murray himself did not hold the United States in high esteem, and it is interesting that Murray once expressed this opinion in a letter to Janet Spens by using terms reminiscent of a phrase used by Thomson, "I quite agree about America; USA is a rather blunt and coarse version of Europe as Rome was of Greece" (22 May 1953: GM 169.147). In his book *The Classical Background of English Literature*, Thomson had said of Plautus and Terence, "there is nothing Roman about them except the language and a certain blunting or coarsening of the Attic spirit" (Thomson 1948, 69–70).

Many British classicists of the period engaged in such casual disparagement of American scholarship and institutions, but few had Thomson's experience of teaching in the trenches. Even an ardent Anglophile like Grace Macurdy was aware that the differences in practice between the American and British educational systems caused problems for both visiting instructors and host institutions, as indicated in her response to Henry Noble MacCracken, president of Vassar, when he suggested that she hire "a young Englishwoman" as a sabbatical replacement:

> She might be very good, though it sometimes takes the English a time to get used to our ways. I should feel more confident if I were going to be here to prevent her being too "Anglican" in her teaching. *We* have to make concessions.
> (2 February 1922: VC MacCracken 27.34; emphasis in original)[4]

She apparently did not feel that this caveat applied to Thomson (see McManus, this volume, for a description of her efforts to secure him as her replacement), but Thomson himself sounds rather "Anglican" in a letter to Murray describing his exasperation at American educational practices:

> I have rather a grudge against Bryn Mawr that I seem to be all the time occupied in either preparing or correcting examinations. Never was such a place for examinations! It seems to me such a bad system.

> And this is combined with a vast amount of mere window-dressing;
> the shallow pretentiousness of the courses in American universities
> is really appalling. It must be the fault partly of the American mind
> and partly of the system. These Bryn Mawr girls—often quite clever
> and charming girls—come up knowing *nothing* accurately. That of
> course is the fault of the schools. It is jolly hard to make Latin inter-
> esting to people who have not read any real literature at all. The girls
> themselves are delightful. I was telling a Horace class about Sappho,
> and one rather pretty maid, who had been listening with all her soul
> in her eyes, held up her hand. "Please, Doctor Thomson, just when
> did that bird live?" "Bird"—not even "bard." O America!
>   (12 March 1922: GM 172.32–33)

While it is true that the college-preparatory education of girls still
lagged somewhat behind that of upper-class boys during this period,
Thomson is emphasizing a general lack of literary background among
American students rather than deficiency in Latin skills. His perception of
this lack, coupled with his later experiences at the University of London,
helped provide the idea and impetus for the "classical influence" books
of his retirement years (Thomson 1948, 1951a, 1952, 1956). Thomson's
most significant and long-lasting American influence, however, was his
close friendship with Grace Macurdy. They met during his year at Harvard, and she obviously caught his attention. As he wrote Murray when
he was preparing to return to the United States,

> I have a great liking and admiration for America; still one agrees
> with Odysseus about the *patris*. And I must say the atmosphere of
> classical study in America is far from stimulating. Really I think the
> most living person I met there was Miss Macurdy of Vassar.
>   (26 August 1921: GM 172.21–22)

His year at Bryn Mawr cemented their friendship, and thereafter she
spent every summer in England with him until World War II prevented
overseas travel. She drew him into her circle of American friends and
kept him abreast of scholarly and educational developments in the
United States.

Macurdy herself was active in curricular programs linking classics
to other disciplines, particularly English. For example, at Vassar she
designed and co-taught a course on "Tragedy: Ancient and Modern" that
coupled the departments of Greek and comparative literature. She also
participated in a project sponsored by the National Council of Teachers
of English to develop syllabi that would correlate English with other
subjects and wrote a section on "The Living Legacy of Greece and Rome"
for their volume on *A Correlated Curriculum* (Macurdy and Weeks 1936).
It is clear that she and Thomson frequently discussed the ways that clas-

sical and English literary study could be linked. In a statement from her manuscript for "The Living Legacy of Greece and Rome" that does not appear in the published version, she wrote:

> In King's College, London University, the head of the Department of Classics, a distinguished scholar and writer, is also a member of the Department of English and gives lectures each year to large classes in the department of English and of Journalism on the Greek Drama and kindred subjects. This has proved highly successful.
> (VC MacCracken 38.16)

Thomson's outreach to English literary studies was not typical for classicists in British universities, but in the United States such efforts were becoming increasingly common as part of a trend in the period following World War I that saw the rise of Classics in Translation, Great Books, and Western Civilization courses in American colleges and universities (see Carnochan 1993; Cross 1995; Lindenberger 1990; Schein 2007). In an article discussing the "culture wars" that are a contemporary offshoot of this postwar development on American campuses, Paul Cartledge notes that these battles are predominantly fought on North American shores but are "potentially of much wider significance: when Cambridge, Mass., sneezes, sooner or later Cambridge, England, catches a cold" (Cartledge 1998, 17). In the early twentieth century, however, the germs typically traveled across the Atlantic in the other direction, as several articles in this volume demonstrate. Thomson was unusual in the degree to which he was influenced by his American experiences and contacts; the seeds of his classical influence books were planted in the United States and nurtured by his continuing friendship with Grace Macurdy.

"CLASSICAL INFLUENCES"

Soon after his retirement from King's College, Thomson proposed to Sir Stanley Unwin a new type of publication:

> I have been indirectly approached by the Clarendon Press with the suggestion that I might consider contributing a volume to the Home University Library on "The Classical Background of English Literature." It is natural to welcome the chance of publication, which I had assumed to be almost non-existent for matter of my kind. But you have the first say in the matter. If I wrote with an eye to possible publication by you, it would be something quite different—fuller and more detailed—than what the H.U.L. requires, and more suited, I should have thought, to the wants of students of English. But you are a better judge than I am of the prospects of such a volume in the

more or less immediate future. In the meantime I must give some
kind of answer to the Oxford people.

(24 February 1946: AUC 280/8)

The idea for such a book was in fact Thomson's own; he himself had
suggested it for the Home University Library in a letter to Gilbert Murray
just ten days previously (14 February 1946: GM 411.1), but apparently
he felt that he needed some bargaining leverage to get Allen & Unwin
interested in the project. Fortunately Unwin replied with an offer of a
contract, and Thomson then sent a more complete description of his
rationale for the book:

> I know a good deal about this particular subject from the practi-
> cal side, as I have not only lectured on it a good deal to English
> Honours students, but I am now the London University examiner
> in the subject. I am also the Moderator of the Classical examina-
> tions at the Matriculation and Higher School Examinations stage.
> It is quite clear to me that, as the study of the original languages
> declines, this "Background" subject is going to increase, slowly but
> steadily. It is already an optional subject for English Honours and it
> is undoubtedly going to be taken up by schools preparing students
> for the university.
>
> It seems to me then that it would be best for me to write with
> these students in mind, though I should hope to interest classical
> students also and the "general public," if it exists, which I sometimes
> doubt. Now what they want is as much instructive detail as they
> can get for their money. . . . Once the book were out, it would be
> recommended by teachers—I think we may count on that—and
> perhaps by the University of London. At any rate it would supply a
> "felt want." If it was the first satisfactory book of the kind, it would
> probably hold the field for quite a longish while. But you will grasp
> my point—it must be reasonably full of matter, and it must not be
> too dear.
>
> If we do agree . . . I shall make a strong effort to let you have the
> ms in time for the Spring of next year. It is important to be first in
> the field. (7 March 1946: AUC 280/8)

Several important points emerge from this letter: Thomson sees this
as a previously unmined area for publication; his purpose is pedagogical
and his primary audience is students, including students at the pre-col-
lege level; he is driven by a sense of urgency, obvious from the repetition
of "first." A later letter to Unwin indicates that American students figure
prominently in his intended audience:

> It is to be hoped the book will sell in America among the countless
> students of English literature at the colleges there. Now about 1942

(I think) there was published in America two volumes of the correspondence between Wendell Holmes, the great American judge, and Sir Frederick Pollock. In one or two of the letters there were very flattering references to my "Greeks and Barbarians" published by you. I do not possess the book and I have forgotten the exact words used by Holmes. But it should not be difficult to get them and I think they would impress American readers, who have a great regard for him. (24 October 1946: AUC 280/8)

He did send Unwin excerpts from the book (Howe 1942, ii:71–82), though it is not clear whether these were ever used in advertisements.

Why was Thomson so keen to move into this new area of publication? His reference to the American audience suggests one important motive, income. When Thomson retired after World War II, he left London to live with his sister in the Berkshire countryside, partly to help her with family troubles (see biographical sketch) and partly because he could not afford to live alone. At this stage in his life, he needed to write books that would sell. Isolation provided another impetus, at first the relative isolation of Berkshire and later the nearly absolute isolation when he was forced by the serious mental illness of his niece to move to the remote Scottish highlands.

A more subtle but no less significant factor was his desire to produce a body of work that would not be viewed as a minor appendage to that of Gilbert Murray (see McManus 2007). That this was on his mind at the time can be discerned by reading between the lines of a comment he makes in the *Classical Background of English Literature*. When pointing out the impact of the printing press, he states that a modern author "may not find—he may not even expect to find—more than a tiny minority of appreciative readers; but at least he has said his say and got it put on permanent record" (1948, 40). *Classical Background* did bring Thomson a new kind of recognition, and he followed up this book with two more detailed studies, *Classical Influences on English Poetry* (1951a) and *Classical Influences on English Prose* (1956). In fact, all of his subsequent publications can be viewed as an effort to create a "permanent record" of the project that he first described to Stanley Unwin in 1946. Murray himself interpreted these books as a new and successful direction for Thomson when he wrote, "I find myself awfully tired and ninety-ish. You are becoming a popular author, with your Penguin Aristotle and all the classical influence books. Macte nova virtute, puer!" (20 March 1956: GM 175.228).

CLASSICAL RECEPTION STUDIES

Thomson was, in fact, able to be "first" in this field, although the manuscript he submitted in December 1946 was not actually published until
February 1948 due to severe paper shortages in postwar Britain. By
October of that year the initial 3,880 copies were nearly gone, and Allen
& Unwin had to begin the laborious process of applying to the Paper
Advisory Committee for a grant of paper to reprint the book (15 October
1948: AUC 378/6); the fact that the second printing was not released
until 1950 indicates how difficult it was to get paper. Meanwhile, on the
other side of the Atlantic another Scottish classicist, Gilbert Highet, who
was an enthusiastic participant in Columbia University's Great Books
course Humanities A (see Ball 1994; Cross 1995; Suits 1990), produced
his own book on this topic, *The Classical Tradition* (1949). This magisterial
tome, its 763 pages testifying to the fact that paper shortages were far less
of a problem in the United States, has given its title to a modern branch of
scholarship and completely eclipsed Thomson's contribution to the field.
For example, in more than five hundred pages Blackwell's *Companion to
the Classical Tradition* devotes only a few words to Thomson, stating that
his books "are slight but can be useful as jumping-off points" (Jenkyns
2007, 278), and Hardwick 2003 does not even include Thomson in the
bibliography. Thus while Highet's contribution to the field is repeatedly
acknowledged, modern scholars do not recognize J. A. K. Thomson as a
direct ancestor of studies of the classical tradition or classical receptions.

A brief overview of Highet's and Thomson's works reveals significantly
different audiences and purposes. Highet does not specify his intended
audience in the book itself, but the dust jacket claims that the book "will
appeal to scholars and to well-informed general readers"; it is clear from
the book's lengthy notes (556–705) that the former were the main targets.[5] Highet states his purpose in the preface: "This book is an outline
of the chief ways in which Greek and Latin influence has moulded the
literatures of western Europe and America" (Highet 1949, vii). Of course
it is much more than an outline, but its vast scope means that few topics
can be covered in great depth. The majority of the book deals with postclassical literature; Highet begins with the "Dark Ages" and discusses the
characteristics of various classical genres and authors in later sections
(particularly in the long chapters devoted to the Renaissance), as prefatory to his analysis of their influence.

In contrast, Thomson's three books (Thomson 1948, 1951a, 1956),
as noted above, were written for students, both the American students
whom he found seriously lacking in literary background and the similarly deficient students he later encountered in London. He clearly states
his purpose in the first of the books:

> It is to help students of English literature who are not themselves
> classical scholars to form a coherent impression of the influence
> exerted by the ancient literatures upon our own. . . . It has been a
> principal aim of the author to supply the reader less with opinions
> than with the kind of information he is likely to want. . . . What he
> does feel the need of, and that, I am told, in an increasing degree,
> is a brief description of classical books he has not had the time or
> opportunity to study for himself. That will explain why a good half
> of a not very large volume is taken up with such a description. But
> two further duties imposed themselves on the author. He had to
> indicate the links between the Greek and Latin writers on the one
> hand and the mediaeval and modern on the other; and he had to
> show how the classics have appeared to each age in its turn. For
> each age has had its own view of them. (Thomson 1948, 8)

The purpose and audience remained the same in his two subsequent
volumes, but these went into greater depth, emphasizing concrete examples and specific quotations from the works described and organizing
the discussion by genres rather than chronology. Because of his intended
audience and his own predilections, Thomson did not include footnotes
or even a bibliography.[6] This absence was lamented by the reviewer in
Classical Philology (Hutton 1950), who obviously had Highet in mind
though he did not mention that book, but journals with a more pedagogical focus gave his books high praise, as this sample from the *Classical
Journal* indicates:

> Although this book is not intended to be a scholarly production, it
> is the kind of book that only a scholar who has devoted his life to a
> study of literature, both ancient and modern, could have produced.
> It fills a real need and can be heartily recommended both to students
> of English literature who are not familiar with classical literature and
> to classical students who may be equally unfamiliar with the vary-
> ing fortune of classical literature in the mediaeval and classical [sic]
> periods. (Law 1949)

From a scholarly perspective, these three books of Thomson may
indeed be "slight"; they are certainly dated and completely untheoretical.
Thomson was a liberal humanist of the Victorian type, and reviewers
correctly pointed out the weakness in his treatment of twentieth-century
literature (Law 1949; Swanson 1957).[7] Nevertheless, these books deserve
a place in the history of classical reception studies as precursors, in some
ways more closely allied to this field than Highet's book.

According to Hardwick and Stray, one of the concerns of classical
reception studies involves "ways in which (partly through education)
both the ancient and the newer works became better known among less
privileged groups, with the newer sometimes acting as an introduction to

the ancient." (Hartwick and Stray 2007b, 3). Thomson's whole purpose in these books is to enable "less privileged" students, those who cannot read Greek or Latin, to assess and evaluate later receptions of ancient works themselves. Because he aims to give them the information and tools to do this, he devotes a much larger proportion of his books than Highet does to descriptions of ancient literature, especially to stylistic qualities that would be difficult or impossible to perceive when reading the works in translation. Although the modern reader is likely to disagree with some of his generalizations about ancient literature (such as the comment about Plautus and Terence quoted above), his descriptions of the more technical aspects of poetic and prose style in Greek and Latin are very clear and would still be useful for students struggling to understand how later English writers encountered and engaged with their classical forebears.

This can be demonstrated briefly by comparing Highet's and Thomson's treatment of Horace. Highet mentions Horace's "precisely arranged four-line stanzas" but dwells most on his differences from Pindar, citing Horace's own contrast between the swan and the bee and arguing that the "two schools, Pindaric and Horatian," are not synonymous with the differences between the "romantic" and the "classical." Here is his summary of the qualities of Horatian lyrics:

> Brief, orderly, tranquil, meditative, they are less intense and rhapsodical but deeper and more memorable than those of Pindar. Cool but moving, sensitive but controlled, elusive but profound, they contain more phrases of unforgettable eloquence and wisdom than any other group of lyrics in European literature.
>
> (Highet 1949, 225–28)

Thomson begins his discussion of Horace by emphasizing the difficulty of measuring his deep influence on English lyric poets due to the fact that "the radical differences that exist between classical and modern verse come out with particular clearness in Horace, because his art emphasizes them." He briefly explains why Horace's typical meters cannot be successfully duplicated in English because of the differences between quantitative and stress verse and because of "the superabundance of little, and yet indispensable words" in English. To demonstrate "the insuperable obstacle of word-order" he quotes in full Horace's Pyrrha ode (1.5) and Milton's rendering of it, pointing out how "Milton is continually being forced by English grammar (which he seems always to be attempting to reduce to Latin rule) to abandon the order of words in Horace." This is his summary of the qualities of Horatian poetry:

> It is a miracle in the art of placing words so that each shall reflect, and have reflected upon it, the utmost significance and poetical

value of which it is capable. We cannot do it in English. . . . Another [element] is a conciseness or economy of words so finely managed that only the student of style observes it. A third element is that classical virtue, quietness of statement controlling deep emotion, although perhaps in Horace the emotion never gets beyond a certain depth. (Thomson 1951a, 147–50)

Highet simply tells the reader what to think of Horace. Thomson, however, in exactly the same number of pages, has given Latinless readers the ability to make their own judgment by providing some sense of the Horace that the English poets knew in the original and of how their reception of his work might be affected by the differences between Latin and English.

The other two aims that Thomson mentions in his preface to *Classical Background* (quoted above) are also congruent with the concerns of modern classical reception studies. Highet tends to present Greek and Roman culture as monolithic (Hardwick 2003, 126), an impression that is intensified because he begins his survey with the postclassical. Thomson, on the other hand, is at pains to trace what is now called "reception within antiquity" (in his words, "the links between the Greek and Latin writers"). In his discussion of ancient epic, for example, he starts by emphasizing that what we see as a beginning, the art of Homer, "can only be understood as a development of oral poetry." After describing the Homeric epics, he discusses Apollonius Rhodius, Vergil, Lucan, and Statius, emphasizing how each reacted to his predecessors, incorporating, adapting, and changing in accordance with the tastes and needs of his own age (Thomson 1948, 39–56).

Thomson was also aware of "the *active* participation of readers (including readers who are themselves creative artists) in a two-way process, backward as well as forward, in which the present and past are in dialogue with each other" (Martindale 2007, 298; emphasis in original). In Thomson's less sophisticated formulation, "It is a cardinal principle, observed throughout this study, that every age looks in the classics for what it likes and takes what suits it" (Thomson 1948, 250). This point is difficult to illustrate briefly since it is distributed throughout the three classical influence books, but the following quotation provides a partial example:

The eighteenth century indeed was almost as much a century of translations as the seventeenth. They were more read no doubt than the originals. Their interest for us is historical as well as literary. Almost better than anything else they show us the classics through eighteenth century eyes. One has only to look at the illustrations in early editions of Pope's Homer to see what kind of figure an Homeric hero presented to the imagination of the artist and perhaps of Pope himself. The actor who took the part of Cato in Addison's play wore a wig. But this only means that eighteenth century men saw themselves in the ancients, and this is what every century does, whatever the degree of its archaeological knowledge.

(Thomson 1948, 220–21)

Thomson was conscious that he was doing something new in these classical influence books, but his untheoretical style and the fact that they were written for students have contributed to their neglect by modern scholars. He did, however, write one reception studies book that had a more scholarly purpose, *Shakespeare and the Classics* (1952). This is in fact the most significant of Thomson's books in the field of reception studies, but its contribution has been not only overlooked but actually misconstrued.

For example, Charles and Michelle Martindale explicitly position their book *Shakespeare and the Uses of Antiquity* as a much-needed replacement for Thomson: "We write on the assumption that the modern student requires something more sophisticated than J. A. K. Thomson's spirited but cheerfully philistine little book *Shakespeare and the Classics* with its no-nonsense neo-Farmerian thesis" (Martindale and Martindale 1990, viii). Martindale and Taylor take over Thomson's title but are only slightly less dismissive in the introduction to their edited collection: "Before that [Martindale and Martindale 1990] one has to go back to J. A. K. Thomson's rather jejune *Shakespeare and the Classics* in the 1950s" (Martindale and Taylor 2004a, 2). In the first of these statements "little" is clearly not an indication of size, since Thomson's book is actually slightly longer and larger than the Martindales' book, and "neo-Farmerian thesis" is definitely misleading since Thomson explicitly states his disagreement with the conclusions of Farmer (1767), though he feels that some of his evidence is valid (Thomson 1952, 30–31).

Furthermore, it would be difficult to find a more inappropriate word for Thomson than "philistine" (though "jejune" comes close). Victorian he may have been, but everyone who knew Thomson recognized his learning and culture. S. A. Handford, his colleague at King's College London, called Thomson "a born scholar . . . absorbed in the profundities of Greek literature and philosophy":

He might have been more in his natural element in one of the older seats of learning a couple of generations ago. His teaching will be remembered best by some of his most gifted pupils, who sat in awed admiration of his deep learning and breadth of culture, in English as well as in the classical languages. (Handford 1959)

It is possible that the modern scholars quoted above were misled by the unsophisticated appearance of Thomson's book, which not only has a limited number of footnotes and no bibliography, but also has no index, no chapter divisions or headings, and a table of contents with the topic listings run together in continuous paragraphs and squeezed onto one page. Archival research helps to explain this unusual appearance, because the postwar paper shortage was still causing serious difficulties for British publishers as late as 1952. Thomson had submitted his completed manuscript to Allen & Unwin in December 1950; the book was typeset by May and ready for printing by October 1951, but no paper was available, so publication was delayed until March 1952. Thomson was extremely frustrated by these delays and he repeatedly wrote urging Stanley Unwin to hasten the book's publication:

> There is much interest in the subject at present, both here and in America. Percy Simpson, the Elizabethan scholar, has written to me about it, saying that he too wishes to write about Shakespeare's learning. There is thus a motive for getting out the book as soon as circumstances permit. (28 December 1950: AUC 478/16)

> I wonder if you are in a position yet to give me some idea of the possibilities of getting my book on "Shakespeare and the Classics" out within a reasonably early date. . . . The trouble is that the longer the book is kept back, the less topical it becomes.
> (8 February 1951: AUC 525/21)

> I am under pressure from other Shakespeare scholars to get the book out as soon as possible, and I have to consider every possibility. I wonder then if you would be good enough to have my ms. sent to the Cambridge University Press . . . which has expressed a desire to see it. (12 February 1951: AUC 525/21)

So the book was published in a format that used as little paper as possible. In the event, Thomson would have been well advised to wait until the book could be presented in a more professional format, since Simpson's piece was not published until 1955 and was merely an essay discussing possible correspondences between passages in Shakespeare and ancient authors. Also, it is likely that Thomson was unable to give the final version of his book the attention it deserved because he was at this time distracted by the serious mental illness of both of his nieces and preoccupied by the complex negotiations between Allen & Unwin and Penguin over his translation of Aristotle's *Ethics* (Thomson 1953; 1955).

Archival research also reveals a much more significant issue than the paper shortage that helps to account for the misinterpretations in the reception of Thomson's book. Thomson had written a good portion of the book before proposing it to Stanley Unwin:

> I have been working for some time on a manuscript dealing mainly with the extent and character of Shakespeare's classical knowledge. It has been read by Dover Wilson, whom I wanted to consult on points outside my competence. He is enthusiastic about it and would like to have it for a series published by the Cambridge University Press ("Shakespeare Problems" edited by Wilson). I ought to say that he is an enthusiastic person, but I think myself there is some good in the stuff. The whole would have to be licked into shape and this would take me perhaps six weeks. I thought of calling the book "Shakespeare and the Schoolmasters"—meaning his academically minded contemporaries. . . . There is of course a sale for Shakespearian books if they are useful and also not unreadable. If you would like the book, that would also be agreeable to me. Why I ask at this point is that for Wilson's series I should be more technical, whereas for a less academic public I would translate the Latin quotations and make things generally lighter.
>
> (7 November 1950: AUC 478/16)

Unwin wrote back that they would like to publish the book but the title would not do; he suggested *Shakespeare's Classical Knowledge,* later changed to *Shakespeare and the Classics.* However, placing the book with Allen & Unwin and changing the title partially sidetracked Thomson from his original purpose, leading to a book with something of a "split personality."

Thomson's main purpose was actually to explore Shakespeare's relationship with "his academically minded contemporaries" and how this affected the development of his art, and the book's intended audience was primarily academic. He characterized the book as "a serious contribution to Shakespearian scholarship" (28 December 1950: AUC 478/16) and urged Unwin to submit it for review to the *Shakespeare Survey* because this journal "carries particular weight with Shakespeare scholars. . . . Its opinion, if favourable, would have great weight with leading scholars, both here and in America" (21 February 1952: AUC 572/10). At Unwin's prompting, however, he allowed himself to be caught up in the topic of how much Latin Shakespeare knew and what original sources he used, which had been recently revived by the two-volume publication of the American scholar T. W. Baldwin, *William Shakespeare's Small Latine & Lesse Greek* (Baldwin 1944; see Wilson 1957 for an overview of the topic). Thus Thomson's preface states, "In estimating the extent of Shakespeare's classical learning I have sought to establish what he certainly did know rather than to discuss what he may have known" (Thomson 1952, 6) and refers to the "general reader" rather than the scholar. Hence, by choosing

Allen & Unwin instead of Wilson's Shakespeare series at Cambridge out of a sense of loyalty to his long-time publisher, Thomson blurred not only the book's thesis, but also its intended audience.

However, removing the long section on "internal evidence" (40–152) dealing with possible borrowings from classical sources in Shakespeare's works in a way that Thomson himself admits is "cursory" (152) gives us the book on "Shakespeare and the Schoolmasters" (comprising a little more than half of the present volume) which Thomson had perhaps already written when he made the proposal to Unwin. If we analyze this as the book Thomson initially intended to publish, we can see that he was trying to move the discussion about Shakespeare and classical literature away from a "classical tradition" model in the direction of what is now called "classical reception studies" (although he did not use these terms). Martindale and Taylor state that the purpose of their *Shakespeare and the Classics* is to "get away from the idea that the dramatist's classicism is primarily a matter of sources, references, allusions" and to show how Shakespeare "was enabled by a variety of classical books to explore such crucial areas of human experience as love, politics, ethics, and history" (Martindale and Taylor 2004a, 2–4). While Thomson never explicitly articulates the purpose of the second half of his book, a careful reading reveals that it is in exactly the same vein as that of Martindale and Taylor. Indeed, Thomson's purpose is even broader, since he also examines the enabling effects of Shakespeare's interaction with his more classically educated contemporaries, a process which Hardwick and Stray (2007b) locate at the core of reception studies:

> The dynamics of creativity in the work of artists and writers, both ancient and modern, also has implications for the relationship between reception and tradition in that writers and artists position themselves in relation to their predecessors and contemporaries and are deeply conscious of being part of a tradition. . . .Yet they also wish to transcend that tradition. How scholars model and discuss that process is at the heart of reception debates. (5)

Although Thomson himself engages in a certain amount of source hunting in the first part of his book for the reasons discussed above, he is actually dismissive of this practice, citing Tennyson's famous disparagement of critics who "will not allow one to say 'Ring the bell' without finding that we have taken it from Sir P. Sidney" (Thomson 1952, 153). Thomson makes it clear that his chief purpose in discussing sources has been to establish that Shakespeare was not a classical scholar, insofar as he was not learned in a way that would be recognized by the standards of his time. Nevertheless, Shakespeare did position himself as a "classicizing author" by his choice of subjects and themes, making it inevitable that "his credentials should be scanned, at least by those who had themselves attempted classical subjects with less applause" (156). Thomson analyzes in some detail the criticisms leveled against Shakespeare by Robert Greene, Thomas Nashe, George Chapman, and Ben Jonson, explaining how the classicism of these men reflected the cultural horizon of the period; he is especially interesting in his examination of how Chapman and Jonson positioned themselves in relation to the ancient authors and how this affected their own writings.

Thomson then turns to the potential effect of these criticisms on Shakespeare: "If we are to understand what the criticism meant to him, we must keep in mind what was said at the beginning of this book about the prestige of the classics in Shakespeare's world. He had to adjust his thoughts and feelings to that" (179). From this perspective he analyzes *Venus and Adonis*, *The Rape of Lucrece*, certain aspects of the sonnets, and *Love's Labour's Lost*, tracing how Shakespeare forged a new style out of the dynamic interplay between his own understanding of the classics and that of his learned contemporaries (in a similar way, Colin Burrow [2004] explores the creative uses Shakespeare makes of the educational methods of the time). As Thomson sums up this point:

> Who will deny that, however little Greek or Latin Shakespeare may have known, he made the most wonderful use of what he did know? So that, in a perfectly real and genuine sense, the classics actually meant more to Shakespeare than to those who had only a book-knowledge of them. (241)

According to Thomson, Shakespeare's close reading of North's *Plutarch* enabled him to move his drama to an entirely new level, and Thomson devotes the long concluding portion of his book to what he presents as a creative encounter, not an influence. He explains how Renaissance ideas led North to misinterpret Plutarch occasionally and how these misinterpretations could prove fruitful for Shakespeare. He argues that Plutarch was for Shakespeare "the channel or medium of the Greek tragic spirit" (243) which taught him to construct unified tragic dramas, to make brilliant use of tragic irony, and to explore the profound effects of character upon destiny (see Nuttall 2004 for a similar argument that Shakespeare picked up the Greek spirit "at a distance" without reading Greek himself).[8] Thomson analyzes *Julius Caesar* as the turning point in this process:

> I believe that it was from Plutarch that Shakespeare learned how to make a tragedy of the kind exemplified in *Hamlet* and *Othello*, *Macbeth* and *Lear*. It was, I think, in the course of writing *Julius Caesar* that he learned it. (242)

This point, too, has been taken up in a modern article (Marshall 2000); as Gordon Braden notes, Cynthia Marshall has actually "recast Thomson's thesis in new terms" (Braden 2004, 189–90). What Braden doesn't mention, however, is that Marshall seems totally unaware of this, since Thomson is never cited in her article.

This brief summary cannot do justice to the full scope of Thomson's arguments, but it should be clear that his emphasis was not on how much or how little Latin Shakespeare knew, but rather on how the perception of Shakespeare's "academically minded contemporaries" that he was not a classical scholar might have affected his work and spurred him to an encounter with classical subjects and themes that proved extremely fruitful for his art. Because of the book's split personality, none of the initial reviewers of *Shakespeare and the Classics* grasped this thesis (Bush 1952; Craig 1953; Jack 1952; Leech 1953; J. O. Thomson 1953). Even J. Dover Wilson, Regius Professor of English at Edinburgh, with whom Thomson had discussed the project in depth, admiringly presents the book as an authoritative statement about "Shakespeare's 'Small Latin'—How Much?" (Wilson 1957). The American Shakespearian scholar Douglas Bush terms Thomson's discussion of Shakespeare's contemporaries "long and dubiously relevant" because he interprets the main purpose of the book as the establishment of "what Shakespeare certainly knew rather than what he might have known" (Bush 1952, 376). Both Bush and the reviewer from the *Times Literary Supplement* (Jack 1952) criticize the book's odd arrangement and the lack of clarity about its target audience; as Bush astutely observes, 'much of the book seems in fact to be addressed to the scholarly reader, and such a reader may wish that Professor Thomson, having taken so much pains, had taken more' (Bush 1952, 377).

All this provides an explanation (though not a justification) for the modern neglect and misinterpretation of the place of Thomson in classical reception studies. For example, none of the recent articles on Shakespeare that I have paralleled with Thomson's book recognize the similarities or take any notice of Thomson's approach to Shakespeare as a forerunner of modern reception studies. This demonstrates the need for more study of what James Porter (2007) calls "the reception of reception":

> Exploring the history of their disciplines is the most natural point of entry to self-reflection and self-examination one could ask for. Such an approach is likely to reveal unexpected continuities with the past, seen now from a more modest vantage-point in the present. (471)

More than fifty years before the foundation of the Classical Reception Studies Network, J. A. K. Thomson was feeling his way toward many of the principles that now characterize classical reception studies. Recognizing this "unexpected continuity with the past" will enrich the history of this field and appropriately acknowledge the work of a pioneer.

J. A. K. THOMSON: BIOGRAPHICAL SKETCH

James Alexander Kerr Thomson (always known as J. A. K.) was born in the coastal town of Stonehaven, Kincardineshire, in northeastern Scotland on 13 June 1879, son of John Craig Thomson, who was a sheriff clerk deputy for the county. He had two older sisters, Janet and Mary. His father was apparently out of the picture by the time he was a young adult because he refers to his responsibility for his mother in a number of letters but never mentions his father. Janet married Andrew Norman Meldrum, a scientist and author, and had three children (Norman, Margaret, and Elizabeth); neither J. A. K. nor his sister Mary ever married.

Thomson was educated at Mackie Academy, a school founded by a local benefactor which had opened in his fourteenth year, and at Aberdeen, from which he graduated in 1900 with first-class honors in classics and the Fullerton Scholarship for the best Classic. He entered Pembroke College, Oxford, as a foundation scholar in 1901, and gained a second in Moderations (1903) and second in *Literae Humaniores* (1905), receiving his B.A. in 1906. From 1906 to 1909 he served as Greek assistant to John Burnet at St Andrews, after which he was a lecturer in Greek history and a university assistant in Greek at Aberdeen from 1910 to 1913 and subsequently examiner for the universities of Aberdeen and Wales for the next several years. In 1908 he had began corresponding with Gilbert Murray, and Murray eventually became his primary mentor and close personal friend.

At the instigation of Murray, the Clarendon Press published Thomson's first book, *Studies in the Odyssey*, in 1914. Rejected as unfit for service in the army because of eye problems, he began teaching again at St Andrews in 1916 for a very small salary to replace instructors serving in the army and continued to write, publishing in 1915 *The Greek Tradition: Essays in the Reconstruction of Ancient Thought* with Allen & Unwin, which was to remain his publisher for the rest of his life. Gilbert Murray, seeking a more permanent position for his protégé, helped Thomson obtain an invitation from Harvard University in 1917 to serve for a year as visiting lecturer, but the war prevented his taking up this post until September 1919; in the two intervening years, he taught at Winchester College.

During his year in the United States, Thomson took a lecture tour around the country, giving talks at Vassar College and at the universities of Michigan and Illinois, and published a long article on "The Religious

Background of the *Prometheus Vinctus*" for *Harvard Studies in Classical Philology* (1920). Upon his return to Scotland in 1920, he was unable to find employment and devoted his time to composing a second book of essays, *Greeks and Barbarians* (1921). In the fall of 1921 he was back in America, teaching for a year at Bryn Mawr as a sabbatical replacement for Arthur H. Wheeler, professor of Latin. During his two years in the United States, Thomson established a close friendship with Grace Harriet Macurdy, professor of Greek at Vassar. They were frequent traveling companions and amassed a joint collection of Greek artifacts that were donated to the Ashmolean Museum at Oxford and the Classical Museum at Vassar after her death in 1946.

When Thomson returned to Scotland in June 1922 at the age of 43, he still had no permanent employment, but with considerable help from Murray he was selected in 1923 to replace W. C. F. Walters as professor of classical literature and chair of the classics department at King's College, London, a position he held until his retirement in 1945. His fourth book, *Irony: An Historical Introduction*, was published in 1926. Gilbert Murray invited Thomson to accompany him on a trip to the Swiss Alps in the summer of 1927, initiating a tradition of annual shared holidays that did not cease until Murray died in 1957.

Thomson's good fortune was soon clouded by health and family problems. After publishing an essay on "Erasmus in England" for a Warburg collection (1932), he lost the vision in his left eye due to a detached retina complicated by a serious infection. An operation by the noted surgeon Sir Stewart Duke-Elder and several difficult hospitalizations eventually restored partial vision in the eye. His nephew, Norman Meldrum, a chemistry student at Cambridge, committed suicide by swallowing chemicals from the lab in 1933, and Norman's father died the following year when he allegedly took a walk along the Edinburgh coast on a stormy night and fell into the sea (apparently a suicide concealed as an accident).

Thomson's fifth book, *The Art of the Logos*, was published in 1935, and he endeavored to repay his debt to Murray by spearheading the effort to produce a volume of *Essays in Honour of Gilbert Murray*, which was presented to Murray on his retirement from Oxford in 1936. Thomson moved to Bristol in 1939 when King's College was relocated there because of the war; while in Bristol he endured several serious blitzes, one of which occurred when he was temporarily in a nursing home because of the threat of another retinal detachment. He was blitzed again in 1942 when the Bristol operations moved to Bath. In 1945 he retired as Professor Emeritus of Classics in the University of London and moved into his sister Janet's home in Pangbourne, Berkshire.

Thomson devoted his retirement years to a new project, writing books for non-classicists on the myriad influences of Greek and Roman literary works upon English literature, beginning with *The Classical Background of English Literature* (1948). He followed this up with *Classical Influences on English Poetry* (1951a) and *Shakespeare and the Classics* (1952). He was elected a fellow of the Royal Society of Literature on the nomination of Sir Stanley Unwin in 1950 but never became a fellow of the British Academy despite several nominations by Murray. On the last of these attempts, Thomson's classical influence books and Murray's continued support won him the votes for fellowship in 1954, but Thomson was notified that he could not be accepted because he had recently turned seventy-four, which was the cut-off age according to new academy rules.

His new-found publishing success was, however, dimmed by more family troubles. In 1950 his niece Elizabeth Meldrum was committed to a mental health institution in Scotland because of repeated suicide attempts; she remained in this institution until her death in 1999. His other niece, Margaret Meldrum, was also suffering from serious depression and anxiety, so much so that Thomson and his sisters moved in 1952 to a remote part of the Scottish highlands (Newtonmore, Inverness-shire) in an effort to help her. This sacrifice ultimately proved futile, since Margaret committed suicide in November of that year by taking sleeping pills and lying across some nearby train tracks at night. Since Margaret Meldrum had been a specialist in ancient Greek philosophy, Thomson had arranged to produce a translation of Aristotle's *Nicomachean Ethics* for both Allen & Unwin (1953) and the Penguin Classics series (1955) in the hope that cooperation in this project would counteract her depression; in the end, he could only dedicate the book to her memory. Ironically, the Penguin Ethics has brought Thomson his most enduring status; it is the only one of his books still in print (in its revised version).

In 1952 A. J. B. Wace and F. H. Stubbings invited Thomson to contribute an introductory chapter on the influence of Homer on European literature for the *Companion to Homer* that they were editing, although the book was not published until 1962, after Thomson's death. He completed his books on the classical tradition with *Classical Influences on English Prose* in 1956. Fittingly, his last publication was the obituary article for Gilbert Murray in the *Proceedings of the British Academy* (1957). Thomson himself died only a short time after his friend, on 6 February 1959, in a nursing home at Kingussie, Scotland.

Chapter 8

"The Anglicizing Way"
Edith Hamilton (1867–1963) and the Twentieth-Century Transformation of Classics in the U.S.A.

ↄ—*Judith P. Hallett*

Much has already been said about how the career of the celebrated American educator and author Edith Hamilton redefines the term "classicist": by myself among others, a decade ago (Hallett 1996–1997, 107–47). But new studies published, and information made available, since then prompt a new look at some questions previously raised about her life and work.[1] One question is how accurately Edith Hamilton's writings represent the classical Greek and Roman world. Another is how she became credentialed as an authoritative representative of that storied realm—as what her longtime devotee John Mason Brown called "an ambassador of an ancient civilization" (Brown 1963, 16–17). A third is how her representation of classical, particularly Greek, antiquity first attracted the notice, and keeps commanding the uncritical attention, of the Kennedy family, whose patriarch actually was an ambassador, and indeed ambassador to Great Britain. In this essay, I will argue that Britain figures significantly in the "diplomatic portfolio" assembled by "Ambassador Plenipotentiary" Edith Hamilton, as a prestigious credentialing mill. To my mind, Edith Hamilton owes a measure of her credibility, and thus the esteem accorded her as a public intellectual in the United States from the

1930s onward, to an identification with what her mid-twentieth-century American cultural milieu evidently regarded as "the best of Britain." She achieved this identification in part through the efforts of several Anglophilic Americans who refashioned and championed her as a voice of timeless Hellenic wisdom, notwithstanding their own limited knowledge of Greco-Roman antiquity. Yet Hamilton herself also sought and received the validation of individuals in and from Britain, among them esteemed classical scholars.

EDITH HAMILTON: SOME BIOGRAPHICAL DETAILS

Some basic details, first about Edith Hamilton's life, then about her influence on the study and perceptions of the classical world in the U.S., should help illuminate the role played by Britain, and by the image of British classics and culture, in both. During the 1950s and 1960s, Edith Hamilton was virtually a household word in the U.S, at least in relatively well-heeled and well-read households. Although her name may no longer be as instantly recognizable as it was at that time, much has occurred since then to add luster to her reputation as a spokesperson for classical studies.

Edith Hamilton earned both B.A. and M.A. degrees in Latin and Greek, at the relatively late age of almost twenty-seven, in 1894, from the all-female Bryn Mawr College near Philadelphia. She then spent a further year there as a fellow in Latin, winning the college's Mary E. Garrett European fellowship in spring 1895. With these funds, Edith and her younger sister Alice, who had just completed her own training as a physician, were both able to travel to Germany—first to Leipzig, then to Munich—for a year of graduate study (Alice Hamilton 1943, 18–19; Reid 1967, 33–37; Bacon 1980, 306–8; Hallett 1996–1997, 109).

Owing to a shortage of family funds, however, Edith Hamilton then abandoned plans to pursue a doctorate in classics. Upon returning to the United States in 1896, she accepted the offer of M. Carey Thomas, president of Bryn Mawr College, to become headmistress at the Bryn Mawr School, a private academy for girls in Thomas' native Baltimore. Alice Hamilton changed her course, too. After spending a year in Baltimore at the Johns Hopkins Medical School, she took up residence at Jane Addams's settlement, Hull House in Chicago, laboring tirelessly with Addams on behalf of social reform and world peace: initially while teaching pathology at the Women's Medical School of Northwestern University, and later as a bacteriologist at the Memorial Institute for Infectious Diseases. In this latter capacity, she pioneered the study of industrial toxicology, which led to her appointment in 1919 as the first woman professor at the Harvard Medical School (Sicherman 1984, 1–10, 97–236).

The first all-female secondary institution in the United States with an exclusively college-preparatory curriculum, the Bryn Mawr School had been founded eleven years earlier, in 1885, by Thomas and her wealthy friend Mary E. Garrett. A classically trained administrator was a valuable asset at the school's helm: Latin was required of everyone; either Greek or German of advanced students. Despite her heavy administrative duties, Edith Hamilton also regularly taught Vergil's *Aeneid* to the senior class (Reid 1967, 38–55; Hallett 1996–1997; Andrea Hamilton 2004, 56–57).

In 1922, after twenty-six years in this position, Hamilton resigned, amid much contentiousness and negative publicity, owing to increasingly difficult relations with Thomas. Along with alienating the affections of Hamilton's longtime companion Lucy Donnelly, a Bryn Mawr College English professor, Thomas—who insisted on micromanaging the Bryn Mawr School from Bryn Mawr College a hundred miles away—had alienated many Bryn Mawr School faculty, parents and alumnae by short-sighted financial decisions. Supporting Hamilton in this controversy, and vehemently attacking Thomas and her policies in the press, were an eminent Baltimore couple: Edith Gittings Reid, a biographer and playwright, and her husband Harry Fielding Reid, a geology professor at Johns Hopkins University (Bacon 1980, 307, 500; Sicherman 1984, 214, 252, 253, 257–60, 269; Horowitz 1994, 429–30; Hallett 1996–1997, 110, 127,130–42; Andrea Hamilton 2004).

After she departed from Baltimore, Hamilton moved to a house that the Reids purchased at Sea Wall, on Mt. Desert Island, Maine, with the Reids' daughter Doris Fielding Reid. A Bryn Mawr School alumna twenty-eight years Edith's junior, Doris had studied music, but never attended college, after leaving the school in 1911. The eldest of the Reids' grandchildren, Dorian Fielding Reid, born in 1917, came to live with Edith and Doris in Maine. Edith legally adopted Dorian in March 1922; the four other Reid grandchildren, offspring of Doris's brother and his first wife, also frequently lived with Edith and Doris when they were growing up. (Reid 1967, 56–64; Bacon 1980, 307: Hallett 1996–1997, 111)

In 1924 Edith and Doris rented the first of several apartments that they occupied in Manhattan, retaining the Maine residence as a summer home. The couple—and the two women were a couple, who made no bones about both their physical and emotional bonds to one another—eventually relocated once more: in 1943, when Doris, who had worked for over a decade at a Wall Street investment firm, was asked to head its Washington, D.C. office. It was in Washington that Edith died, on 31 May

1963, a few months shy of her ninety-sixth birthday (Reid 1967, 89–102; Bacon 1980, 307–8; Sicherman 1984, 407–11; Hallett 1996–1997, 111–12, 121 n. 29, 127–30). In the forty-one years between her retirement from the Bryn Mawr School and her death, Edith Hamilton never taught Latin again. She never appears to have taught Greek in a formal institutional setting at all. During this period, moreover, she published only one article in a learned classics journal: namely "The Classics," in *Classical World* in 1957, at the age of ninety. Barely four pages long, it has only one footnote, by Edward A. Robinson of Fordham University, the *CW* editor.[2]

Yet this is no ordinary footnote. Robinson identifies this paper as an address that "Miss Hamilton" gave, in New York City, in April 1957, at the fiftieth anniversary meeting of the Classical Association of the Atlantic States (CAAS), which publishes *CW*. Noting that she was elected an honorary member of CAAS on this occasion, he states that she "assuredly needs no formal introduction to classical readers. Her *Greek Way*, her *Roman Way*, and numerous other publications have themselves become classics in the interpretive literature of our field." Robinson then asserts that readers "of the present paper and Miss Hamilton's latest book, *The Echo of Greece* . . . would, we think, greatly enjoy a charming interview on the occasion of her trip to New York," headlined "Nineteen and a Half Minutes" as reported in the May 11 *New Yorker*.

The *New Yorker* paid her heed for good reason. During those last forty-one years of her life, Edith Hamilton produced several renowned, critically and commercially successful, books about classical and Biblical antiquity. In addition to the three cited by Robinson, which appeared in 1930, 1932, and 1957 respectively, W. W. Norton published five others: *Prophets of Israel* in 1936; *Three Greek Plays: Prometheus Bound, Agamemnon, The Trojan Women* in 1937; *Witness to the Truth: Christ and His Interpreters* in 1948, *Spokesmen for God* in 1949, and *The Ever-Present Past* (posthumously) in 1964 ("Books by Edith Hamilton" in Reid 1967, Bacon 1980, 308; Hallett 1996–1997, 111).

Perhaps her best-known book, *Mythology*, subtitled *Timeless Tales of Gods and Heroes*, came out in 1942, and continues to be a bestseller. Often assigned in elementary, secondary, and even university classrooms, it is one of the reasons I myself became a classicist. Little, Brown commissioned *Mythology* from Edith as the twentieth-century successor to another volume of mass appeal, *Bulfinch's Mythology*, which was written in 1855 for a general audience (Reid 1967, 81–83; Bacon 1980, 308; Cleary 1994; Hallett 1996–1997, 108)

Along with these books Hamilton penned a steady stream of articles and reviews in a variety of respected popular venues.[3] In 1961, at the age of ninety-four, she published a coedited volume—*The Collected Dialogues of Plato*—in the Princeton University Press Bollingen Series with a Washington D.C. attorney, Huntington Cairns. He composed the introductory essay; Edith furnished prefatory notes to each text (of Plato's letters as well as his dialogues); together they selected English renditions of Plato's writings by over a dozen different translators, ranging from Benjamin Jowett to their own contemporaries (Reid 1967, 94, 125–26; Cairns Papers, Library of Congress).

Her renown assumed various forms: honorary doctorates from such elite private colleges and universities as Yale University, the University of Pennsylvania, Goucher College, and the University of Rochester; the Jane Addams Medal for Distinguished Service from Rockford College; election to the American Academy of Arts and Letters; invitations to deliver high-profile public lectures and appear on radio and television programs. To recognize her contributions toward fostering Hellenic culture, King Paul of Greece awarded her the Gold Cross of the Order of Benefaction in the summer of 1957. The award ceremony, at which she was proclaimed an honorary citizen of Athens, took place in the ancient theater of Herodes Atticus; her translation of Aeschylus's *Prometheus Bound* was then performed (Reid 1967, 103–18; Bacon 1980, 308; Hallett 1996–1997, 112).[4]

HAMILTON'S IMPACT AND INFLUENCE IN THE UNITED STATES

Edith Hamilton was not only widely read, and revered, in mid-century America as a modern-day emissary from the enlightening domain of classical antiquity. Her achievements in the 1930s and early 1940s also paved the way for other successful American endeavors to popularize and legitimate the study of ancient Greek and Roman culture in English translation, both within and outside of the academy. From the 1950s onward, the Scottish-born and British-trained Gilbert Highet, a serious classical scholar who occupied a named professorship of Latin at Columbia University, reached mass audiences through a weekly radio broadcast. Along with serving as chief literary critic for *Harper's Magazine*, and chair of the editorial board of *Horizon*, Highet helped to shape American reading habits by his membership on the Book-of-the-Month Club Board of Judges. Such activities not only brought Highet, and the discipline of classics, visibility and influence. Vocationally speaking, they also subliminally signalled that teaching classics was an estimable calling for a learned man, requiring urbanity and sophistication as well as toil and erudition (Ball 1994; Hallett 1996–1997, 118–19; on Highet, see also McManus on J. A. K. Thomson in this volume).

More influential still were the efforts to integrate classics, and for the most part classics-in-translation, into a broadly based brand of higher education for the huge influx of college students taking advantage of the 1944 GI Bill, which funded thirty-six months of schooling for U.S. military veterans (Olson 1974). Highet's colleague at Columbia, Moses Hadas, and two Columbia classics Ph.D.s then teaching in New York's public colleges—Naphtali Lewis and Meyer Reinhold—deserve major credit for these curricular reforms. They dramatically changed how, where, when, why, and to whom classics is taught in the United States (Benario 1994; Briggs 2002).

As McManus's essay on J. A. K. Thomson in this volume notes, courses on classics in translation, great books, and Western civilization had emerged in a number of American colleges and universities after the first World War. But men such as Hadas, Lewis, and Reinhold—and the materials in English translation that they produced—inaugurated a range of courses in English translation, on both ancient Greek and Roman civilization and classical literary texts, which evolved into staples of undergraduate liberal arts education nationwide. They thereby helped ensure the survival of classical studies as a viable university subject: attracting healthy enrollments and appealing to a wide spectrum of students. Such courses, needless to say, also ensured a market for Edith Hamilton's books, especially *Mythology*.

Hamilton's renown also came from, and came with, men (and a few women) who exercised influence of diverse kinds on the American cultural scene, and cherished her pronouncements on the classical world as profoundly meaningful, gospel truth. During her nineteen years in New York, these disciples were largely from the realm of literary publishing: Rosamund Gilder and Dorothea McCollester of the *Theatre Arts Monthly* staff; John Mason Brown, drama critic for the *New York Evening Post* and later a columnist and editor for the *Saturday Review*; Brown's friend Elling Aannestad, an editor at W. W. Norton. During the Washington years she and Doris began to socialize with prominent artists and writers, too: Robert Frost, Stephen Spender, Robert Lowell, and most notably Ezra Pound, in those days institutionalized at St. Elizabeth's Hospital. Their circle expanded to embrace molders of public opinion, and political luminaries, chief among them Cairns, a protégé of both the legendary journalist H. L. Mencken and the philanthropist Paul Mellon (Reid 1967, 79–86, 91–94; Bacon 1980, 308; Lindquist 1990, 7–8; Mellon 1992, 307–10 368–70; Hallett 1996–1997, 122, 126, 143).

Most important, in the years immediately after Hamilton's own death and his brother's assassination in 1963, her words about the ancient Greeks memorably echoed in public utterances by Senator Robert F. Kennedy of New York. On 4 April 1968, while campaigning for the

Democratic presidential nomination in Indianapolis, RFK learned the news of Martin Luther King's death. He attempted to console a grieving African American audience with lines from Hamilton's translation of the *Agamemnon*, saying: "My favorite poet is Aeschylus. He wrote: 'And even in our sleep, pain which cannot forget falls drop by drop upon the heart, until, in our own despair, against our will, comes wisdom through the awful grace of God.'" (Schlesinger 1979, 617–18; Hallett 1996–1997, 144–47).

Kennedy concluded this speech by entreating "Let us dedicate ourselves to what the Greeks wrote so many years ago: 'to tame the savageness of man and make gentle the life of the world.'" This phrase, too, was Edith Hamilton's, first surfacing in her *Classical World* article (where she prefaced it by the statement "There was said to have been an old inscription at Delphi, which stated [this] as man's aim"), then in a *Saturday Evening Post* essay reprinted in *The Ever-Present Past*. Although Kennedy did not offer an ancient source for this phrase, an invitation to a large public event on 6 June 1993, commemorating the twenty-fifth anniversary of his death at his Arlington National Cemetery gravesite, attributes it (wrongly) to Aeschylus.

A 1998 collection of quotes from RFK's daybook journal and speeches, edited by his son Maxwell Taylor Kennedy, also takes its title from this phrase: *Make Gentle the Life of This World: The Vision of Robert F. Kennedy*. The collection contains several quotes from Edith Hamilton's writings as well as her translations of lines from various Greek poets. The introduction, referring to "the Greek translations that so moved him," describes RFK's "well-thumbed and underlined copy of *The Echo of Greece* by Edith Hamilton." In a section entitled "Education," an excerpt from Kennedy's own 1967 book *To Seek A Newer World* concludes a quote on this topic by noting, "This speaker was not part of a Berkeley rally; it was Edith Hamilton, one of our greatest classicists"; the text credits also cite Hamilton's *The Greek Way* (Kennedy 1998, xvii, 90–91, 180).

HAMILTON'S CREDIBILITY AND CREDENTIALING: THE ROLE OF BRITAIN

Such, then, is some basic background on Edith Hamilton "the classicist," and on the impact of her very public engagement with, and representation of, the classical world. Let us now examine the intertwined issues of her credibility and credentialing, and the role of Britain and its classicists in both. Since this public engagement occurred only after Hamilton began a totally new career as a popularizing author, at the age of sixty, we should first consider how she was launched so successfully and authoritatively on her so-called ambassadorship before exploring how Britain figured in this launching.

Our main source on Edith Hamilton's career change, and much else about her, is a 1967 memoir by her partner Doris Fielding Reid. Doris asserts that, while running their household in New York and functioning as a parental presence to young Dorian, Edith routinely and compellingly related sanitized versions of tales from classical and Biblical antiquity to him and the other Reid grandchildren. These story-telling activities, Doris implies, developed into more adult entertainments, impromptu translations and explications of Athenian drama, whenever Edith would socialize with their friends from *Theatre Arts Monthly*. Doris claims that these friends then persuaded Edith to share her ideas with their readers, and that—with some additional nudging from another friend, Elling Aannestad at W. W. Norton—Edith's writing simply took off from there, instantly capturing the hearts of the American reading public (Reid 1967, 61–63, 66–69, 78–80; Hallett 1996–1997, 133).

Like much else in Reid's memoir, this account seems to oversimplify the events that prompted this professional transition. Studies of Edith and her family, such as Barbara Sicherman's magisterial *Alice Hamilton: A Life in Letters*, have noted the troubling contradictions between Doris Reid's assertions and the actual evidence about Edith's life and work, problematizing in particular Doris's assertions about what actual evidence there is.[5] Some of this evidence Doris herself deposited in the Princeton University Library: extensive correspondence attesting to the aggressive promotion and packaging of Edith and her writings by John Mason Brown and Storer Lunt, W. W. Norton's president. Even Doris admits that when asked what made her start writing, Edith said, "I was bullied into it" (Reid 1967, 69; and in Hamilton 1964, 13).

Nor does Doris explain how Edith Hamilton managed to pass off on an unsuspecting public what are euphemistically termed "idiosyncratic" interpretations of ancient classical texts and their contexts. Hamilton's translations abound with errors, such as her use of the singular, Christian, "God" for "gods" (Bacon 1980, 307). Her statements frequently lack documentation from ancient texts, rarely if ever cite modern scholarly authorities, and rely on highly arbitrary selections of evidence (Sicherman 1991, 483–84). What is more, she often and unfairly disparages the Romans as a despotic, Orientally flavored society while uncritically extolling "the Greeks," by which she means the classical Athenians.

As an instance, one might cite Hamilton's contention, in *The Greek Way*, that "when Greece died . . . play, too, died out of the world . . . [Roman games] were fathered by the Orient." To support this claim, she adduces the brutality of Anchises's funeral games in Vergil's epic *Aeneid*.

Yet she does not, as fairness and historical accuracy demand, acknowledge the brutality of the Homeric scenario inspiring Vergil, Patroclus's funeral games in the *Iliad*.[6] Comparing Hamilton's interpretation of Greek mythology with that of Robert Graves, Sheila Murnaghan has shown how Hamilton's *Mythology* "whitewashes" the violence and irrationality in Greek mythic narratives in order to dissociate the Greeks from primitive peoples, and how Hamilton privileges classical Athenian poets as sources on mythology because they (unlike the unrefined Hesiod and cynical Ovid) "believed in what they wrote" (Murnaghan 2005).

Of relevance to these issues of credentialing and credibility is a recent discussion by Joseph Casazza. It elucidates the source of the phrase, beloved of Robert F. Kennedy, which Hamilton attributed to an old, putative, unnamed Delphic inscription defining man's aspirations: "To tame the savageness of man and make gentle the light of the world." Casazza convincingly argues that Hamilton concocted it from two totally different sentences in Gilbert Murray's 1907 book, *The Rise of the Greek Epic*.

There Murray quotes the first-century BCE Dionysius of Halicarnassus as "sum[ming] up the praises of the Athenians by saying, in the very language of an old Delphian decree, that they 'made gentle the life of the world.'" But Murray also quotes and translates part of this actual decree from Delphi, dated to 125 BCE. Its words praise Athens because "she won mankind from the life of the wild beasts to gentleness"; these words clearly inspired Hamilton's "to tame the savageness of man," as they did Murray's (and Dionysus's) "made gentle the life of the world." Hamilton, though, has represented a statement from Roman times as "old," and changed it from the indicative past tense into a purpose clause (Casazza 2003).

In pondering how Edith Hamilton got, and still gets, away with misrepresentations of this magnitude, it is instructive to compare the highly favorable public reactions to her writings with the less enthusiastic reception accorded another, later, also elderly, American public intellectual who interpreted Greek, indeed Athenian, antiquity for a wider audience, namely, the radical journalist I.F. Stone, in his best-selling 1988 book, *The Trial of Socrates*, published when Stone was 81. In his 1992 biography, *Izzy*, Robert Cottrell remarks that the reviews were "not altogether complimentary, and some proved to be downright scathing." Cottrell continues, "The [book] was declared to be no work of scholarship and Stone fearfully naïve about any number of philosophical matters." A Yale University classics professor writing for *Commentary* "found Stone's Athens to be a 'mythical' one; his analysis of the 'vulgarly reductionistic' sort; and his general reading of Socrates' intentions 'ludicrous.'" (Cottrell 1992, 313).

To be sure, Hamilton enjoyed her heyday at a different time, before the advent of classics-in-translation had transformed teaching and learning about the ancient Greco-Roman world throughout American higher education. Other factors worked in Hamilton's favor, too: her female gender, her WASP (in contrast to Stone's Jewish) ethnicity, her close connections with arbiters of taste in the cultivated literary world, and the ways in which her writings and image were marketed. Hamilton herself took an active role in this marketing campaign. Much credit must go to her lucid, accessible prose, which wears her learning lightly.[7] She was also fond of deprecating her own abilities and achievements. Perhaps she adopted this self-effacing pose as a self-defensive strategy. Doris reports that early in her writing career Edith was wounded by a critical letter from an unidentified English classicist who faulted her for writing an "unscholarly idealization of ancient Greece." Even Doris concedes that "if one means by a 'scholar' one whose books would not be read except by another student in the same line, then Edith was not a scholar."[8]

Yet Doris insists that if by the word scholar one means "a person of real ability who has studied a subject over many years and knows it as few could better," the term scholar fully applies to Edith. To prove her superior, long-term knowledge of her subject, Edith stressed her close familiarity with the ancient texts in the original languages, rarely consulting commentaries or critical studies, much less translations. By way of contrast, Stone had come late to learning Greek, and did not keep his reliance on Loeb Classical Library volumes and other *vade mecums* a secret.[9]

But also central to Hamilton's self-validation as a legitimate authority on the classics were the subtle linkages forged between herself and British culture: in her writing, by her advocates, and through her rare interactions with professional classicists. Describing a girls' preparatory school much like Baltimore's Bryn Mawr in his 2002 novel *Middlesex*, Jeffrey Eugenides observes that "in America, England is where you go to wash yourself of ethnicity."[10] The text of Edith's 1957 *Classical World* article—uniquely directed at an audience of classicists—vividly illustrates this phenomenon, by "Anglicizing" the classics to argue for their timeless value.

Her opening allusion, to a long-ago conversation with "the greatest Greek scholar our country has produced, Professor Gildersleeve of the Johns Hopkins," gratuitously notes that "he was just back from a celebration held for him at Oxford," and spells *honoured* in the British fashion, with a "u."[11] The only other two classicists she mentions are British: Sir Richard Livingstone and Gilbert Murray.[12] To exemplify the intelligibility missing in contemporary literature she extols Tennyson's poems; she quotes Matthew Arnold's statement about the Greeks' "unclouded clearness of mind" while taking jabs at the "gobbledegook" of U.S. government jargon. Next to this bleached-out, elitist vision of why classics matters to her contemporaries is the masthead listing the eleven members of *Classical World*'s editorial board, men (and one woman) actually keeping Hamilton's "subject" alive in both secondary schools and universities for a demographically and ethnically diverse, post-*GI Bill*, student body. Many taught at urban, or public, institutions; several are Jewish; Robinson, the editor, was an Irish Catholic teaching at a Catholic university.[13]

As for her advocates, a number of those who promoted Edith as a spokesperson for classical civilization at the same time fostered her associations with England and her Anglicizing ways. It warrants repeated emphasis that none of them had done much, if any, formal study of the classics. Doris's writings about Edith are particularly striking in this regard. Her preface to *A Treasury of Edith Hamilton* concludes by quoting a passage from *The Roman Way*. It justifies Hamilton's intense focus on literary texts as historical sources by stating "When we read Anthony Trollope or W. S. Gilbert we get an incomparably better view of what mid-Victorian England was like than any given by the historians." In addition to stressing the roots of Edith's ancestors in the British Isles, and enumerating in detail the British authors Edith adored as a child, Doris's memoir calls attention to a visit the couple made in 1958 to see a "close family friend," the Nobel Prize winning physicist Sir George Thomson, then master of Corpus Christi, Cambridge (Reid 1969, 7; 1967, 17, 20–23, 29–30, 130).

Doris came by this Anglophilia from her own mother, Hamilton's contemporary and friend Edith Gittings Reid, who eventually joined their household after she was widowed in 1944. When Doris left the Bryn Mawr School in 1911, at the age of sixteen, she and her mother took up residence near the Thomsons in Cambridge, England, for the winter while her brother studied for an undergraduate degree at Magdalene College. Doris and her family had also visited the Thomsons in England in 1905 and 1910. Over the next few years she returned to the U.K. on several occasions, often with her mother (G. P. Thomson 1966, 16–17, 27, 33, 46).

Thomson's father, Sir Joseph, also a Nobel laureate in physics, was a longtime colleague of Edith Gittings Reid's geologist husband. Her own writings celebrated individuals who had made their mark on British science: in 1922 she published a play about the British nurse Florence Nightingale commemorating the centenary of Nightingale's birth; in the 1930s she published biographies of two Johns Hopkins medical professors—Sir William Osler, who later became the Regius Chair of medicine at Oxford, and William Sydney Thayer—with Oxford University Press. Edith Reid's British connections numbered literary luminaries as well. An episode in the Lucia novels by her friend E. F. Benson was reputedly inspired by Doris's antics while sailing off the coast of Maine.[14] As correspondence by Alice Hamilton and others testifies, it was Edith Reid's insistence that Edith Hamilton stay with her and Doris in England through early December 1921, and miss the first few months of the academic year, that precipitated Hamilton's rupture with M. Carey Thomas and resignation from the Bryn Mawr School (Sicherman 1984, 257–58; Hallett, 1996–1997, 134).

John Mason Brown and Huntington Cairns—Edith's closest male friends and most fervent promoters—also strongly identified with British culture, and met with approval from Edith in their pro-British remarks and endeavors. Brown served in England as a naval officer in World War II, accompanied the British forces as an observer during the invasion of Italy, and made frequent visits to the U.K. in the postwar years (Brown 1944, 31–46; Stevens 1974, 140–41, 192–93, 229–40). In a 2 November 1944 letter to Brown, now in the Princeton University library, Edith responds with delight to an article he wrote about his British experiences, singling out his remark that "[t]he average cultured Englishman at any age seemed about a century older than the equivalent American." Brown's connections with the British theatrical scene may help account for the interest in Edith's translation of The Trojan Women by Michael Cacoyannis, who studied and lived in England from 1939 through 1951, and who used her translation—terming it superior to Gilbert Murray's—both when staging the play on Broadway in 1963 and in filming it eight years later.[15]

The special rapport between Cairns, son of a Scottish immigrant and proud recipient of an honorary degree from St Andrews, and Paul Mellon, a major collector of British art and passionate aficionado of British culture, also merits mention. Both men took an active part in founding the Harvard University Center for Hellenic Studies, a few blocks from Edith's home in Washington. Most of the Plato translations that Cairns and Edith chose for their Bollingen volume were by academics from the U.K.. Cairns's papers (1993) in the Library of Congress include a considerable amount of correspondence with British cultural eminences: Sir Kenneth Clark, Cyril Connolly, Bertrand Russell, Arnold Toynbee, and Robert Graves.[16]

Both Brown and Cairns, moreover, were among those who hosted Graves during his 1957 tour of the United States. A 1959 letter to Edith from Agnes Meyer, whose husband had been publisher (and then chaired the board) of the Washington Post, eagerly anticipates a public forum at which Graves and Edith are slated to speak in January 1960. While Graves's biographers do not mention this event, they report that on the 1957 tour Graves did meet with Cairns as well as with another good friend of Edith's, Robert Richman, director of the Institute of Contemporary Art. Graves appeared with Brown and the stripper Gypsy Rose Lee on a television program about the meaning of words.[17]

Edith Hamilton also invoked, and benefited from the endorsements of, prominent British classical scholars. By way of contrast, save for Gildersleeve, the German émigré Werner Jaeger and her Bryn Mawr College professor Paul Shorey, her writings never mention their American counterparts.[18] So, too, other than the encomiastic Robinson, few American classical scholars recognized her as a professional colleague. As we have seen, she lionized Gilbert Murray: reverentially reviewing and quoting and misquoting from his writings; reportedly protesting that Murray, and not she, deserved the Greek accolades in 1957.[19] Sir Richard Livingstone, accorded brief mention in the *Classical World* essay, figures elsewhere in her writings as well. In *The Greek Way*, she uses Murray's translations of Euripides and Aristophanes and Livingstone's translation of a Pindaric ode; she also bases a comparison between Aristophanes' frank criticisms of Athenian war policy, and the restrictions on free speech during World War I, on Livingstone's *The Greek Genius and Its Meaning to Us* (Hamilton 1963, 8, 320, 321, 325, 326). While Murray and Livingstone never seem to have written or even referred to her, C. M. Bowra furnished glowing commendations for *The Greek Way*, representing its scholarly limitations in a positive, albeit somewhat sexist, light by attributing them to her "feminine intuition." "Miss Hamilton," he remarks,

> started from the best, the right, the only possible point—the actual texts of Greek literature. These she knew from the inside, not through translations and commentaries but through the original words, which are remarkable for their clarity and elegance and force. With this knowledge she was able to turn her feminine intuition in many directions, to adapt herself easily and almost unconsciously to the writers whom she studied, and to extract from their work what appealed most deeply to her and seemed to be the most significant. (Hamilton 1963, xvii)

And although Gilbert Highet never mentions any of Edith Hamilton's work in his scholarly writing, he provided a blurb for the *Ever-Present Past*; she provided a blurb on the dust jacket of his *Poets in a Landscape,* and he must have been involved in the relentless promotion of her books by the Book of the Month Club.[20]

Efforts to legitimate the authority of Edith Hamilton and her work by associating both with England were ironic, and in some ways necessary, because Edith's European ties were with Germany. Not only did she study there, she was born there: near Dresden, in 1867, since her mother's Southern-sympathizing, sugar-selling family had fled there from the

States during the Civil War. She studied German for many years as a girl in Fort Wayne, Indiana, often invoked German writers, and subscribed to a Hellenocentric, Athenocentric, vision of classical antiquity heavily influenced by German thought. This vision itself was not without its ironies. She had been a graduate fellow in Latin at Bryn Mawr College, had taught only Latin at the Bryn Mawr School, and was sponsored in Munich by Professor Eduard Woelfflin, editor of the *Thesaurus Linguae Latinae* (Reid 1967, 16, 24, 26–27, 32; Bacon 1980, 306–7; Sicherman 1984, 17–18, 89; Hallett 1996–1997, 108–9, 128). The two world wars, however, made it difficult for Hamilton to sustain or celebrate this German connection, especially because she, unlike her sister Alice, was apparently not interested in trying to rescue and resettle Jewish colleagues from Nazi-occupied Germany (Sicherman 1984, 332–34, 338, 340–44).

EDITH HAMILTON AND THE KENNEDY FAMILY

Accounting for, and indeed documenting the extent of, Edith Hamilton's appeal for the Kennedy family is not without its complications. But her, and their, British connections also play a significant role here: although immensely proud of their Irish roots, the Kennedys are a notably Anglophilic clan. The memoir of John F. Kennedy's presidency, *A Thousand Days*, by Arthur M. Schlesinger Jr., devotes several pages to JFK's "love of England," according special attention to his senior thesis at Harvard University, published as a book, *Why England Slept*, in 1940. Its title brashly alludes to Winston Churchill's collection of speeches, *While England Slept*. Schlesinger also mentions that JFK inserted two quotations about the death of a British soldier, Raymond Asquith, in France in 1915 in the notebook from 1945 he kept about the deaths of his brother Joseph and his brother-in-law, William Cavendish, Marquess of Hartington, eldest son of the Duke of Devonshire—one from Churchill and the other from John Buchan's *Pilgrim's Way*. His sister Kathleen, widow of "Billy Hartington," was planning to wed the eighth Earl Fitzwilliam when both were killed in a 1948 plane crash (Schlesinger 1965, 81–87).

A striking number of the quotes prized by Robert F. Kennedy, and included in his son's *Make Gentle the Life of This World*, are from English writers, including the lengthy poetic epilogue, from Alfred, Lord Tennyson's *Ulysses* (Kennedy 1998, 165–67), which was also read at the service commemorating the twenty-fifth anniversary of RFK's death. Michael Beran observes that while John F. Kennedy "loved David Cecil's evocations of the country homes of eighteenth-century Whig nobility," "it was Bobby, not Jack, who realized Cecil's splendid vision in his own life, in a house" "alive with the effort and hurry of politics." In pursuit of this vision, RFK asked Arthur M. Schlesinger Jr., who would later write biographies of himself and his brother, to organize a series of educational seminars at his home and at the White House. These "all-star intellectual galas" featured two academic luminaries from Oxford, the political scientist Sir Isaiah Berlin and the philosopher A. J. Ayer. Mindful that his sister's brief union with Hartington had enabled the Kennedys "to marry into one of the great Whig families in England," Bobby, like his father, the ambassador to Great Britain, "never forgot the family's aristocratic connection," "naming their first child Kathleen Hartington" (Beran 1998, 37–43).

Robert Kennedy's biographers have contended that he first discovered the writings of Edith Hamilton, and through her the Greeks, several months after his brother's death in November 1963. They attribute his interest in her and her topic to his brother's widow Jacqueline Bouvier Kennedy, who gave him her copy of *The Greek Way* when both were staying at Paul Mellon's home in Antigua (Schlesinger 1978, 617–18; Beran 1998, 90–91). Testimony from other sources, however, calls this contention into question. John White, another Anglophilic intimate of Edith Hamilton's and a one-time suitor of Jacqueline's, took credit for introducing Jackie, and ultimately RFK, to Edith's rendition of the lines from Aeschylus's *Agamemnon* about pain dripping upon the heart, after the death of Jackie's infant son Patrick in August 1963 (Heymann 1989, 397). Kathleen (Hartington) Kennedy Townsend, Robert F. Kennedy's eldest daughter, has attested that he was already a devoted Hamilton reader in the 1950s.

Jacqueline's own familiarity with Edith Hamilton and her writings may well have predated the summer of 1963. She studied Latin from 1942 through 1944 at the Holton-Arms School, then located around the corner from Edith's home in Washington, D.C., with a beloved teacher, Helen Shearman, who later chaperoned her and her sister on a trip to Europe. Jackie then attended Miss Porter's School in Connecticut, which boasted Edith and Alice Hamilton as their most distinguished graduates (Heymann 1989, 54, 69–70; Hallett 1996–1997, 114–15). Jackie's friendship with the Greek shipping tycoon Aristotle Onassis—who entertained her on his yacht in October 1963, a month before her husband's assassination, and whom she married after RFK's death in 1968—also needs to be considered in determining when and how she might have become an Edith Hamilton devotee (Hallett 1996–1997, 146).

It is worth mentioning in this context that at his final press conference on 31 October 1963, shortly after Jackie's return from her Greek holiday with Aristotle Onassis, JFK responded to a question about why he was seeking reelection by observing: "As far as the job of President goes, it is rewarding and I have given before to this group the definition of happiness of the Greeks, and I will define it again. It is full use of your powers along lines of excellence. I find, therefore, the Presidency provides some happiness" (John F. Kennedy Presidential Library and Museum, News Conference, 63).

This definition, from Aristotle's *Nicomachean Ethics* 1.13, was much invoked by Edith Hamilton. In *The Greek Way* she remarks that "the exercise of vital powers along lines of excellence is a life affording them scope is an old Greek definition of happiness," At the seventy-fifth anniversary of the Bryn Mawr School in 1960 she concluded her speech with this "bit of Aristotle I always like to quote," maintaining "He says it is a definition of happiness . . . but I think it also is what education should strive for" (Hamilton 1963, 20; Reid 1969, 122). JFK did not attribute the quote to Aristotle, and he may well have come across this statement in another source. But he, too, may have been a Hamilton reader.

A recent, sensationalistic book by the British journalist Peter Evans purports to illuminate the interconnections between Jacqueline Kennedy Onassis, Aristotle Onassis, John F. Kennedy, Robert F. Kennedy, and Edith Hamilton. Evans, who contends that Onassis bankrolled the assassination of RFK in June 1968, claims that Onassis and Jackie became lovers on that October 1963 cruise and that afterwards he sent her "books, including Edith Hamilton's *The Greek Way*." Indeed, Evans states that it was this copy of the book that Jackie later gave to RFK (Evans 2004, 121–23).

There is no evidence that Onassis knew Edith Hamilton personally. But he was a friend of the Hollywood mogul Spyros Skouras, a Greek immigrant who had been a member of the honorary committee when Edith received her honorary Athenian citizenship in 1957 (Reid 1967, 106). Evans further alleges that Skouras had motivated the fiercely competitive Onassis to pursue Jackie Kennedy by apprising him of extramarital dalliances by both John and Robert Kennedy with Marilyn Monroe, at one time Skouras's lover too. Whatever the truth of Evans's statements, he has given his book the title of a Greek mythological figure, Nemesis, and its chapter about Onassis's role in the events immediately following JFK's assassination the title of Hamilton's *The Greek Way* (Evans 2004, 64–66, 114–23).

However the Kennedy family first became acquainted with Edith Hamilton's writing, it was ultimately the prestige commanded by British culture in the circles that Edith Hamilton frequented which accounted for the Anglicizing of her words and work. Her identification with Britain in turn helped to legitimate her as the most prominent American spokesperson for the timeless relevance of classical Greek values in the mid-twentieth century. Such an unorthodox means of legitimation proved crucial because Hamilton, and those who fostered her career as an expert witness on the classical past, did not set much store by traditional modes of conveying specialized knowledge and of establishing authority. That her writings inspired impressionable readers to pursue classics as a learned profession is another ironic aspect of her phenomenal success. Yet another irony is that Hamilton's fame is largely limited to America's shores. Her popularizing, Anglicizing writings have yet to receive much attention in Britain itself.[21]

Notes

Introduction

1   See, e.g., the Earl of Cromer's *Ancient and Modern Imperialism* (1910). There is a useful survey in Vance 1997, 222–46. On the classical status of English literature in the Empire see e.g., Viswanathan 1989.

2   The notion of internal colonialism was advanced by Hechter (1975), which provoked considerable debate both within and without Britain. It should be remembered that Ireland was part of the United Kingdom between 1800 and 1922. We regret that an original contributor to the volume was unable to provide a chapter on classics in Ireland at the conference.

3   On Adam, see Robinson 2005.

4   Cf. Stray 2007b.

5   Similarly, there was and is a cultural politics of regionalism in the United States. The three U.S. classicists discussed in this volume came from different parts of the country—the South, New England, and the Midwest. Yet all ended up in the New York/Washington "power corridor."

6   See Agard 1953, 147–48. He there quotes the claim by Edward Everett, professor of Greek at Harvard, himself German-trained, that the

universities in America "have nothing to learn from England, but everything to learn from Germany."

7   See R. A. Ackerman, "The Cambridge Ritualists (act. 1900–1914)," *Oxford Dictionary of National Biography* (online edition: Oxford University Press, October 2007, http://www.oxforddnb.com/view/theme/ 95519, accessed 26 October 2007).

8   Shorey's attitude was not merely a reaction to the global politics of World War I. In a 1911 article in the *Nation*, Shorey had been bitterly critical of German scholarship as sloppy and narrow, assuring him a frosty reception when he arrived in Berlin as the Theodore Roosevelt lecturer in 1913–1914. See Briggs and Kopff 1995, 466–69.

9   British publishers of textbooks as well as scholarly studies in the field of classics are well aware that the U.S.A. forms the largest single market for books in English.

10   See the essays on these and other topics in Stray (ed.) 2007.

11   At the 5 May 1956 meeting of the New York Classical Club, Highet saw to it that a resolution honoring Murray on his ninetieth birthday was passed. Murray replied by expressing his admiration for "the amount of work" that Highet had "got through in America" and "the amount of real enlightenment that [Highet] must have brought to intelligent readers." See Ball, forthcoming.

Chapter 1

1   Glover 1943, 95. The seventy-mile long river Tweed marks the traditional, but often contested, border between Scotland and England. The major town at the mouth of the river, Berwick-upon-Tweed, has had a very checkered career; between 1147 and 1482 it changed hands eleven times, between the Scots and the English. "Berwick has always had a curiously anomalous position, and was often listed separately in official documents (although the story that it was omitted from the Treaty of Versailles in 1919 and hence is technically still at war with Germany is apocryphal)." Gardiner and Wenborn 1995, 77.

2   I know of only one doctoral thesis on this subject: G. M. Sutton, "The History of Teaching of Classics in Scotland until 1872" (University of St Andrews, 1956). The eighteenth century is slightly better served with A. J. Murray's Ph.D. thesis "The Influence of Dr. Alexander Adam, Rector of the High School of Edinburgh, upon the Culture and Political Opinion in Scotland and the United Kingdom During the Enlightenment" (Open University, 1991).

3   The 1826 Commission found that at King's College Junior Latin was given two hours, but at Glasgow ten; but Junior Greek at King's was given ten hours, at Glasgow five.

4   *Evidence Oral and Documentary*, 1:1. [Hereafter: *Evidence.*]

5   Of the seventeen originally appointed seven were very senior Scottish lawyers or advocates. The rest were either members of the Scottish aristocracy or leading figures in the Church of Scotland.

6   The oddity of this chronology does not need to be underlined but is far from easy to explain. It seems clear that one of the reasons why the proposed reforms did not occur when the legislation was brought forward is that the friends of "reform" lacked the ammunition that the four volumes of *Evidence* would have provided. Amongst the reasons that can be brought forward to explain this hiatus are the following: Lord Liverpool's government, which had appointed the Royal Commission, was replaced in August 1827 by Lord Goderich's administration, with Peel no longer at the Home Office, then in January 1828 Lord Wellington was made prime minister, with Peel restored to his previous cabinet post. In November 1830 Lord Grey formed a radical Whig administration with Peel out of government and Lord Melbourne as the Whigs' home secretary. This administration in turn was replaced in July 1834, with Melbourne now as prime minister and Viscount Duncannon in charge of home affairs. In December 1834 this government fell; Peel formed his first administration and Goulburn took over as home secretary. Then in April 1835 Peel was replaced as prime minister by Lord Melbourne, who presided over the two failed attempts to bring in a bill to reform Scotland's universities; this was all the more fascinating since his home secretary was Lord John Russell, a product of the benches at the University of Edinburgh. Clearly one reason for the confusion was the succession of administrations, who perhaps saw reform of Scotland's ancient universities as a very low priority in a time of turbulent economic and parliamentary reform. Then also, the death of King George III in 1830 required a new royal warrant to continue the work of the commissioners. But a much more practical reason may have been simply the fire in 1834 which destroyed not just the old Palace of Westminster but also many parliamentary records. Under Sir Charles Barry's designs Parliament arose again, like the phoenix, and presumably records were recovered or not from the debris and then, and, perhaps only then, could the oral testimony from Scotland's professors be put into print. Whatever the cause, the delay was of the greatest significance to both friends and foes of reform.

7   This proposal, supported by Sir Robert Peel, was never acted upon.

8   It is difficult, reading some of the contemporary material, not to conclude that a smaller country like Scotland simply could not need, or be allowed to retain, so many more universities than England: Oxford and Cambridge were the model.

9   In 1836 he was elected Lord Rector of Glasgow University. This unique Scottish university post was an elective one, the voters being the matriculated students of the university. The rector, who usually served for three years, was intended to be the students' voice and defender in the Senatus of the university. The men who had served as rectors at Glasgow make an impressive list: Burke, Disraeli, Palmerston, Gladstone, and Lords Macaulay, Cockburn, and Curzon. Lord Rosebery has the unique distinction of being elected rector to every one of Scotland's ancient universities.

10   Humanity, Greek, mathematics, natural philosophy, and moral philosophy.

11   He was under the care of his elder brother, himself only twelve.

12   Perhaps the best example of this process at work is the education of James George Frazer who, after a brilliant undergraduate career at the University of Glasgow, went to Trinity College, Cambridge, not by the more familiar and expected route, as a Snell exhibitioner, to the "Scottish college at Oxford (Balliol)." His Free Church father clearly felt the dangers of Anglo-Catholic Oxford were too great for his son, even in the 1870s.

13   In 1827 John Keble, fellow of Oriel, published *The Christian Year*, a hugely popular collection of Anglo-Catholic verses. His sermon before the University of Oxford on 14 July 1833 is usually regarded as the beginning of the "Oxford Movement." John Henry Newman's conversion to Roman Catholicism in 1845 was regarded with very little favor or sympathy in Presbyterian Scotland.

14   Posts both in the universities of Scotland and her schools were invariably made on the basis of *ad vitam aut culpam* ("until the death or until a great misdeed"). This had predictable consequences for schools and colleges: it was extremely difficult to correct a very poor appointment.

15   Alexander Monro *Primus* was appointed in 1721, aged twenty-six.

16   A revised second edition was published in 1964 but in essence this only dealt with minor corrections.

17   Davie 1961, foreword.

18   Davie 1961, 3.

19   The memory of Burns is important here: none who cared about Scotland's poet could forget that his poetic work, in "Scots," published in the Kilmarnock edition (1786), had to be translated into English, for the Edinburgh edition a year later, to meet the needs of a more "respectable" audience.

20   Davie 1961, 5. The concept of betrayal of Scotland by "the men above" has a particular resonance in Scottish popular history: the surrender of William Wallace to the English, the Act of Union, the collapse of the 1745 Rebellion, and the Highland Clearances were often seen as examples of the perfidy of some Scottish aristocrats.

21   Davie 1961, 4.

22   Davie 1961, 7.

23   If Davie's book has a hero, it is probably the Scottish metaphysician and doctor Sir William Hamilton, whose dramatic profile greets the reader looking like Sir Henry Irving playing Hamlet, facing the title page, in the hardback edition of *The Democratic Intellect*. By the early twentieth century, figures like Hamilton and his fellow metaphysician J. F. Ferrier had been marginalized: there never was any great taste for metaphysics in the philosophy departments of English universities.

24   Headmaster of the recently established Edinburgh Academy.

25   Professor of Greek at Glasgow, appointed like Gilbert Murray at the age of twenty-three.

26   Davie either did not know or simply chose to omit just how much contempt Sandford had for Oxford teaching; see Sandford's own philippic, *Letter to Rev. P. Elmsley* (1822).

27   Davie 1961, 31.

28   Davie has not been without his critics, some of them merely dismissive: "Davie's wilful analysis," in Humes and Paterson 1983, preface. Others, like R. D. Anderson, are more judicious: he praises Davie's "remarkable book," but queries some of the details in the thesis; for example, he argues that philosophy was not *primus inter pares* in the Scottish degree program (1983, 25). Sometimes Davie has to be rescued from his supporters: Craig Beveridge and Ronald Turnbull, in their *The Eclipse of Scottish Culture*, see parallels between the Scots and the Algerians under French colonial rule: the inhabitants of Charlotte Square in Edinburgh and Park Circus in Glasgow are apparently the wretched of the earth.

29   Davie never claimed the phrase "democratic intellect" as his own. He said it was first coined by Sir Walter Elliot (1888–1958), a Tory MP and man of many parts much regarded in Scotland. He was elected rector of Glasgow and Aberdeen.

30   In May 2007, the Scottish National Party gained more seats in the (devolved) Scottish Parliament than the ruling Labour Party.

31   This was the basis for a very popular major exhibition in Edinburgh in 1986 which was sponsored by the Saltire Society and curated by David Daiches, *The Scottish Enlightenment 1730–1790: A Hotbed of Genius*. Earlier, in 1971, another major exhibition in Edinburgh to coincide with the festival was opened, *Sir Water Scott 1771–1971: A Bicentenary Exhibition*.

32   Anderson 1985, 94.

33   Anderson 1985, 93–94.

34   Smiles 1859, 284–85. What the Livingstone extract illustrates is that the real barrier to the lad of parts who wanted to enter university was not income or religion but Latin. The Scottish universities assumed that all entrants had received at least three or four years' tuition in Latin. Greek was often taught from scratch. The grammar Livingstone would have been using was Thomas Ruddiman's *Rudiments of the Latin Tongue* (1714), possibly the cheapest and most successful Latin grammar ever published; it flourished in one form or another for over a hundred fifty years.

35   He shared his birthplace, Haddington, with John Knox.

36   Briggs 1970, 118.

37   In the early years of the last century the Edinburgh publisher T. N. Foulis had considerable success with titles such as Nicholas Dickson's *The Kirk and its Worthies* (1912), Francis Watt's *The Book of Edinburgh Anecdotes* (1913), and in the same year, D. Macleod Malloch's *The Book of Glasgow Anecdotes* and T. Radcliffe Barnett's *The Makers of the Kirk* (1920). They also produced very successfully an edition of Dean Ramsay's *Reminiscences of Scottish Life and Character*, which by 1920 had gone through sixteen editions. This book, first published in 1857, ran through twenty-one editions before the author's death in 1872; it remains the *locus classicus* for this genre of literature.

38   Thomas Chalmers (1780–1847), theologian, preacher and philanthropist: leader of the Great Disruption and regarded by many in his lifetime as the moral conscience of Scotland.

39   "The 'History' has been translated into German, Polish, Danish, Swedish, Italian, French, Dutch, Spanish, Hungarian, Russian, Bohemian

and Persian," *Dictionary of National Biography* (hereafter *DNB*) 12 (1937–1938): 416.

40   Vol. 1 (Everyman Edition, 1907), 58. It must be said that Macaulay is far less sympathetic to the Catholic and especially the Irish-Catholic cause: see vol. 2, chap. 12.

41   The commissioners ordered a notice to be put up at "the public entrances to the College of Edinburgh, similarly upon the gate at the College of Glasgow . . . the public entrance to the Common Hall at the University of St Andrews and on the public entrances to King's College and Marischal (stating) His Majesty's Commissioners for the Visitation of the Universities of Scotland . . . are ready to hear all concerned in regard to all matters relating to the University and the College. ... Any communications duly authenticated may be sent to their secretary, 29 Queen Street, Edinburgh," *Evidence* 1:15.

42   For example Glasgow, Edinburgh's mighty rival and nearest in student population size, saw only thirty-three witnesses called in a nine-day period. It is the depth of the interrogations at Edinburgh that seem so striking. In 1826 Edinburgh had 1905 matriculated students; Glasgow had 1256, Marischal 738, King's 235, and St Andrews 223. The commissioners spent five days at Aberdeen and St Andrews.

43   In England they would have been called headmasters.

44   Rev. James Melvin, rector of Aberdeen Grammar School and part-time humanity lecturer at Marischal, was briefly questioned.

45   One puzzling feature of the Edinburgh hearings is the absence of any substantial testimony from one the university's finest academic adornments, Sir William Hamilton. This noted metaphysician was professor of civil history, a noncompulsory discipline at Edinburgh. Hamilton's defeat in 1820 in the election to the chair of moral philosophy by John Wilson [Christopher North] was final proof, if proof were needed in Scottish Whig circles, of the utter Tory corruption of the Edinburgh corporation. Again, Sir Walter Scott seems to have been very active in the promotion of the case for the intellectually inferior Wilson. Hamilton, who as a Snell exhibitioner at Balliol was described as "the most learned Aristotelian in Oxford," appeared before the commission, but "the Evidence not printed on account of the extensive alteration made by him thereon, when sent for verbal correction, to be re-examined" (*Evidence* 1:9). He was not recalled, and the 1831 Final Report gives a fairly anodyne summary of his views.

46   Baird was married to the daughter of Edinburgh's Lord Provost. The title "Very Reverend" indicates that he was a former moderator of the general assembly of the Church of Scotland, the highest ecclesiastical post in the Kirk.

47   *Evidence* 1:98.

48   *Evidence* 1:96–97.

49   *Evidence* 1:101.

50   *Evidence* 1:485–86.

51   *Evidence* 1:510.

52   *Evidence* 1:511.

53   *Evidence* 1:513.

54   *Evidence* 1:512.

55   Dunbar had been tutor to the Fettes family.

56   Edinburgh's session began on the last Wednesday in October, i.e., five weeks before Pillans's interrogation.

57   It should not be forgotten that the holidays Pillans mentions lasted six months.

58   *Evidence* 1:428.

59   From 1824 to 1825 one hundred fifty-three students were matriculated for this class.

60   This text, written by an Edinburgh schoolmaster, was in essence an expanded version, with clear acknowledgment, of Ruddiman's *Rudiments of Latin Grammar* (1714), the bedrock of Latin teaching in Scottish schools.

61   *Evidence* 1:430.

62   It is worth noting Professor Leslie's [mathematics] jaundiced view: "I disapprove of the system of monitors, and am convinced that there is much deception in the machinery that has lately been put in motion," *Evidence* 1:133.

63   *Evidence* 1:431.

64   *Evidence* 1:435.

65   *Evidence* 1:436.

66   *Evidence* 1:437.

67   The *DNB* noted that Francis Jeffrey, when he went to Queen's College, Oxford in 1791, lost his Old Scottish but acquired in its place an unpleasing English accent: a "high keyed accent and sharp pronunciation."

68   *Evidence* 1:439.

69   The texts appear to be largely extracts from Shakespeare.

70   Pillans's hostility to the Scots tongue would have annoyed at least one commissioner if he had been present at the hearing on 4 December: Sir Walter Scott. The Wizard of the North pours scorn on the "English" method of pronouncing Latin: "January 25th . . . the mode of pronunciation approved by Buchanan and Milton and practised by all nations excepting the English . . . is certainly the best. . . . I wish the cocknified pedant who first disturbed it by reading Emo for Amo and quy for qui had choked in the attempt." *The Journal of Sir Walter Scott* (1939), 305. But Scott's enthusiasm for this way of pronouncing Latin must be set against the fact that the new Edinburgh Academy boasted in its "Statement by the Directors" that there would be "a Master for English who shall have a pure English accent," something unheard of in Scottish schools. The reason given was "to remedy a defect in the education of boys in Edinburgh, who are suffered to neglect the cultivation of their native language and literature" (*Statement by the Directors of Edinburgh Academy* [1824]: 11; National Library of Scotland ABS 2.99 34/4). Scott was a key supporter of the new school.

71   He was also the university librarian.

72   He in fact continued in post until 1835 and then became principal aged ninety-one. He died two years later. His remarkable situation raised a serious issue: the inability of professors to retire due to the lack of an adequate pension. Hence the sale of offices. At Glasgow Principal Macfarlane in his evidence was involved in an exchange

about the problem of infirm and or incompetent professors. He was asked if there were any professors that "are not competent to teach as well as formerly." He agreed and said there were two such cases: the professor of practical medicine "is from age incapable of teaching—this is the second session in which he has been allowed to employ another person to lecture for him. But the temporary intervention of an individual reading *his lectures* is not found to be effectual for the instruction of pupils" (emphasis mine). The second professor found wanting was James Millar, professor of mathematics, who was not infirm but unable to keep good order in the lecture hall: ". . . a total want of the power of exerting authority in his class by exerting discipline among his students; the Faculty has been repeatedly obliged to intervene since I have been Principal" (*Evidence* 2:134). Millar had been in post for forty years and owed his position to the fact that his father had been professor of law at Glasgow. The 1831 report urged Millar to retire, and said he owed his position to his father's eminence. MacFarlane went on to tell the commission that the only power the faculty had to dismiss anyone was in cases of "gross malversation." But MacFarlane himself was not above criticism: he was publicly criticized for holding both the post of principal and the living of the High Church of Glasgow. He seems to have courted controversy—he was moderator to the General Assembly in 1843 when the Great Disruption occurred.

73   One of his colleagues, Patrick Forbes (humanity), believed Jack was clinically insane. See Lee Papers, 3434.330 (National Library of Scotland).

74   *Evidence* 4:9.

75   The commissioners must have found it difficult on occasion to penetrate the fog of medievalism that surrounded appointments at King's. This, for example, is how the "civilist" is appointed: "The Civilist is elected by the Rector, Procuratores Nationum, the Principal Mediciner, Humanist, Subprincipal, three Regents and the Professor of Divinity and Oriental Languages" (*Evidence* 4:183). It is very difficult to be certain, but the post of civilist seems to involve someone with expertise in civil law as opposed to "canonists" who were expert in ecclesiastical law.

76   *Evidence* 4:10.

77   *Evidence* 4:11.

78   *Evidence* 1:243.

79   *Evidence* 1:245.

80   *Evidence* 1:273.

81   *Evidence* 1:279.

82   *Evidence* 1:252.

83   *Evidence* 1:45.

84   *Journal of the House of Lords*, 28 June 1834.

85   *Journal of the House of Lords*, 28 June 1836, 494.

86   *Journal of the House of Lords*, 28 June.

87   *Journal of the House of Lords*, 28 June.

88   *Journal of the House of Lords*, 7 July.

89   Davie 1961, 36.

90   This may well be explained by the promise made in 1835 to give a government grant of £15,000 to Marischal to rebuild the college. Marischal lay within the city's boundaries; King's College did not.

91   This term refers to the events that took place on 18 May 1843 at the opening of the General Assembly of the Church of Scotland. After the opening prayers, the retiring moderator, Reverend David Welsh, stated that there had been "an infringement on the Constitution of the General assembly," and led over 450 ministers out of St Andrew's church, down George Street, past the thousands on the street, to Tanfield Hall in Canonmills, where a Deed of Demission was signed and the Free Church of Scotland was established. The issue was who should appoint a minister: the crown or the heritor (landowner), or the congregation. These clergymen were turning their backs on their careers, income, and homes on moral principle. This was the "most important domestic event in Scotland during the nineteenth century." Michael Fry, in Brown and Fry 1993, viii.

92   A jibe rarely heard in Scotland concerns the definition of a Scottish boomerang: "it never comes back but perpetually sings of return."

93   A. E. Housman wrote, "I am not a pessimist but a pejorist (as George Eliot said she was not an optimist but a meliorist)." Burnett 2007, 2:329.

94   This department was created as a result of government attempts to recognize Scotland's role within the United Kingdom. In 1885 the new post of secretary of state for Scotland had been created. This was based in London until 1939.

95   George Davie died on 20 March 2007, two days after his ninety-fifth birthday. I would like this chapter to be a tribute to this remarkable Scot.

Chapter 2

1   L. Edwards 1865, 136; reprinted in L. Edwards [1867], 180–81.

2   For a biography, see T. L. Evans 1967, or more briefly, the article by Brynley F. Roberts in *Oxford Dictionary of National Biography*, 2004, volume 17: 951–2.

3   T. C. Edwards 1901, 193.

4   T. C. Edwards, 1901, 486: Lewis Edwards, letter to the Rev. Owen Thomas, 9 May 1856.

5   L. Edwards 1849, 350; L. Edwards [1867], 24.

6   "Dyben yr ysgrif hon yw galw sylw at yr anghenrheidrwydd am ychwaneg o ysgolion ieithyddol yn Nghymru, sef ysgolion i gyfranu dysgeidiaeth ieithyddol drwyadl yn yr ieithoedd Lladin a Groeg" (L. Edwards 1849, 347; L. Edwards [1867], 20).

7   *Reports* (1847). In 1848 a shorter version was published, in one volume, as well as a Welsh translation.

8   On Williams, see D. Evans [1939]. For his motion to the House of Commons, 10 March 1846, ibid., 82.

9   J. C. Symons, in *Reports* (1847), Part II: 1.

10   *Reports* (1847), Part III: 49.
11   *Reports* (1847), Part III: 51.
12   *Reports* (1847) Part I: 227.
13   For studies of education in Wales, see J. G. Williams 1993; G. E. Jones 1997; G. E. Jones and G.W. Roderick 2003.
14   See P. Morgan 1984.
15   *Reports* (1847), Part II: 62.
16   *Reports* (1847), Part II: 66.
17   *Reports* (1847), Part I: 489.
18   G. Williams 1979, 105.
19   "No episode did more to rouse nonconformist bodies from their political quietude. The 'treachery' of the Blue Books was to be handed down in oral tradition as the censure of a nation, the Glencoe and the Amritsar of Welsh history" (K. O. Morgan 1980, 16).
20   Millward 1991; H. T. Edwards 1991.
21   Jenkins 1957, 205. On the beginnings and history of *Y Traethodydd*, which is happily still published as a quarterly by the Caernarfon-based Gwasg Pantycelyn, see J. E. C. Williams 1981, 1995. Until 1880 names of contributors were not given in issues of *Y Traethodydd*. A list of authors, from the beginning until 1879, was published in *Y Traethodydd* 35 (1880): 5–24.
22   L. Edwards 1848a; L. Edwards 1848b. The essays were reprinted in L. Edwards [1867], 374–405, 406–21.
23   *Reports* (1847), Part I: 3.
24   The two passages by Lewis Edwards, quoted at the beginning of this essay, first appeared in *Y Traethodydd*. See nn. 1 and 5 above.
25   L. Edwards 1852.
26   L. Edwards [1867], 492–504.
27   J. Morgan 1857.
28   T. C. Edwards 1868; G. Ellis 1877–1879.
29   The assertion in Llewellyn-Jones 2002, 6, that "W. J.Gruffydd's translation of Sophocles' *Antigone* of 1950 . . . is regarded as the definitive (and first) poetic translation of a Greek drama" needs to be corrected. Gruffydd's translation is certainly remarkable. It may, arguably, be definitive. It is certainly not the first attempt in Welsh at a "poetic translation."
30   "Hwyrach y syna ambell i Gymro efengylaidd fod gan Bagan syniadau mor gywir am 'pa beth sydd *iawn*'—nid 'pa beth sydd fuddiol' " (O. Jones 1866, 173).
31   "Meddyliasom ninnau y gallai fod yr un mor fuddiol i'r Cymro uniaith gael gweled ambell i ddernyn o weithoedd y beirdd Groegaidd mewn gwisg Gymreig, fel y gallo gael rhyw syniad am yr hyn a ddarllenir gan ein dynion ieuainc yn yr Athrofâu, ac a ystyrir yn orchestion llênyddol y byd" (O. Jones 1866, 173).
32   R. Ll. Owen 1868.
33   R. Ll. Owen 1899.
34   Peter 1867, 1868.
35   R. T. Jenkins 1932–1936, 148.
36   See further C. Davies 1987.
37   See H.T. Edwards 1990.

38   On Hugh Owen and the Eisteddfod, see H. T. Edwards, 1980, 53–112;
      H. T. Edwards 1990, 23–25.
39   R. M. Lewis 1928.
40   Euripides, *Alcestis* (1887).
41   See further C. Davies 1995b: 211–13.
42   W. Davies 1989, 60, 84–86.
43   Norwood 1920.
44   Norwood 1909.
45   Gruffydd 1950. See also n. 29 above.
46   Gruffydd and Roberts, 1900.
47   O. G. Owen, W. J. Gruffydd 1950, E. Williams 1902, 62.
48   C. Davies 1995a: 126.
49   *Reports* (1847) Part II: 66.

Chapter 3

1   This paper was read at a conference on classics in nineteenth- and
      twentieth-century Britain, Hay-on-Wye, 29 June 2005. I am grateful to
      Christopher Stray and Anton Powell who organized the conference and
      made it a pleasant and enriching experience.
2   Cf. Stray 1998, 250–51, for the disadvantages to a classicist of being
      female and not being educated at Oxford or Cambridge.
3   My colleague at the University of Toronto Scarborough, Ann Bodding-
      ton (Lady Margaret Hall 1951) has told me that she was warned at
      Oxford not to use Freeman's books.
4   Notices of Freeman: *Lady's Who's Who 1938/39; Who was Who? 1951–
      1960*: 396; *Times of London* death notice (22 February 1959) and obitu-
      ary (24 February 1959); *Western Mail*, obituary (23 February 1959).
5   I owe this information to Prof. Ceri Davies, whose father was one of
      Freeman's students, and who has given me assistance in many details
      and been a great encouragement. Freeman was proud of her doctorate
      and styled herself Dr. Kathleen Freeman on publications after it was
      awarded.
6   For Freeman's complete bibliography, cf. Irwin 2004a, 2005.
7   *Quarrelling with Lois* (1928); *This Love* (1929); *The Huge Shipwreck*
      (1934), and *Adventure from the Grave* (1936).
8   Freeman used other pseudonyms: Clare St. Donat, Caroline Cory (per-
      haps referring to herself as the *kore* [daughter] of Charles, her father's
      name), and Stuart Mary Wick.
9   Several years before the decipherment of Linear B by Michael Ventris in
      1952. Cf. Chadwick 1958.
10   Freeman, correspondence with the Society of Authors: letter from Free-
      man, 17 September 1947; response from society, 22 September 1947;
      letter to Mary Fitt, 16 March 1948; response from Freeman to society,
      18 March 1948.
11   The quotation appears on the back cover of several Penguin editions of
      her mysteries.

12   I have found only five published sonnets, the three mentioned above published in 1924 and "Failure" and "Gratitude," in *Adelphi* (1925).

13   Cf. *Encyclopedia Britannica* (15th ed. 1974, *Micropaedia*, vol. 4, p. 162) s.v. "Mary Fitton." See further below on the name of the house owned jointly by Freeman and Clopet, "Lark's Rise."

14   Among those recommending publication were Gilbert Norwood, Benjamin Farrington, T. S. Eliot (specifically the article on Pindar), H. J. W. Tillyard, and Cyril Bailey.

15   Stephens 1986, 206 and Aaron 1999, 274 assume that she was born in Cardiff. My information about place of birth and father's occupation comes from her birth certificate.

16   They were still in Yardley in the 1901 census. Freeman's father was alive in 1926 when she signed a copy of *Martin Hanner* for him, rather distantly "To Chas. H. Freeman (father) from Kathleen Freeman, with love, March 1926." (I am grateful to Mark Everett of Barnes, who owns this copy and sent me a photocopy of the signature.) And *Where's Mr Bellamy?* under the pseudonym Stuart Mary Wick (1948) is dedicated to (her mother) Catharine Mawdesley "instead of flowers."

17   Cf. the obituary in the *Western Mail* (23 February 1959); Mathias 2001, 77.

18   Information from Canton School for Girls Website.

19   The whole preface makes interesting reading for her opinion about Greek language instruction. See discussion below.

20   D. Lamb, in Todd, *DBC* 2:555–56 (D. Gill); W. Lamb, *DBC* 2:556–57 (D. Gill); Benton, *DBC* 1:73–74 (L. Zarmati); Toynbee, *DBC* 3:981–83 (S. Dyson), and Dale, *DBC* 1:223–24 (L. Parker).

21   Most lived to a ripe old age (Benton 98, Toynbee 88, and Dorothy Lamb 80) though Winifred Lamb died at 69, and Dale, whose health was never robust, at 66. Dorothy Lamb was married twice and Dale once.

22   Charles Henry's birth was registered in March 1867; her grandfather Charles Freener's death in June 1885, making Charles Henry about 18 when his father died.

23   Sisters Bessie (older) and Annie (younger). My conclusion is based on his age at his father's death and his occupation as listed on Kathleen's birth certificate.

24   Todd, *DBC* 2:721 (C. Collard).

25   For his complete bibliography, cf. White 1952, 85–94.

26   Letter dated 26 October 1954, University of Toronto Archives, B70-002-021.

27   I am grateful to Prof. Ceri Davies for dates and titles.

28   Cf. the appreciation of Richardson by J. V. Luce (1993). I am grateful to Richardson's daughter Hilary Richardson for information about her father and for the reference to Luce.

29   Cf. his address "The Classical Association: The First Fifty Years" (1954).

30   Cf. Cyril Bailey (1931).

31   One of them, J. Gwyn Griffiths, dedicated his Welsh translation of Aristotle's *Poetics* to her memory (1978). I am grateful to Prof. Ceri Davies for this reference.

32   The fruit of those years of interaction with her students is seen in *The Pre-Socratic Philosophers: A Companion* (1946).

33 Norwood's verse translations and acting editions: Plautus *Mostellaria* (1908), Euripides *Iphigeneia at Aulis* (1909), Aristophanes *Acharnians* (1911); cf. White 1952, xi.

34 Selections of her translations from Greek drama (not entire plays) were published in *The Greek Way.*

35 Lilian(e) Marie Catherine Clopet (b. Berwick upon Tweed, 13 December 1901, d. Newport, Gwent, 5 November 1987) MB BCh (1930 Wales) MRCS Eng, LRCP Lond. (1928). MB BCh (bachelor of surgery) was awarded together as a medical degree. Clopet's bibliography is given on p. 204.

36 It has been suggested that the name of the house might have been borrowed from Flora Thompson (1939) *Lark* [not Lark's] *Rise*, but the house name predates Thompson's book by at least four years. *The Medical Register* (1935) gives Lark's Rise as Dr. Clopet's place of residence.

37 From her novels: Austria (*Murder Mars the Tour*, 1936); Madrid, Paris, Berlin, Moscow, Zürich, and Geneva (*Bulls like Death*, 1937); Paris and the south of France (*Doctor Underground*, 1956); and the island of "Acanthos," Greece (*The Late Uncle Max*, 1957). Two children's books show further travels: *The Shifting Sands* (1958) set in Beirut and the Arabian Desert, and *The Great River* (1959) in China.

38 Quoted on the back cover of *Three Sisters Flew Home*, reissued by Penguin in 1953.

39 The same techniques, though not ancient authors, were used in her third book of anti-Nazi propaganda, *What they said at the time: a survey of the causes of the second world war and the hopes for lasting peace, as exhibited in the utterance of the world's leaders and some others from 1917–1944* (Freeman 1945).

40 The inclusion in her *Who's Who* entry is an indication of the importance Freeman attributed to this work and her pride in it.

41 She had a gift for modern as well as ancient languages; she knew Italian, French, and German well. She translated Untersteiner's *I sofisti* from Italian and used Diels-Kranz's *Fragmente der Vorsokratiker* for her *Companion*. She translated modern Greek songs in *The Greek Way.* Some of her material on the Attic orators was translated into Welsh and broadcast on the BBC, but whether translated by her or someone else is not known.

42 *Who was Who?* 1951–1960, 396.

43 From Hippocrates *Corpus Hippocraticum Med.*, *Praeceptiones* 6.6, Littré.

44 *Murder of Herodes*, 43–53; *The Edge of the Chair*, Joan Kahn (ed.) (New York, 1967), 278–88; *The Graveyard Shift*, Joan Kahn (ed.) (New York, 1970), 11–22.

45 "Scandal" in anon 1952, 115–33.

46 For the original, see Theocritus 11.5–6.

47 She apparently drew the city plans included in *Greek City States.*

48 Handwritten letter from Freeman to the Society of Authors, 8.7.54. Archives, British Library.

49 She was impressed with Austen's refusal (in her letters) to consider suicide as a way to escape ill health, undoubtedly a reflection of her own health concerns.

50   Dedicated to "Liliane."

51   E.g., the myth of Theseus in *MizMaze* (1959).

52   In *Clues to Christabel* (1944) the heroine wrote a letter in classical Greek, intelligible only to her friend George with whom she had studied Greek.

53   Cf. Mynors 1966 for awareness of the importance of communicating with the nonspecialist.

54   I knew one of these and learned from his experience what the society could mean: A. E. Kemp, naval veteran, ordained in the Church of England but not a university graduate, found the intellectual challenge and congenial discussion he longed for in the Philosophical Society.

55   Murray wrote the foreword for *Fighting Words from the Greeks* (1952). She inscribed "To Professor Gilbert Murray with every good wish, from Mary Fitt" (dated 8.3.54) on a copy of *The Man Who Shot Birds.*

56   A thorough discussion of this period of the society's history by Robert Hill (2000) is available online at http://www.the-philosopher.co.uk/philhist.htm.

57   I have not included the correspondence over the society in the *Times* in 1954 because there is no evidence that Freeman was still involved at that time.

58   Cf. Hill 2000, chap. 3: the "Board has included two professional philosophers, one Doctor of Divinity, one M.A; one medical doctor and psychologist, one reputed artist, an Archdeacon, and an antiquarian, all of them Fellows acclaimed by other Fellows of the society."

59   At the dinner in his honor, Gilbert Murray claimed to be relieved that Society members were not "real philosophers" and Freeman gently rebuked him with a lesson on "amateurs."

60   The article appeared subsequently as the first and last chapters of *Greek City States.*

61   In an interview with Gwendoline Butler, Melling reports that the publisher Michael Joseph took on Butler as an author "just after Mary Fitt killed herself" (Michael Joseph published five books written by Butler as Jennie Melville between 1962 and 1966.) In fact, Freeman's death certificate gives the cause of death as: "I. (a) congestive cardiac failure, (b) thyrotoxia [sic] heart disease; II. essential hypertension."

Chapter 4

1   Letter to C. P. Ilbert, 17 September 1882 (Abbott and Campbell 1899, 138).

2   Woodruff 1953, 15. Philip Woodruff was the pseudonym of Philip Mason (1906–1999), who graduated with a first-class degree from Balliol College, Oxford, and placed first in the examination for the Indian Civil Service in 1927.

3   Majeed 1999. The prime minister's remark came in parliament in 1922 (House of Commons, *Parliamentary Debates* 157 [1922] col. 1513). Lloyd George's insistence on the British character of the ICS and his

emphasis on its privileged status is consistent with much of the official discourse on the ICS in the nineteenth and early twentieth centuries.

4   Majeed 1999, 106.

5   Moore 1964; Compton 1967, 1968; Dewey 1973, with 1993; Roach 1971, chaps. 8 and 9; cf. Armstrong 1973. See also Tietze Larson 1999 and the scattered references in Brock and Curthoys 2000, Index, s.v. "Indian Civil Service."

6   Symonds 1991, 185–93; Stray 1998, 53–54.

7   In theory, the civil service was opened to Indians already in 1833 with the passage of the Charter Act (see 3 & 4 Will. IV, c. 85, sec. 87). In practice, the administration was less open, and no Indian became a civil servant until 1864.

8   In the period from 1864 to 1886, twelve Indians altogether gained admission to the ICS, including Satyendranath Tagore. There is a useful table of the twelve ICS natives in *Report of [India] Public Service Commission, 1886–87, PP* 48 (1888), Cd. 5327, paragraph 61.

9   Said 1993, 114.

10 See Wellesley's Minute ("Minute in Council at Fort William, Dated the 18th August 1800, by the Marquis Wellesley, K.P. containing His Reasons for the Establishment of a College at Calcutta"), in the *Asiatic Annual Register* for the year 1802, "State Papers" i–xxvii; also reprinted in the collection of Wellesley's dispatches edited by M. Martin (1886, 2:325–55), and in the *Selection* edited by S. J. Owen (1877).

11 China Factory Records 1803–1804 (Oriental and India Office Collections [OIOC]: G/12/145): 214.

12 OIOC: J/2/1, 2–16.

13 Cohn 1987, 520–21.

14 See e.g., the *East-India Register and Directory* for 1843, xix. Throughout the existence of the college, the *East-India Register and Directory* printed the regulations for entering students as well as the names of teachers, students, and prize winners for each year. In contrast to the volume for 1843, the *Register and Directory* for 1808 stipulates a smaller range of authors and subjects for candidates: "Candidates for admission into the College are expected to be well grounded in arithmetic, and qualified to be examined in *Caesar* and *Virgil*, the *Greek Testament*, and *Xenophon*" (xxix; emphasis in original).

15 There is some evidence concerning the crammers who helped students get into Haileybury. One of them was E. E. Rowsell, who was himself unable to get admission to Haileybury; instead, he went to St. John's College, Cambridge, after which he began preparing students for entrance. See Cohn 1987, 334.

16 Stephens, in Lowell 1900, 258.

17 Cohn 1987, 536, gives details concerning "the educational institutions from which students presented certificates before entering Haileybury." The figures are somewhat different toward the end of Haileybury's existence. Using the information given for 1852 to 1856 by the *Committee of College References* (OIOC, vols. 80–88), Compton (1968, 279–80) calculates that about 33 percent of the students at Haileybury had come from the nine major public schools (Charterhouse, Eton, Harrow, Merchant Taylors', Rugby, St. Paul's, Shrewsbury, Westminster, and

Winchester) and another 17.8 percent from the newer public schools. He notes that 6 percent had been "educated neither privately nor at public school." He also mentions, however, a "very high proportion of successful competitioners—rarely less than a half—who had been to grammar or proprietary schools."

18 Cohn 1987, 526.

19 *Oxford Dictionary of National Biography*, s.v. "Henley, Samuel (1740–1815)." The third principal, Charles Webb Le Bas, had a habit of coining new words derived from Greek and Latin when he needed to deal with students. On one occasion, he reprimanded a boy, whom he had caught throwing stones in the quadrangle, by saying to him, "Sir, I perceive you are a lithobolizer. Are you not aware that lithobolizing is prohibited? Go, Sir, and never lithobolize any more, or punishment will overtake you!" (*Memorials of Old Haileybury College*, 1894, 149).

20 The prospectus of the college from 1806 gives a few details about the lectures for "Classical & General Literature." See "A preliminary view of the establishment of the Honourable East-India Company in Hertford-shire for the education of young persons appointed to the civil service in India" (East India College, 1806); OIOC: IOR J/1/21 folios 514–21, also reprinted in the *East-India Register and Directory* for 1808 and in *Memorials of Old Haileybury College,* 243–52.

21 Crook 1964.

22 *The Haileybury Observer*, vols. 1–9 (OIOC: ST 287); there are extracts, which are often modified without notice, in *Memorials of Old Haileybury College*, 270–304. The references below are to the texts published in bound volumes by W. H. Allen and Co. from 1842 onward. The motto that appeared on the first issue (dated 9 October 1839) was taken from Horace, *Satires* 1.4.103–5. See also Stephens, in Lowell 1900, 292.

23 *The Haileybury Observer*, vol. 1, pt. 2 (30 September 1840): 5.

24 *The Haileybury Observer*, vol. 1, pt. 1 (9 October 1839): 2. Or consider this extract from a later piece by the same hand (vol. 1, pt. 1 [16 October 1839[: 15):

> At Lecture, may some tough Greek play,
> Defy your best exertion;
> And, still worse yet, may you always get
> The hardest piece in Persian.

25 See "Pugna Amwellensis," in *The Haileybury Observer,* vol. 1, pt. 2 (7 October 1840): 14.

26 *The Haileybury Observer*, vol. 1, pt. 2 (28 October 1840): 38.

27 See e.g., *The Haileybury Observer*, vol. 1, pt. 2 (30 September 1840): 7–8; and 24 (14 October 1840); and vol. 1, pt. 3 (3 February 1841): 7.

28 Merivale 1898, 52.

29 The official records include the names of prize-winning students and the subjects for which they received their awards. For the examination of 1806, for example, see OIOC: J/1/96.

30 Instruction, however, in the vernacular languages was available at the College of Fort William, in Calcutta, which by this time had basically turned into a language training school for the company; see Lord Minto's remarks to this effect in *Public Disputation of the Students of the College of Fort William in Bengal, before the Rt. Hon. Lord Minto, Governor*

General of Bengal and Visitor of the College; together with His Lordship's Discourse. 15th September 1810 (Calcutta, 1811) (OIOC: IOL, P/T 3890). On the annual prize-day at Fort William, some of the students made disputations and speeches in Indian languages, and a visiting dignitary would follow the students with a speech of his own. On one occasion, the viceroy made two speeches, "of which the second, somewhat tactlessly, was in praise of Greek" (Blunt 1937, 194).

31 Against this value placed on Sanskrit learning in the official syllabus, however, there is the case of Jonathan Scott, who was the first person appointed to a professorship in oriental languages at Haileybury. He resigned his appointment in 1805 before taking it up on the grounds that he ought to have received a higher salary than the other professors since there were few professors of Oriental subjects in Britain at the time: see Cohn 1987, 528–29.

32 The East India Company Charter Act of 1813 gave the Court of Directors the right to establish and alter the regulations for students at Haileybury (53 Geo. III, c. 155, sec. 44).

33 Cohn 1987, 544.

34 Campbell 1853, 264; cf. Cohn 1987, 532. Monier Monier-Williams himself also questioned the place of Sanskrit in the curriculum at Haileybury (*Memorials of Old Haileybury College,* 52–53 n. 4).

35 See Ghosal 1944, 316–21; Penner 1974, 47–50. However, the success of the Haileybury vision lingered on in other contexts, for example, in the view summarized in Lowell (1900), vii, that "the writer [H. Morse Stephens] has been irresistibly led by his study of those methods to the conclusion that the only practicable plan for the United States to adopt is that of a college not altogether unlike Haileybury."

36 Malthus 1817, 99–100.

37 Trevelyan 1978, 2:270.

38 *Hansard's Parliamentary Debates,* 3rd ser., 19 (1833): 503–35; see esp. 525–26 (= Keith 1922, 1:252–54). For the response to the speech, see Moore 1964, 246.

39 Kiernan 1995, 41. On "Macaulay's Studies at Calcutta," see Trevelyan 1978, 2:443–50.

40 Keith 1922, 1:252.

41 For the minute, see OIOC: F/4/1846, No. 77633, 127–46; repr. in Zastoupil and Moir 1999, document 14. See also Woodruff 1954, 352, for Plato's would-be response.

42 Keith 1922, 1:265.

43 Keith 1922, 1:265.

44 Letter to Gladstone, 23 July 1853 (OIOC: Sir Charles Wood Papers, MSS. Eur. F. 78, 51B); partly quoted in Moore 1964, 250–51.

45 Moore 1964. Some of these figures were satirized by Anthony Trollope in *The Three Clerks,* where Jowett appears as Mr. Jobbles and Charles Trevelyan as Sir Gregory Hardlines. For a discussion of the novel and its relationship to the evolving Victorian culture of large-scale examinations, see Shuman 2000.

46 In *Memorials of Old Haileybury College,* 38, Monier Monier-Williams recalls the advice he received from Robert Scott when the former was about to leave Oxford for Haileybury: " 'Remember,' he said, 'that when

you reach India you will probably be sent to some remote province, where you will be like a light set on a hill. Millions will watch your conduct and take their ideas of Christianity from your actions and words.'"

47   See Jowett's letter to Gladstone, 14 December 1853, *Gladstone Papers*, British Library, Additional MS. 44376, folios 210–15. Jowett's letter echoes a letter that he had received from Trevelyan, in October 1853, in which the latter had said that the examinations would "replace our two great Universities, & especially Oxford, *in relation* with the active life of the country, & lead to a great improvement in the course of study & in the application of the rewards they have to offer" (Trevelyan Letter Books, Bodleian Library, Oxford; also quoted in Moore 1964, 254). Jowett's letter to Gladstone contains a telling shift in emphasis from Oxbridge to Oxford alone.

48   For the impact of Macaulay's Committee and a discussion of the marking schemes it proposed, see Majeed 1999, 91–98.

49   *PP* 1854–55 (40), 114. The ICS recruit's need to excel in Greek and Latin verse is part of the joke in George Trevelyan's *Competition Wallah*. See Trevelyan 1864, 18.

50   The place given to mathematics reflects the prominence it had at Cambridge. The dominance of mathematics at the university was semi-anomalous until the 1860s. Concerning the sciences, it should be noted that "natural sciences" and "moral sciences" (see table 1) are terms specific to Cambridge and the title of triposes, both first examined in 1851. See Searby 1997, 191–92, and chap. 6. (I am grateful to Chris Stray for this information.)

51   Before 1906, candidates were free to take as many subjects as they liked, and no subject was obligatory. However, "smattering" was discouraged, and, in effect, the examiners set aside a student's marks in a subject if they fell below a certain minimum. From 1906 onward, candidates could offer any of the subjects, "provided that the maximum number of marks that can be obtained from the subjects chosen is limited to 6,000." Chris Stray writes that the system of providing a list of subjects and letting candidates choose what to offer is characteristically Oxonian and goes back to the early days of the honors examination set up by the 1800 Examinations Statute; see Walsh, in Brock and Curthoys 2000, 311.

52   For instance, between 1865 and 1872, only six of the 362 candidates who were selected in the open competition failed their final examination, while five failed probation on health grounds, and none failed on the basis of "character." See *PP* 55 (1876), Cd. 1446: 319 (43).

53   For the latter's role in the ICS, see Sidgwick and Sidgwick (1906) 373, 502–3.

54   Symonds 1991, 191.

55   See Compton 1968.

56   *The Selection and Training of Candidates for the Indian Civil Service*, PP 55 (1876), Cd. 1446, 283–85 (7–9).

57   Abbott and Campbell 1897, 2:136.

58   *The Selection and Training of Candidates for the Indian Civil Service*, PP 55 (1876), Cd. 1446, 285–88 (9–12).

59   *The Selection and Training of Candidates for the Indian Civil Service, PP* 55 (1876), Cd. 1446, 316 (40).

60   *The Selection and Training of Candidates for the Indian Civil Service, PP* 55 (1876), Cd. 1446, 566 (290).

61   *The Selection and Training of Candidates for the Indian Civil Service, PP* 55 (1876), Cd. 1446, 496 (220).

62   *The Selection and Training of Candidates for the Indian Civil Service, PP* 55 (1876), Cd. 1446, 503 (227).

63   *The Selection and Training of Candidates for the Indian Civil Service, PP* 55 (1876), Cd. 1446, 578 (302).

64   The reduction in marks for Greek and Latin was slight but definite. It may perhaps be explained by Salisbury's own biography, given that, in a speech delivered to students at King's College, London, he described "versification in the dead languages" as "the most perfectly useless accomplishment to which the human mind can be turned." See "Lord Salisbury at King's College," *The Times*, 4 July 1883. It would be interesting to learn why Greek counted for fewer marks than Latin in the new scheme.

65   The effect on Indians of this policy would not have troubled much Salisbury, who, in 1877, indicated that if too many Indians were able to secure positions in the administration by competition, the government would be obliged to control their intake. See *Oxford Dictionary of National Biography*, s.v. "Cecil, Robert Arthur Talbot Gascoyne, third marquess of Salisbury (1830–1903)."

66   *Hansard's Parliamentary Debates*, 3rd ser., 235 (1877): 454. The remarks were delivered on 28 June 1877.

67   For the percentages, see Dewey 1973, 276.

68   See Abbott and Campbell 1897, 2:135–42, 348–51.

69   Jowett's views on the ICS probationers can be traced through his letters in Abbott and Campbell 1899, 138–58.

70   Abbott and Campbell 1899, 151–55.

71   *Report of [India] Public Service Commission, 1886–87 (PP* 48 [1888], Cd. 5327), 40 (dissenting members on 42).

72   *Report of [India] Public Service Commission, 1886–87 (PP* 48 [1888], Cd. 5327), 45.

73   *Report of [India] Public Service Commission, 1886–87 (PP* 48 [1888], Cd. 5327), 46.

74   *Report of [India] Public Service Commission, 1886–87 (PP* 48 [1888], Cd. 5327), 46.

75   For one Indian's criticism of the Commission, see Roy 1888.

76   Dewey 1973, 274.

77   The splitting of each subject into separate literature and history papers parallels the separation that took place in the reformed Cambridge tripos of the 1880s; see Stray 1998, 147–49.

78   For much of the nineteenth and twentieth centuries, Oxford undergraduates typically could choose philosophy or ancient history in the Final Honor School in *Literae Humaniores* ("Greats"). 1968 was the first year in which a student at Oxford was able to study Greek and Latin literature, which was previously only available in Moderations ("Mods"), in the Final Honor School.

79	The percentage figures are based on Dewey 1973, 276.
80	Lowell 1900, 36.
81	These figures are based on information provided by Stanley Leathes for the Islington Commission, *PP* 24 (1914): 678–85; cf. Honda 1996.
82	Symonds 1991, 306–7.
83	Symonds 2002, 98–99.
84	Symonds 2002, 97.
85	Symonds 2002, 98.
86	Cotton 1909, 1, also quoted in Symonds 2002, 97.
87	Quoted in Symonds 2003, 53.
88	Symonds 1991, 191.
89	Symonds 1991, 191–92.
90	OIOC: L/P&J/6/330, File 1774. An additional note to the OIOC file provides Godley's name.
91	OIOC: L/P&J/6/360, File 2135. The author's initials are not fully legible, but I read them as "AG."
92	"The I.C.S. Examination," *Oxford Magazine* (25 October 1893), 23–25; quotation on p. 23.
93	*Oxford Magazine,* 25 October 1893, 23.
94	"Powis square" is a reference to Walter Wren's crammer, which was situated there in London.
95	*Oxford Magazine,* 25 October 1893, 24.
96	*Oxford Magazine,* 25 October 1893, 24.
97	'The Master at Breakfast', *Oxford Magazine,* 25 October 1893, 25–26; quotation on p.26.
98	OIOC: L/P&J/6/360, File 2122.
99	OIOC: L/P&J/6/696, File 2517.
100	OIOC: L/P&J/6/698, File 2716.
101	Quoted in Potter 1986, 86. By this time, the number of undergraduates who showed interest in ICS careers also seems to decline at both Oxford and Cambridge. On 7 December 1920, the Board of Indian Civil Service Studies at Cambridge sent a note to the India Office, 'So far as we can see at present we think the number of Cambridge European candidates for the Open Competition for the Indian Civil Service in August 1921 will be in all probability a mere fraction of those who competed in pre-war days.'
102	OIOC: J&P/3557/1922 in L/P&J/6/1812.
103	See e.g. the memorandum entitled "Statement relating to the arrangements made in the University of Oxford for the reception and training of Selected Candidates for the Indian Civil Service," JLSD, Box 7: IV/B/2: i.
104	JLSD, Box 7: IV/B/7.
105	See e.g. nos. v and vi, JLSD, Box 7: IV/B/2.
106	Draft of letter dated 13 March 1898, JLSD, Box 7: IV/C/1.
107	Strachan-Davidson to Godley (14 June 1904), quoted in Symonds 1991, 190.
108	For the proposal and the satire, see JLSD, Box 7: IV/C/2.
109	Mackail 1925, 80.
110	*Report of the Royal Commission on the Public Services in India*, Appendix, vol. 10, *PP* 24 (1914), Cd. 7583, 576, Questions 55050 and 55051.

Strachan-Davidson did also say that he could "see no objection to Sanskrit and Arabic being marked up to Latin and Greek" in the open competition (Question 55047).

111   Mackail 1925, 88.

112   For Jebb in particular, see the letter of 13 June 1904 sent by S. H. Butcher to Strachan-Davidson, JLSD, Box 7: IV/B/1, and also Box 7: IV/B/2, xxi and xxvi.

113   JLSD, Box 7: IV/B/2, xii.

114   See the correspondence with R. Latta (professor of logic and rhetoric at the University of Glasgow), JLSD, Box 7: IV/B/1, and the "Memorial" from the Scottish universities, Box 7: IV/B/2, xiii.

115   See "Changes in the Civil Service Competition," *Oxford Magazine* (26 October 1904), a copy of which also appears in JLSD, Box 7: IV/B/2, xxx.

116   Symonds 1991, 192–93.

117   Rahim 1982, 37.

118   Potter 1986, 32–33. The Indian figures are based on the India Office and Burma Office List for 1938 and the comparative salaries on Schiff 1939, 145–47.

119   Malabari 1895, 135.

120   Aravamudan 2003, 196. Aurobindo's training in Greek and Latin must have helped him when he composed "a five-thousand-line unfinished poetic treatment on the Trojan War in quantitative hexameters, entitled "Ilion," and published a vast corpus of dramatic and narrative poetry recreating classical Greek and Hindu myth" (201–2). When Aurobindo was put on trial in Alipore in 1908, one of the presiding magistrates was someone who had obtained fewer marks than he had in the Greek examination.

121   Letter by Godley to Hamilton (15 December 1899), OIOC: L/P&J/6/527, File 2360. Letter by Curzon to Hamilton (23 April 1900), OIOC: Correspondence of Lord George Francis Hamilton, MSS Eur. D 510/5: Private Correspondence India, Curzon to Hamilton, vol. 17, folio 7. Curzon's letter is quoted, inaccurately, in Sharma 2001, 224.

122   See e.g. OIOC: IOR/M/1/161 = P&J (B) 1769 and OIOC: L/P&J/6/527, File 2360.

123   The recommendations concerning Sanskrit and Arabic can be found in the volumes of evidence published by the Islington Commission as the appendices to its *Report of the Royal Commission on the Public Services in India* (esp. PP [1914] vols. 21–24). See e.g., the statements given in Bombay in March 1913: *Report of the Royal Commission on the Public Services in India*, Appendix, vol. 6, PP 22 (1914), Cd. 7579, Questions 26047, 26291–301, 26482–84 (R. P. Paranjpye); 27035, 27046, 27089, 27260–62 (Aga Sultan Muhammad Shah, the Aga Khan); 27349 (Lalubhai Samaldas Mehta); 30237 (Raghunath Vyankaji Sabnis); 32891, 32971 (Narsinh Chintaman Kelkar); 33231 (Sir Chinubhai Madhavlal). Compare the evidence of some English officers who testified to the greater value of Greek and Latin over Sanskrit; see e.g., *Report of the Royal Commission on the Public Services in India*, Appendix, vol. 2, PP 21 (1914), Cd. 7293, 248, Question 3352.

124   *Report of the Royal Commission on the Public Services in India,* Appendix, vol. 10, *PP* 24 (1914), Cd. 7382, 47–48, Question 48488.

125   *Report of the Royal Commission on the Public Services in India,* Appendix, vol. 8, *PP* 23 (1914), Cd. 7296, 657, Question 41355.

126   See e.g. *Report of the Royal Commission on the Public Services in India,* Appendix, vol. 2, *PP* 21 (1914), Cd. 7293, 435–36, Question 6861.

127   *Report of the Royal Commission on the Public Services in India,* Appendix, vol. 6, *PP* 22 (1914), Cd. 7579, 821, Question 31502.

128   Dutt, in Satthianadhan 1890, i.

129   Dutt, in Satthianadhan 1890, ii.

130   By contrast, in a mid-century guide book for Cambridge students, Henry Latham makes this same point as a reason for his charges to opt *for* Greek and Latin in the open competition: "Not only does this branch supply a great proportion of the marks of the successful candidates, but it has the additional advantage of not requiring to be specially *got up* before an Examination. A good classic has, to a great degree, his knowledge always about him, and can therefore better spare the valuable time just before the Examination which is wanted for those subjects which, to be of any use in the Examination, must be quite fresh in the memory" (Latham 1863, 239).

131   See Viswanathan 1989.

132   See Honda 1996.

133   At about that time, the scheme of the London examination also changed. In the new system, subjects (there were now sixty-seven) were divided into two groups, A and B. All six subjects in A were compulsory, of which one had to be an "auxiliary language" (Greek or Latin was acceptable). From B, the student had to choose a number of subjects from the long list, which included Greek and Roman topics and, by the 1930s, also two papers in classical archaeology. It was Percy Gardner, professor of classical archaeology in Oxford, who campaigned for the introduction of archaeology as a subject in the civil service examinations; see Symonds 1991, 193. On Gardner's ineffective attempts to make archaeology a major option in Greats, see Walsh, in Brock and Curthoys 2000, 325–26.

134   See also Majeed 1999, 100–6.

135   Bhabha 1994, 86, 89.

136   See e.g., a letter by Sir Charles Wood to Trevelyan (16 October 1864): "The clever well crammed youths from Irish Universities or Commercial schools obtain the highest marks & go to Bengal. The University men who are *gentlemen* go to Madras. We have added more marks for Greek & Latin by way of giving them a turn, but the story is a very good exemplification of what I mean. It is difficult to say this in public, for I should have half a dozen wild Irishmen on my shoulders & as many middle class examination students, but that makes all the more reason for not giving into anything which might lead to similar results" (OIOC: Sir Charles Wood Papers, MSS. Eur. F. 78, Letter Book 18). See also Lord Lytton's assessment in 1879 of the relative merit of Irish, English, and Scottish elements in the Indian Civil Service: letter from Lytton to James Caird, 1–11 March 1879 (OIOC: H/796, folios 249–51). For the

performance of students from Aberdeen University at the ICS examinations, see Hargreaves 1994, 99–102.

137   The relationship between Nari Rustomji, who studied Classics as an undergraduate at Cambridge, and Sir Harold Dennehy is described in Rustomji 1971, 32–33, 53; cf. Potter 1977, 878–79.

138   For the class background of ICS recruits from 1860–1874, see Kirk-Greene 2000, 99, with Spangenberg 1976. For 1892–1902, according to the forms completed by successful British candidates, 27 or 5.6 percent came from the aristocracy (peers, landowners, etc.), 290 or 60.4 percent from the educated middle classes (civil servants, clergymen, lawyers, medical professions, educational professions), 104 or 21.7 percent from other middle classes (the police, bankers, industry, etc.), and 51 or 10.6 percent from the working class. For 1903 to 1914, 13 or 3.4 percent came from the aristocracy, 236 or 61.9 percent from the educated middle classes, 82 or 21.5 percent from other middle classes, and 47 or 12.3 percent from the working class. On the class background of the recruits, see also Honda 1996.

139   Sinha 1995, 103.

140   Sinha 1995, 103.

141   *The Selection and Training of Candidates for the Indian Civil Service, PP* 55 (1876), Cd. 1446, 524 (248).

142   Sinha 1995, 104.

Chapter 5

1   In addition to *Soldier and Scholar*, see Briggs 1987 and Miller 1930. For bibliography, see Briggs 1992, 326–36.

2   South Carolina felt itself particularly aggrieved when Congress passed the so-called "Tariff of Abominations," in 1828 and 1832, which hit the textiles exported to Europe by South Carolina especially hard. South Carolina's claim that a state could nullify an act of the federal congress provoked a constitutional crisis, ultimately calmed by President Andrew Jackson.

3   Finch's brother Richard enlisted in the Third New York Regiment of the Line and Finch buried a cousin, Daniel Gildersleeve, at Valley Forge in 1778. See W. H. Gildersleeve 1941, 240.

4   *Charleston Courier* (9 November 1833).

5   "Sir Walter had so large a hand in making Southern character, as it existed before the war, that he is in great measure responsible for the war" (Mark Twain, *Life on the Mississippi* [1883], chap. 46). See Krause 1967, 182–83.

6   His diary from 1847 in the Johns Hopkins archives lists eighty-five books read during his year at Jefferson College.

7   "Thy mighty Scholiast, whose unweary'd pains / Made Horace dull, and humbled Milton's strains. / Turn what they will to Verse, their toil is vain, / Critics like me shall make it Prose again" (*The Dunciad*, 24.210–13).

8   Particularly South Carolina's William Gilmore Sims, with *Lays of the Palmetto* (1848): see Johannsen 1985, 212–13.

9   Students from both within and without Britain traditionally came to Oxford and Cambridge to take second first degrees, e.g. Rhodes Scholars.

10   Arnold's "Higher Schools and the Universities of Germany" (1874) pointed to disadvantages of the English system. Blackie's approach based the study of ancient Greek syntax on modern Greek, which filled Gildersleeve with "disgust." Blackie, *On the Living Language of the Greeks* (1853); Briggs 1992, 34.

11   For example, B. L. Gildersleeve 1878, 1896, and 1879.

12   I am very grateful to Christopher Stray for enlightening me on this difference.

13   Jebb contributed a correspondence on *Antigone* to *AJP* 12 (1891): 256–58; Campbell, "Notes on the 'Agamemnon' of Aeschylus," *AJP* 1 (1880): 427–39 and correspondence in 3 (1882): 128–29; Ellis contributed one article per year to the first sixteen volumes of *AJP*. Lindsay contributed "The St. Gall Glossary" to *AJP* 38 (1917): 349–69; Housman, "On Two Corruptions in the *Persae* of Aeschylus," *AJP* 9 (1888): 317–25.

Chapter 6

1   The few published accounts of Macurdy's life and work (Pounder 1999, Pomeroy 1994, and Erck 1971) are all brief sketches; only Pomeroy, the shortest of the three, is free of errors.

2   The abbreviation GM will be used throughout to refer to the Bodleian Library, Oxford, MSS Gilbert Murray, with box and folio number.

3   The abbreviation VC will be used throughout to refer to the Vassar College Libraries, Archives and Special Collections. Citations include collection name with box and folder number (if such numbers are used in the collection). I would like to thank Nancy MacKechnie, former Curator of Rare Books and Manuscripts; Dean Rogers, Special Collections Assistant; and Elizabeth Daniels, Vassar Historian, for their help.

4   For more information on Harrison, see especially Robinson 2002; Beard 2000; Lloyd-Jones 1996 and 2004; Stewart 1959.

5   Eschbach 1993 provides the fullest comparison of the two countries, but she does not sufficiently stress the importance of the professional academic opportunities for women provided by the American women's colleges. For more information on America, see Horowitz 1993 and Solomon 1985; for England, see Vicinus 1985, 121–62 and Shils and Blacker 1996 on Cambridge.

6   The abbreviation UL will be used throughout to refer to the Senate House Library, University of London, The University Archives, with reference numbers.

7   Lily Ross Taylor (Broughton 1990) and Jane Ellen Harrison (Schlesier 1990), whose careers are in many ways diametric opposites, are the only women included in *Classical Scholarship: A Biographical Ency-*

clopedia; for more information on Taylor as an "honorary male," see McManus 1997, 32–34.

8   Julia Josephine Thomas Irvine (Cornell B.A. 1875 and M.A. 1876), professor of Greek at Wellesley College, served as president of the college from 1894 to 1899. Since she was not related to William Frederick Cody ("Buffalo Bill"), the students were probably jesting, but they cleverly chose a strategy calculated to appeal to Macurdy. It is not surprising that Macurdy was something of a "bluestocking" at this time; given her economic and social background, her college degree and current position could have been obtained only by an intense and single-minded focus on academic achievement.

9   Leach's biographers seriously downplay this part of her life. Briggs calls it "the single, if minor, blemish" of Leach's life and career (Briggs 1996–1997, 105). Halporn relegates the whole conflict to a footnote; although he notes Leach's "strong personal animus" toward Macurdy, he lists her academic charges against Macurdy as though they were true (Halporn 1999, 130, n. 6). Zwart actually read the correspondence, but she chose to minimize the conflict by calling it an "inability to get along," though she acknowledges that Leach "could be distressingly inflexible" (Zwart 1971, 380). The notes she took while reading the correspondence tell a different story; here she characterizes Leach as "an unhappy and disturbed woman—obsessed with GH Macurdy issue" (Schlesinger Library, Radcliffe Institute, Harvard University, *Notable American Women* files, MC 230, Box 52).

10   Zwart 1971, 380, echoed by Briggs 1996–1997, 101, includes only the phrase "remarkably handsome and fine looking" from this letter, inadvertently demonstrating how misleading it can be to take a quotation out of context.

11   Harrison has coined a feminine singular form of the Greek word *Chorizontes* ("Separators"), a masculine plural term used to characterize ancient Homeric scholars from Alexandria who argued for separate authorship of the *Iliad* and *Odyssey*.

12   Interview by author, 6 December 1997, Poughkeepsie, N.Y.

13   Harrison's shawls and spangled dresses frequently caught the audience's notice during her public lectures (one boy famously compared her to "a beautiful green beetle"), but in her case this was part of a "careful attention to theatrical effect" (Robinson 2002, 80).

14   James Alexander Kerr Thomson (always known as J. A. K.) published numerous books and articles on classical topics, but there is very little information about his life in print; see my article in this volume and McManus 2007.

15   The abbreviation ASCSA will be used throughout to refer to the Blegen Library Archives, American School of Classical Studies at Athens, identified by collection with box and folder number. I would like to thank the archivist, Dr. Natalia Vogeikoff-Brogan, for her assistance.

16   For Michael Ivanovich Rostovtzeff, see Calder 1994 and Fears 1990; for William Scott Ferguson, see Kopff 1994; for William Woodthorpe Tarn, see Adcock and Reynolds 2004 and Potter 2004; Macurdy used the abbreviation *CAH* to refer to the *Cambridge Ancient History*.

Chapter 7

1   Since there are no published accounts of Thomson's life and work, I have appended a brief biographical sketch to this article; see also McManus 2007 and McManus, this volume.

2   The abbreviation GM will be used throughout to refer to the Bodleian Library, Oxford, MSS Gilbert Murray, with box and folio number.

3   The abbreviation AUC will be used throughout to refer to the Department of Special Collections, Reading University Library, Allen & Unwin Collection, with reference number. I would like to thank Michael Bott, Keeper of Archives and Manuscripts, for his help with this collection.

4   The abbreviation VC will be used throughout to refer to the Vassar College Libraries, Archives and Special Collections. Citations include collection name with box and folder number.

5   Thomson's eminently fair review of Highet emphasizes this fact (and its implicit difference from his own work): "It is probable that classical scholars will find most of what specially concerns them in the great mass of notes which compose the latter part of the volume. They are full of exact observation ranging over an exceptionally wide field of study and reading. . . . *The Classical Tradition* is much more than a handbook; it is a work of original thought and constructive art" (1951b, 45). However, since he himself had been scrupulous about carefully reading everything he discussed in his books, he privately expressed to Murray some reservations about Highet's "immense book": "It is very readable and learned—only he <u>cannot</u> have read all the books he criticises. What makes it very difficult to review is its heterogeneous and rather eccentric character" (28 November 1949: GM 175.18–19; emphasis in original).

6   This was Thomson's practice even in his earlier books. As he explained in the preface to *The Art of the Logos,* "When an author has long reflected on his subject everything he has read is apt to influence his thinking about it. A bibliography becomes misleading or impossible" (1926, 7–8).

7   In a letter to Thomson commenting on their shared literary tastes, Gilbert Murray made the following telling observation: "What a weary business old age normally is, or at any rate extreme old age. . . . I am sure one of the troubles is that all one's tastes become out of fashion. You love the poetry and the painting which you knew as a young man, and are rather repelled by the work of those who find it a bore" (10 April 1957: GM 175.249).

8   Even some of their language is similar: "I am suggesting that Shakespeare had a faculty for driving through the available un-Greek transmitting text to whatever lay on the other side" (Nuttall 2004, 214); "Thus did Shakespeare penetrate through the Latin to the Greek influence" (Thomson 1952, 254).

Chapter 8

1   These studies include Beran 1998, Briggs 2002, Casazza 2003, Evans 2004, Andrea Hamilton 2004, and Murnaghan 2005; newly available materials include Kennedy 1998, G. D. Thomson 1966, and interviews with Edith Hamilton's adopted son Dorian Fielding Reid in 2005, 2006, and 2007.

2   In the first essay of *The Ever-Present Past*, Reid reprinted substantial portions of the *Classical World* article without acknowledging *Classical World*; she claims that this essay appeared under the title "The Lessons of the Past" in the September 27, 1958 *Saturday Evening Post*. Another essay in this volume—"Plato"—"was an address given before the Classical Association of the Atlantic States, 29 April 1960. Previously unpublished."

3   Among the publications in which the essays in *The Ever-Present Past* previously appeared are *The Saturday Evening Post, Theatre Arts Monthly, The New York Times Book Review, Saturday Review, The Atlantic Monthly, Vogue,* and *Greek Heritage.*

4   Hamilton's "Address to the Athenians," delivered at the award ceremony, also appears in Reid 1964, 188–89.

5   For the unreliability of Reid's memoir, see Sicherman 1984, 420–21 ("is not accurate in all details"); Bacon 1980, 308 ("The fullest, but still very selective, account"); Hallett 1996–1997, 117–18, n. 19 (challenging the publisher's note to Reid, and its claim that Hamilton's correspondence to and from others had not survived). Reid never, for example, mentions Edith's long association with Lucy Donnelly.

6   See Hallett 1996–1997, 124–25. Sentences from this passage are also reprinted in Reid 1969, 22, in a section entitled "Mind and Spirit."

7   See the assessment of Bacon 1980, 307–8: "[her] prose was vivid and graceful, and salted with the same quotations and moral exhortations that inspired students at the Bryn Mawr School. . . . Her life was ruled by a passionately nonconformist vision that was the source of her phenomenal strength and vitality and her almost magical appeal as public figure and author."

8   Reid 1967, 153–54; also 66 ("She had little or no interest in books *about* Greece").

9   Reid 1967, 66 ("For decades her absorption and joy had been to read, in the original text, the Greek tragedians, she had no interest in translations. . . . Equally well-worn volumes of the great writers of that ancient period were also her daily companions. Plato, Homer, Thucydides, Herodotus, and the rest she had studied and absorbed and loved since her early youth"). For Stone's reliance on commentaries and Loeb Classical Library translations, see Patner 1988, 164 ("When you're working alone, without a teacher, you need a lot of commentaries"), 165–68.

10   Eugenides 2002, 337. As Andrea Hamilton 2004, 39–40 notes, the Bryn Mawr School "actively sought to insulate its students from the 'wrong' kinds of people," particularly Jews: although Mary Garrett "wanted the school open to Jews," "Thomas wanted the numbers kept

low." Among the English "traditions" adopted by the Bryn Mawr School in Hamilton's day—from 1907 through 1933—was engaging Samuel Arthur King, an Englishman who taught elocution at Bryn Mawr College, to visit Baltimore each month, "lecture on enunciation, and give corrective exercises." See Beirne 1970, 53–54.

11   For Gildersleeve (1831–1924), who taught at Johns Hopkins from 1876 through 1915, see Briggs 1994a in Briggs 1994b, 213–18: he received honorary D.Litt. degrees from Cambridge and Oxford in 1905. Elsewhere in the essay Hamilton spells the word "labor" without the "u."

12   For Murray (1866–1957), see Fowler 1990. For Livingstone (1880–1960), see Stray 2004.

13   For E. A. Robinson (1910–1972), see Clack 1994, 532–33. The other editorial board members were Louis Feldman (Yeshiva); Irving Kizner (Hunter College High School); Herbert Benario (Columbia); LeRoy Campbell (Brooklyn College); Evelyn Harrison (Columbia); Samuel Lieberman (Queens College); Robert D. Murray Jr. (Princeton); Martin Ostwald (Columbia); John F. Reilly (LaSalle Military Academy); J. Hilton Turner (Westminster College). For Murray (1919–1975), see McKay 1994; many of the other board members are alive and professionally active at the time of this writing.

14   For Edith Gittings Reid and her writings, see Reid 1967, 59, and Harry Fielding Reid Papers; for Sir Joseph and Sir George Thomson, see J. J. Thomson 1936 and G. P. Thomson 1966. For Edith Reid's friendship with Benson (and his use of an episode about Doris and the "Unseaworthy Door" in Maine as the inspiration for the "famous impromptu ocean voyage of the two ladies above an upturned kitchen table" in his 1931 *Mapp and Lucia*), see White 1970. White's article also calls attention to Hamilton's British literary tastes: Sir Thomas Browne, Lewis Carroll, detective story writers such as Agatha Christie, Dorothy Sayers, and Josephine Tey "who chronicled upper class crime."

15   For Cacoyannis, his British connections, and his productions of *The Trojan Women*, see Katz 2001, 207. Although Reid included a favorable review of the 1963 Broadway production in the materials deposited at Princeton, she never mentions it, or him, in her 1967 book: a surprising omission in view of the space she devotes to Hamilton's 1957 Greek honors, and to the immense popularity of Cacoyannis's *Zorba the Greek* in 1964.

16   See the index to the Cairns papers in the Library of Congress, 2001; Lindquist 1990, 6–37; Mellon 1963.

17   The letter from Agnes Meyer, dated 21 December 1959, is from the Hamilton Family Papers. For the role of Cairns and Brown in Graves's 1956 U.S. tours, see Smith 1982, 478–501 (which mentions both Cairns and Brown, but refers to the former as director of the National Gallery of New York); Graves 1995, 266–69 (which mentions Brown and Richman, but not Cairns); and Seymour 1995, 364–65 (which only mentions Gypsy Rose Lee). For Richman, see also Reid 1967, 121–23.

18   For Hamilton's "mutual admiration society" with Jaeger, whose large library—as Lindquist 1990, 53, notes—was purchased by Harvard for the Center for Hellenic Studies, see Hallett 1996–1997, 121–23

and Reid 1967, 135. She uses Shorey's translation of Pindar, referring to him in her notes as "Professor Paul Shorey," in *The Greek Way*, but never mentions him—although she does mention Gilbert Murray—in her CAAS address on Plato (Hamilton 1963, 323; 1964, 38).

19   For her admiration of Murray, see also Hallett 1996–1997, 123; Reid 1967, 111. It seems to have predated her relationship with Doris, and may well go back to the years when she was coupled with Lucy Donnelly. Donnelly was a close friend and correspondent of Bertrand Russell, and well acquainted with Gilbert Murray, married to Russell's cousin. The *Bryn Mawr Alumnae Bulletin* 18 (July 1936) quotes tributes from both Russell and Murray on the occasion of Donnelly's retirement, in which the former states that he has known her for nearly forty-two years. Notes to *The Greek Way* also cite books by two other scholars from the U.K., *The Legacy of Greece* by D. A. W. Thompson, and *Tragedy* by W. Macneile Dixon (Hamilton 1963, 321, 325)

20   For Bowra's imprimatur, see also Reid 1967, 156; Highet's blurb for *The Ever-Present Past* appears on the dust jacket to Reid 1967; Hamilton's blurb for *Poets in a Landscape* (New York 1957) is on the dust jacket for the fourth printing (1967).

21   Special thanks to my research associate Wayne Millan; Elizabeth Di Cataldo of the Bryn Mawr School Archives; Kathleen Kennedy Townsend, and friends and family of Edith Hamilton: Alice Reid Abbott, Preston Brown, Dorrit Pfeiffer Castle and Tom Castle, Sheila K. Dickison, Donald Lateiner, Janet M. Martin, John S. McDaniel, Maura McKnight, Sheila Murnaghan, Beth Pfeiffer, the late Elizabeth Reid Pfeiffer, Nicholas Rauh, Dorian Fielding Reid, and Sir John Thomson. Gratitude is also due to Eleanor Winsor Leach, my host at Indiana University, where I presented an earlier version of this paper in March 2006, and John McLucas and Allaire Stallsmith of Towson University, where I presented another version in April 2007.

Bibliography

Introduction

Agard, W. (1953) "Classical Scholarship," in M. Curti (ed.), *American Scholarship in the Twentieth Century* (Harvard University Press), 146–67.

Ball, R. (forthcoming) "The Correspondence of Gilbert Highet and Helen MacInnes with Classical Scholars and Other Notable Individuals," *Classical World*.

Briggs, W. W., and E. C. Kopff. (1995) *The Roosevelt Lectures of Paul Shorey (1913–1914)*, trans. and annotated by E. C. Reinke (Olms).

Cromer, Earl of. (1910) *Ancient and Modern Imperialism* (John Murray).

Goff, B. (ed.) (2005) *Classics and Colonialism* (Duckworth).

Hardwick, L. P., and C. Gillespie. (eds.) (2007) *Classics in Post-Colonial Worlds* (Oxford University Press).

Hechter, M. (1975) *Internal Colonialism: The Celtic Fringe in British National Development, 1536–1966* (Routledge & Kegan Paul).

McManus, B. F. (1997) *Classics and Feminism* (Twayne Publishers).

197

Robinson, D. B. (2005) "James Adam 'in the Arena of the South': An Aberdeen Platonist in Cambridge," in C. A. Stray (ed.), *The Owl of Minerva, Proceedings of the Cambridge Philological Society*, suppl. vol. 28:47–68.

Shorey, P. (1911) "American Scholarship," *The Nation*, 11 May, 466–69.

———. (1919) "Fifty Years of Classical Scholarship in America," *Transactions of the American Philological Association* 50:33–61.

Stray, C. A. (2007a) Review of J. G. W. Henderson's *Oxford Reds: Classic Commentaries on Latin Classics* (Duckworth, 2005); *Journal of Roman Studies* 97:45–46.

———. (2007b) "Non-identical Twins: Classics at Oxford and Cambridge," in C. A. Stray (ed.), *Oxford Classics: Teaching and Learning 1800–2000* (Duckworth).

———. (ed.) (2007c) *Gilbert Murray Reassessed: Hellenism, Theatre, and International Politics* (Oxford University Press).

Symonds, R. A. (1986) *Oxford and Empire: The Last Lost Cause?* (Macmillan).

Vance, N. (1997) *The Victorians and Ancient Rome* (Blackwell).

Viswanathan, G. (1989) *Masks of Empire: Literary Study and British Rule in India* (Columbia University Press).

Chapter 1

Anderson, R. D. (1983) *Education and Opportunity in Victorian Scotland: Schools and Universities* (Oxford University Press).

———. (1985) "In Search of the Lad of Parts: the Mythical History of Scottish Education," *History Workshop: A Journal of Socialist and Feminist Historians* 19:82–104.

———. (1995) *Education and the Scottish People 1750–1918* (Oxford University Press).

Anderson, W. E. K. (ed.) (1972) *The Journal of Sir Walter Scott* (Clarendon Press).

Beveridge, Craig, and Ronald Turnbull. (1983) *The Eclipse of Scottish Culture* (Polygon).

Briggs, A. (1970) "Samuel Smiles and the Gospel of Work," in *Victorian People: A Reassessment of Persons and Themes*, rev. ed. (University of Chicago Press).

Brown, S. J., and M. Fry. (eds.) (1993) *Scotland in the Age of the Disruption* (Edinburgh University Press).

Burnett, A. (ed.) (2007) *The Letters of A. E. Housman*, 2 vols. (Oxford University Press).

Davie G. E. (1961) *The Democratic Intellect* (Edinburgh University Press).

(1837) *Evidence Oral and Documentary Taken and Received by the Commissioners for Visiting the Universities of Scotland:* Volume I, *University of Edinburgh;* Volume II, *University of Glasgow;* Volume III, *University of St Andrews;* Volume IV, *University of Aberdeen* [King's College and Marischal College].

Gardiner, J., and N. Wenborn. (eds.) (1995) *The History Today Companion to British History* (Collins & Brown).

Glover, T. R. (1943) *Cambridge Retrospect* (Cambridge University Press).

Humes, W. M., and H. M. Paterson. (1983) *Scottish Culture and Scottish Education* (John Donald).

Journal of the House of Lords (1509–) (HMSO).

Macaulay, Lord. (1907) *The History of England from the Accession of James II*, 2 vols. (Everyman Edition).

Sandford, Sir Daniel Keyte. (1822) *Letter to Rev. P. Elmsley in Answer to the Appeal made to Professor Sandford as the Umpire between the University of Oxford and the Edinburgh Review* (Munday & Slatter).

Smiles, S. (1859) *Self-Help* (John Murray).

Tait, J. G. (ed.) (1939) *The Journal of Sir Walter Scott, 1825–26* (Oliver and Boyd).

Chapter 2

Davies, C. (1987) "Lewis Edwards, Oes Victoria, a'r byd clasurol," *Y Traethodydd* 142:115–30.

———. (1995a) *Welsh Literature and the Classical Tradition* (University of Wales Press).

———. (1995b) "Y Traethodydd 1845–1995: cyfieithu'r clasuron Groeg a Lladin i'r Gymraeg rhwng tua 1850 a 1890," *Y Traethodydd* 150:201–14.

Davies, R. R., R. A. Griffiths, I. G. Jones, K. O. Morgan. (eds.) (1984) *Welsh Society and Nationhood: Historical Essays Presented to Glanmor Williams* (University of Wales Press).

Davies, W. (1989) *The Curriculum and Organization of the County Interme-diate Schools, 1880–1926* (University of Wales Press).

Edwards, H. T. (1980) *"Gŵyl Gwalia"; yr Eisteddfod Genedlaethol yn Oes Aur Victoria 1858–1868* (Gwasg Gomer).

———. (1990) *The Eisteddfod* (University of Wales Press).

———. (1991) "Y Prifeirdd wedi'r Brad," in P. Morgan (ed.) (1991), 166–200.

Edwards, L. (1848a) "Adroddiadau y Dirprwywyr," *Y Traethodydd* 4: 24–51.

———. (1848b) "Addysg yng Nghymru," *Y Traethodydd* 4:112–36.

———. (1849) "Ysgolion ieithyddol i'r Cymry," *Y Traethodydd* 5:347–55.

———. (1852) "Hector ac Andromache," *Y Traethodydd* 8:448–52.

———. (1865) "Yr hen brifysgolion a'r brifysgol i Gymru," *Y Traethodydd* 20:133–43.

———. ([1867]) *Traethodau Llenyddol* (Hughes & Son).

Edwards, T. C. (1868) "Gwladwriaeth Plato," *Y Traethodydd* 23:99–115; 222–37; 399–409.

———. (1901) *Bywyd a Llythyrau y Parch. Lewis Edwards, DD* (Isaac Foulkes).

Ellis, G. (1877–1879) "Gwleidyddiaeth Aristotle," *Y Traethodydd* 31:473–85; 32:105–18, 273–83; 33:31–45.

Euripides, *Alcestis*. (1887) *Yr Alcestis gan Euripides. Chwareugerdd Roegaidd wedi ei throsi i'r Gymraeg gan (a) Proffeswr D. Rowlands, B.A. (Dewi Môn) a'r (b) Parch.D.E.Edwardes, M.A.* (Cymdeithas yr Eisteddfod Genhedlaethol).

Evans, D. ([1939]) *The Life and Work of William Williams, MP for Coventry 1835–1847, MP for Lambeth 1850–1865* (Gomerian Press)

Evans, T. L. (1967) *Lewis Edwards, ei fywyd a'i waith* (John Penry).

Gruffydd, W. J. (trans.) (1950) *Antigone Sophocles* (University of Wales Press).

Gruffydd, W. J., and R. S. Roberts. (1900) *Telynegion* (Jarvis & Foster).

Jenkins, R. T. (1932–1936) "John Peter (Ioan Pedr), 1833–1877," *Journal of the Welsh Bibliographical Society* 4:137–68.

———. (1957) *Ymyl y ddalen* (Hughes & Son).

Jones, G. E. (1997) *The Education of a Nation* (University of Wales Press).

Jones, G. E,. and G. W. Roderick. (2003) *History of Education in Wales* (University of Wales Press).

Jones, O. (1866) "Antigonë gan Sophoclës," *Y Traethodydd* 21:171–202.

Lewis, R. M. (1928) *Iliad Homer: Cyfieithiadau gan R.Morris Lewis, gyda chwanegiadau, rhagair a nodiadau gan T.Gwynn Jones* (Hughes & Son).

Llewellyn-Jones, L. (2002) "Trasidei [*sic*] Gymraeg: Is There a Classical Tradition in Welsh Language Drama?" Open University Seminar Series 2002, The Reception of the Texts and Images of Ancient Greece in Late Twentieth-century Drama and Poetry in English, http://www2.open.ac.uk/ClassicalStudies/GreekPlays/Seminar02/LLJ Lewis.htm.

Millward, E. G. (1991) "Pob gwybodaeth fuddiol," in P. Morgan (ed.) (1991), 146–65.

Morgan, J. (1857) "Hanes athroniaeth," *Y Traethodydd* 13:5–37; 257–75; 415–37.

Morgan, K. O. (1980) *Wales in British Politics*, 3rd ed. (University of Wales Press).

Morgan, P. (1984) "From Long Knives to Blue Books," in R. R. Davies, et al. (eds.) (1984), 199–215.

———. (ed.) (1991) *Brad y Llyfrau Gleision: ysgrifau ar Hanes Cymru* (Gwasg Gomer).

Norwood, G. (ed.) (1909) *The Iphigeneia at Aulis of Euripides. An abridged acting edition. Arranged, translated and enacted by "The Frogs" Classical Society of University College, Cardiff* (Sherratt & Hughes).

———. (1920) *Greek Tragedy* (Methuen).

Owen, O. G., W. J. Gruffydd, and E. Williams. (1902) *Eisteddfod Genedlaethol Bangor, 1902: Yr Awdl, Y Bryddest a'r Telynegion (ail-oreu)* (Swyddfa'r, Caernarfon 'Genedl').

Owen, R. Ll. (1868) "Horas a Lydia," *Y Traethodydd* 23:497.

———. (1899) *Hanes Athroniaeth y Groegiaid* (R. E. Jones & Bros., Conway).

Peter, J. (1867) "Virgil—Prif-fardd y Rhufeiniaid," *Y Traethodydd* 22: 309–22.

———. (1868) "Yr Aeneid," *Y Traethodydd* 23:23–37.

Reports (1847) *Reports of the Commissioners of Inquiry into the State of Education in Wales, appointed by the Committee of Council on Education.* HMSO. (London).

Williams, G. (1979) *Religion, Language and Nationality in Wales* (University of Wales Press).

Williams, J. E. C. (1981) "Hanes Y Traethodydd," *Y Traethodydd* 136:34–49.

———. (1995) "Y Traethodydd 1845–1995: hanes y cychwyn," *Y Traethodydd* 150:5–45.

Williams, J. G. (1993) *The University Movement in Wales* (University of Wales Press).

Chapter 3

BIBLIOGRAPHY OF KATHLEEN FREEMAN (CLASSICAL WRITINGS)

1923

"The Dramatic Technique of the Oedipus Coloneus," *Classical Review* 38:50–54.

1926

The Work and Life of Solon, with a translation of his poems (Cardiff, University of Wales Press Board).

1935

"Anaxagoras," *Greece & Rome* 4:65–75.

1936

"Copper Fly," *Greece & Rome* 6, 18–30.

1938

"Epicurus—A Social Experiment," *Greece & Rome* 7:156–68.

"Portrait of a Millionaire—Callias, son of Hipponicus," *Greece & Rome* 8:20–35.

1939

"Pindar: The Function and Technique of Poetry," *Greece & Rome* 8:144–59.

1940

"Plato: the Use of Inspiration," *Greece & Rome* 9:137–49.

1941

"Thourioi," *Greece & Rome* 10:49–64.

1945

"Vincent, or the Donkey," *Greece & Rome* 14:33–41.

1946

The Pre-socratic Philosophers: A Companion to Diels, Fragmente der Vorsokratiker (Oxford, Blackwell).

The Murder of Herodes and Other Trials from the Athenian Law Courts (London, MacDonald).

1947

Gown and Shroud. A novel (London, Macdonald).

The Greek Way: An Anthology. Translations from Verse and Prose (London, MacDonald).

1947/48

Ancilla to the Pre-socratic Philosophers: A Complete Translation of the Fragments in Diels, Fragmente der Vorsokratiker (Oxford, Blackwell; Cambridge, Mass., Harvard University Press).

1948

"The Lesson of Ancient Greece," *World Affairs* n.s. 2:233–42.

The Philoctetes of Sophocles: A Modern Version (London, Muller).

1949

"The Idea of God in the Pre-socratic Philosophers," *The Philosopher* n.s. 1:67–77, 87.

"A Brief Survey of Philosophy for Students with a List of the Chief Books Advised for Reading," *The Philosopher* n.s. 1:109–18.

1950

Greek City States (London, Macdonald; New York, W.W. Norton).

"Murder in Athens," *London Mystery Magazine* 6:32–45.

1951

"The Concept of Man in the Greek Philosophers," *The Philosopher* n.s. 3:2–11, 30–39.

Dinner Address in Honour of Gilbert Murray, *The Philosopher* n.s. 3:88, 98–99.

"Mystery in Athens," *London Mystery Magazine* 10:26–42.

"Scandal in Athens," *London Mystery Magazine* 12:72–85.

1952

Annual luncheon address, *The Philosopher* n.s. 4:101–6.

"The Mystery of the Choreutes," in M. E. White (ed.) *Studies in Honour of Gilbert Norwood*, 85–94.

God, Man and State: Greek Concepts (London, Macdonald).

1954

The Paths of Justice (London, Lutterworth Press).

Everyday Things in Ancient Greece (London, Batsford). A one-volume revision of *Everyday Things in Homeric Greece, Everyday Things in Archaic*

Greece, and *Everyday Things in Classical Greece* by C. H. Quennell and Marjorie Quennell 1929–1932.

The Sophists. Translation of Mario Untersteiner, *I sofisti* (Oxford, Blackwell).

1957

[As Mary Fitt] *Man of Justice: The Story of Solon.* A children's book (Edinburgh, Thomas Nelson & Sons).

KATHLEEN FREEMAN (NON-CLASSICAL WRITINGS)

1924 (poetry)

"Candour" and "Liberation," *The Golden Hind* 2.8:17.

"Friendship," *Adelphi* 1.10:922.

1925 (poetry)

"Failure" and "Gratitude," *Adelphi* 2.11:922.

1926

The Intruder and Other Stories (London, Cape).

Martin Hanner. A Comedy (London and New York, Cape & Harcourt Brace).

1928

Quarrelling with Lois (London, Cape).

1929

This Love (London, Cape).

1934

The Huge Shipwreck (London, Dent).

1936

Adventure from the Grave (London, Davies).

Murder Mars the Tour (as Mary Fitt) (London, Nicholson & Watson).

Three Sisters Flew Home (as Mary Fitt) (London, Nicholson & Watson).

1937

Bulls Like Death (as Mary Fitt) (London, Nicholson & Watson).

1941

Ir Has All Happened Before. What the Greeks Thought of Their Nazis (London, Muller).

1943

Voices of Freedom (London, Muller).

1944

Clues to Christabel (as Mary Fitt) (London, Michael Joseph).

1945

What They Said at the Time: A survey of the causes of the second world war and the hopes for a lasting peace, as exhibited in the utterance of the world's leaders and some others form 1917–1944 (London, Muller)

1948

And Where's Mr Bellamy? (as Stuart Mark Wick) (London, Hutchinson).

1952

Fighting Words from the Greeks for Today's Struggle (Boston, Beacon Pres).

1954

The Man Who Shot Birds, and Other Tales of Mystery and Detection (as Mary Fitt) (London, Macdonald).

1956

T'other Miss Austin (London, Macdonald). [A study of Jane Austen]

Doctor Underground (as Caroline Cory) (London, Macdonald).

1957

The Late Uncle Max (as Mary Fitt) (London, Macdonald).

1958

The Shifting Sands (as Mary Fitt) (London, Thomas Nelson & Sons). [A children's story]

1959

Mizmaze (as Mary Fitt) (London, Michael Joseph).

The Great River (as Mary Fitt) (London, Thomas Nelson & Sons). [A children's story]

MATERIAL IN ARCHIVES (UNPUBLISHED)

Correspondence between Freeman and the Society of Authors, 1947–1954, British Library Add MSS 63243, Society of Authors Archive, vols. 38ff., 165.2ff.:10–43.

Correspondence. Freeman—Dent Publishers, March/April 1939. Archives, University of North Carolina.

Norwood papers, University of Toronto Archives.

BBC Wales Archives, Cardiff. Kathleen Freeman, *Llysoedd Groeg* (The Greek courts) 1 (1948) *Y Tri Drws* (The three doors) 28, 4; 2 (1948) *Yr Olewydden Gysegredig* (The sacred olive tree) 12, 5.

Bibliography of Liliane Clopet

n.d.

Three Plays for Children, containing *The Wolf-Emperor*: 4–11; *The Magic Candle*: 15–22; *Purl and Plain*: 25–35.

1937–1939, 1950s

Children's hour talks on BBC Cardiff.

1938

The Crypt. Play in one act. (Cardiff, Napiers).

1939

Julie Destin. Play in one act. (Cardiff, Napiers).

1944

Once upon a Time, illustrated by W. Heath Robinson (London: Frederick Muller). It contains four stories: "The Tale of the Apothecary's Assistant"; "The Scarlet Boots"; "The House with the Glass Key"; "The Woodcutter and his Three Sons." Dedicated "To KF, for whom I wrote them."

1950–1952

Several short stories for children in *London Mystery Magazine*.

1954

Doctor Dear (London: Michael Joseph). Writing as Mary Bethune.

Selected Bibliography

Aaron, Jane. (ed.) (1999) *A View across the Valley: Short Stories by Women from Wales c. 1850–1950* (Honno, South Glamorgan, Wales). Contains Freeman's short story "The Coward" on pp. 95–106 and a note about Freeman on p. 274.

Anon. (ed.) (1952) *Mystery: Anthology of the Mysterious in Fact and Fiction* (London: Hulton).

Atkinson, Frank. (1987) *Dictionary of Literary Pseudonyms* (Library Association).

Bailey, Cyril. (1931) "Ad Lectores," *Greece & Rome* 1:1–2.

Canton School for Girls. www.chrisb.4ce.co.uk/schools_site/school (accessed September 26, 2003; site no longer available).

Chadwick, John. (1958) *The Decipherment of Linear B* (Cambridge University Press).

"Mary Fitton." (1974) *Encyclopedia Britannica*, 15th ed. *Micropaedia*, vol. 4, p. 162.

Griffiths, J. Gwyn. (1978; reissued 2001) *Barddoneg Aristotles: cyfiethiad gyda rhagymadrodd a nodiadau* (Gwasg Prifysgol Cymru, Caerdydd).

Hill, Robert, Alan Holloway, Justin Woods, and Martin Cohen. (2000) "A Philosophical Kindergarten. The History of the Philosophical Society of England," in *The Philosopher* 87, chap. 3, "New Beginnings and Controversies," http://atschool.eduweb.co.uk/cite/staff/philosopher/Chap3.htm.

Irwin, M. E. (2004a) "Bibliography of Kathleen Freeman," *Quaderni di Storia* 59:247–59.

———. (2004b) "Kathleen Freeman," in Todd et al. (eds.), *DBC* 1:343–44.

———. (2005) "Kathleen Freeman 1897–1959," www.utsc.utoronto.ca/~irwin/KathleenFreeman/KathleenFreeman.htm).

Kahn, J. (ed.) (1967) *The Edge of A Chair* (Harper & Row).

———. (1970) *The Graveyard Shift* (Dell)

Keating, H. R. F. (1996) "Mary Fitt," in J. P. Pederson and T. Benbow-Pfalzgraf (eds.) *St. James Guide to Crime and Mystery Writers*, 4th ed. (St. James Press), 353–55.

Kirk, G. S., and J. Raven. (1957) *The Presocratic Philosophers: A Critical History with a Selection of Texts* (Cambridge University Press).

Littré, E. (1861) *Oeuvres complètes d'Hippocrate*, vol. 9 (Bailliere).

Luce, J. V. (1993) "L.J.D. Richardson," *Hermathena* 154:5–9.

Mathias, Roland G. (2001) "Kathleen Freeman," in R. T. Jenkins, E. D. Jones, and B. F. Roberts (eds.), *Dictionary of Welsh Biography 1941–1970* (Honourable Society of Cymmrodorion), 77.

Melling, John Kennedy. (n.d.) "Elegant Death. Gwendoline Butler Interview," www.crimetime.co.uk/interviews/gwendolinebutler.php.

Mynors, R. A. B. (1966) "Classics Pure and Applied," Presidential address to the Classical Association, delivered at Cardiff, 13 April (John Murray).

Norwood, Gilbert. (1908) *The Riddle of the Bacchae* (Manchester University Press).

Richardson, L. J. D. (1926) *The Indian Mutiny of 1857, After Herodotus*, revised and augmented (Basil Blackwell).

———. (1941) "Agma, a Forgotten Greek Letter," *Hermathena* 57:57–69.

———. (1947) "A Little Classics is a Dangerous Thing," *Greece & Rome* 16:41.

————. (1954) "The Classical Association: The First Fifty Years," Jubilee address delivered at the fiftieth annual general meeting of the association held at University College, London, 7–10 April (John Murray).

Ryle, Gilbert. (1949) *The Concept of Mind* (Hutchinson).

Stephens, Meic. (ed.) (1986) *The Oxford Companion to the Literature of Wales* (Oxford University Press in association with Yr Academi Gymreig).

Stray, C. (1998) *Classics Transformed: Schools, Universities, and Society in England, 1830–1960* (Clarendon Press).

Todd, Robert, et al. (eds.) (2004) *Dictionary of British Classicists*, 3 vols. (Thoemmes-Continuum). [= *DBC*]

White, M. E. (ed.) (1952) "Bibliography of Gilbert Norwood," in *Studies in Honour of Gilbert Norwood, Phoenix*, suppl. vol. 1, xi–xviii.

Williams, J. Gwynn. (1997) *The University of Wales 1839–1939. A History of the University of Wales* (University of Wales Press).

Chapter 4

JLSD   Papers of James Leigh Strachan-Davidson, Balliol College Library, Balliol College, Oxford.

OIOC   Oriental and India Office Collections, British Library, London.

PP   *Parliamentary Papers* (House of Commons).

Abbott, E., and L. Campbell. (1897) *The Life and Letters of Benjamin Jowett, M.A. Master of Balliol College, Oxford*, 2 vols. (John Murray).

————. (eds.) (1899) *Letters of Benjamin Jowett, M.A. Master of Balliol College, Oxford* (John Murray).

Aravamudan, S. (2003) "The Colonial Logic of Late Romanticism," *The South Atlantic Quarterly* 102, 179–214.

Armstrong, J. A. (1973) *The European Administrative Elite* (Princeton University Press).

Bhabha, H. (1994) *The Location of Culture* (Routledge).

Blunt, E. A. H. (1937) *The I.C.S.: The Indian Civil Service* (Faber).

Brock, M. G., and M. C. Curthoys. (eds.) (2000) *The History of the University of Oxford*, vol. 7: *Nineteenth-century Oxford*, part 2 (Oxford University Press).

Campbell, G. (1853) *Modern India: A Sketch of the System of Civil Government. With Some Account of the Natives and Native Institutions*, 2nd ed., rev. and corr. (John Murray).

Cohn, B. S. (1987) "The Recruitment and Training of British Civil Servants in India," in B. S. Cohn (ed.), *An Anthropologist among the Historians and Other Essays* (Delhi), 500–53.

Compton, J. M. (1967) "Indians and the Indian Civil Service 1853–79: A Study in National Agitation and Imperial Embarrassment," *Journal of the Royal Asiatic Society*, 99–113.

———. (1968) "Open Competition and the Indian Civil Service, 1854–1876," *English Historical Review* 83:265–84.

Cotton, J. J. (1909) *A Book of Corpus Verses* (Blackwell).

Crook, J. M. (1964) *Haileybury and the Greek Revival. The Architecture of William Wilkins, R.A.*, repr. from *The Haileyburian and I.S.C. Chronicle* (Dept. of History, University of Leicester).

Dewey, C. (1973) "The Education of a Ruling Caste: The Indian Civil Service in the Era of Competitive Examination," *English Historical Review* 88:262–85.

———. (1993) *Anglo-Indian Attitudes: The Mind of the Indian Civil Service* (Hambledon).

Ghosal, A. K. (1944) *Civil Service in India under the East India Company: A Study in Administrative Development* (Calcutta University Press).

Hargreaves, J. D. (1994) *Academe and Empire: Some Overseas Connections of Aberdeen University 1860–1970*. Quincentennial Studies in the History of the University of Aberdeen (Aberdeen University Press).

Honda, T. (1996) "Indian Civil Servants, 1892–1937: An Age of Transition," D. Phil. thesis, University of Oxford.

Keith, A. B. (ed.) (1922) *Speeches and Documents on Indian Policy 1750–1921*, 2 vols. (Oxford University Press).

Kiernan, V. G. (1995) *The Lords of Human Kind: European Attitudes to Other Cultures in the Imperial Age*, repr. of 1969 ed. with a new preface (Serif).

Kirk-Greene, A. H. M. (2000) *Britain's Imperial Administrators, 1858–1966* (Macmillan).

Latham, H. (1863) "Examinations for the Civil Service in India," in *The Student's Guide to the University of Cambridge* (Deighton, Bell), 236–59.

Lowell, A. L. (1900) *Colonial Civil Service: The Selection and Training of Colonial Officials in England, Holland, and France. With an Account of the East India College at Haileybury (1806–1857) by H. Morse Stephens* (Macmillan).

Mackail, J. W. (1925) *James Leigh Strachan-Davidson, Master of Balliol. A Memoir* (Oxford University Press).

Majeed, J. (1999) "Comparativism and References to Rome in British Imperial Attitudes to India," in C. Edwards (ed.) *Roman Presences: Receptions of Rome in European Culture, 1789–1945* (Cambridge University Press), 88–109.

Malabari, B. M. (1895) *The Indian Eye on English Life or Rambles of a Pilgrim Reformer*, 3rd ed. (Apollo Printing Works).

Malthus, T. R. (1817) *Statements respecting the East-India College with an appeal to facts, in refutation of the charges lately brought against it, in the Court of Proprietors* (John Murray).

Martin, M. (ed.) (1836–1837) *The Despatches, Minutes and Correspondence of the Marquess Wellesley during his Administration in India*, 5 vols. (W. H. Allen).

(1894) *Memorials of Old Haileybury College by Frederick Charles Danvers, Sir M. Monier-Williams, Sir Steuart Colvin Bayley, Percy Wigram, the late Brand Sapte and Many Contributors* (Constable).

Merivale, J. A. (ed.) (1898) *Autobiography & Letters of Charles Merivale, Dean of Ely* (printed for private circulation).

Moore, R. J. (1964) "The Abolition of Patronage in the Indian Civil Service and the Closure of Haileybury College," *Historical Journal* 7:246–57.

Owen, S. J. (ed.) (1877) *A Selection from the Despatches, Treaties, and Other Papers of the Marquess Wellesley, K. G., during his Government of India* (Clarendon Press).

Penner, P. (1974) "Haileybury: School for Anglo-Indian Statesmanship," *Bengal Past & Present* 93:39–58.

Potter, D. C. (1977) "The Shaping of Young Recruits in the Indian Civil Service," *Indian Journal of Public Administration* 23:875–87.

———. (1986) *India's Political Administrators 1919–1983* (Oxford University Press).

Rahim, M. A. (1982) "Indian Members of the Covenanted Civil Service, 1854–1913: A Study of their Status and Role in British-Indian Administration," *Bengal Past & Present* 101:34–44.

Roach, J. (1971) *Public Examinations in England, 1850–1900* (Cambridge University Press).

Roy, P. C. (1888) *Indian Civil Service Reform. A Digest and Criticism of the Report of the Public Service Commission* (T. Fisher Unwin).

Rustomji, N. (1971) *Enchanted Frontiers: Sikkim, Bhutan and India's North-Eastern Borderland* (Oxford University Press).

Said, E. W. (1993) *Culture and Imperialism* (Chatto & Windus).

Satthianadhan, S. (1890) *Four Years in an English University.* With a Chapter on the Indian Civil Service Examination by A. C. Dutt (Srinivasa).

Schiff, L. M. (1939) *The Present Condition of India: A Study in Social Relationships* (Quality Press).

Searby, P. (1997) *A History of the University of Cambridge*, vol. 3, *1750–1870* (Cambridge University Press).

Sharma, M. (2001) *Indianization of the Civil Services in British India (1858–1935)* (Manak).

Shuman, C. (2000) *Pedagogical Economies: The Examination and the Victorian Literary Man* (Stanford University Press).

Sidgwick, A., and E. M. Sidgwick. (1906) *Henry Sidgwick: A Memoir* (Macmillan).

Sinha, M. (1995) *Colonial Masculinity: The "Manly Englishman" and the "Effeminate Bengali" in the Late Nineteenth Century* (Manchester University Press).

Spangenberg, B. (1976) *British Bureaucracy in India: Status, Policy and the I.C.S. in the Late 19th Century* (Manohar Book Service).

Stray, C. (1998) *Classics Transformed: Schools, Universities, and Society in England, 1830–1960* (Clarendon Press).

Symonds, R. (1991) *Oxford and Empire. The Last Lost Cause?* corr. ed. (Clarendon Press).

———. (2002) *The Fox, The Bees and the Pelican: Worthies and Noteworthies of Corpus Christi College, Oxford* (Corpus Christi College).

———. (2003) "'To Do What One Liked with the World': The Early Letters of Malcolm Hailey to P. S. Allen from India," *The Pelican Record* 41:50–64.

Tietze Larson, V. (1999) "Classics and the Acquisition and Validation of Power in Britain's 'Imperial Century' (1815–1914)," *International Journal of the Classical Tradition*, 185–225.

Trevelyan, G. O. (1864) *The Competition Wallah* (Macmillan).

———. (1978) *The Life and Letters of Lord Macaulay*, repr. 2 vols. in 1; (Oxford University Press; repr. of London, 1876).

Viswanathan, G. (1989) *Masks of Conquest: Literary Study and British Rule in India* (Columbia University Press).

Woodruff, P. [= P. Mason] (1953) *The Men Who Ruled India: The Founders* (Cape).

————. (1954) *The Men Who Ruled India: The Guardians* (Cape).

Zastoupil, L., and M. Moir. (eds.) (1999) *The Great Indian Education Debate: Documents Relating to the Orientalist-Anglicist Controversy, 1781–1843* (Curzon).

Chapter 5

Berwanger, Eugene H. (1994) *The British Foreign Service and the American Civil War* (University of Kentucky Press).

Briggs, Ward W. (ed.) (1987) *The Letters of Basil Lanneau Gildersleeve* (The Johns Hopkins University Press).

————. (ed.) (1992) *The Selected Classical Papers of Basil Lanneau Gildersleeve* (Scholars Press).

————. (ed.) (1998) *Soldier and Scholar: Basil Lanneau Gildersleeve and the Civil War* (University of Virginia Press).

————. (2002) "'Second-Hand Superiority': Basil Lanneau Gildersleeve and the English," *Polis* 19:1–2, 109–23.

Bruce, Philip Alexander (1921) *History of the University of Virginia 1819–1919* (Macmillan).

Gildersleeve, Basil Lanneau (1847) *Diary*, Johns Hopkins Archives.

————. (1854) "Necessity of the Classics," *Southern Quarterly Review* 26, n.s. 10:145–67, here cited in Briggs (1992), 3–19.

————. (1867) "Limits of Culture," *Southern Review* (Baltimore) 2.4:421–48, repr. in his *Essays and Studies*, 3–40, here cited in Briggs (1992), 20–39.

————. (1878) "Classics and Colleges," *Princeton Review* 54:67–95, repr. in his *Essays and Studies*, 43–84; excerpted in Briggs (1992), 105–12.

————. (1879) "University Work in America and Classical Philology," *Princeton Review* 55:511–36, repr. in his *Essays and Studies*, 87–123, here cited in Briggs (1992), 113–32.

————. (ed.) (1885) *Pindar. The Olympian and Pythian Odes* (Harper & Bros.) xii.

————. (1890) *Essays and Studies* (N. Murray).

——. (1892) "The Creed of the Old South," *Atlantic Monthly* 69:75–87.

——. (1896) "Classical Studies in America," *Atlantic Monthly* 78:728–37, repr. in Briggs 1992, 142–53.

——. (1897) "A Southerner in the Peloponnesian War," *Atlantic Monthly* 80:330–42.

——. (1901) "Oscillations and Nutations of Philological Studies," *Johns Hopkins University Circulars* no. 151:45–50.

——. (1909) *Hellas and Hesperia: Or, the Vitality of Greek Studies in America* (Henry Holt).

Gildersleeve, Willard Harvey. (1941) *Gildersleeve Pioneers* (Tuttle Publishing).

Hawkins, Hugh. (1960) *Pioneer: A History of the Johns Hopkins University, 1874–1889* (Cornell University Press).

Johannsen, Robert W. (1985) *To the Halls of Montezuma: The Mexican War in the American Imagination* (Oxford University Press).

Krause, Sydney J. (1967) *Mark Twain as Critic* (The Johns Hopkins University Press).

Miller, Charles William Emil. (ed.) (1930) *Selections from the Brief Mention of Basil Lanneau Gildersleeve* (The Johns Hopkins University Press).

Mowbray Susie R., and Charles S. Norwood. (1985) *Bazile Lanneau of Charleston 1746–1833; A Family History* (Hilburn Printing).

Reinhold, Meyer. (1976) "The Silver Age of Classical Studies in America, 1790–1830," in John H. D'Arms and John W. Eadie (ed.) *Ancient and Modern: Essays in Honor of Gerald F. Else* (Ann Arbor: Center for the Coordination of Ancient and Modern Studies), 181–213, repr. in *Classica Americana: The Greek and Roman Heritage in the United States* (Wayne State University Press, 1984), 174–203.

Stray, Christopher. (1999) "The First Century of the Classical Tripos (1822–1922): High Culture and the Politics of Curriculum," in his *Classics in 19th and 20th Century Cambridge: Curriculum, Culture and Community* (Cambridge Philological Society), 1–14.

Chapter 6

Adcock, F. E., and K. D. Reynolds. (2004) "Tarn, Sir William Woodthorpe," in Matthew and Harrison (2004), 53:789–90.

Beard, M. (2000) *The Invention of Jane Harrison* (Harvard University Press).

Bellinger, A. R. (1933) Review of Macurdy 1932, *American Historical Review* 38:359.

Bonner, C. (1927) Review of Macurdy 1925, *Classical Philology* 22:438–39.

Briggs, W. W. (ed.) (1994) *Biographical Dictionary of North American Classicists* (Greenwood Press).

———. (1996–1997) "Abby Leach (1855–1918)," *Classical World* 90:97–107.

———. (1999) "Goodwin, William Watson," in Garraty and Carnes (1999) 9:274–75.

Briggs, W. W., and W. M. Calder. (eds.) (1990) *Classical Scholarship: A Biographical Encyclopedia* (Garland).

Broughton, T. R. (1990) "Lily Ross Taylor," in Briggs and Calder (1990), 454–61.

Calder, W. M. (1994) "Rostovtzeff, Michael," in Briggs (1994), 541–47.

Erck, T. H. (1971) "Macurdy, Grace Harriet," in James (1971), 2:480–81.

Eschbach, E. S. (1993) *The Higher Education of Women in England and America, 1865–1920* (Garland).

Fears, J. R. (1990) "M. Rostovtzeff," in Briggs and Calder (1990), 405–18.

Fowler, R. L. (1990) "Ulrich von Wilamowitz-Moellendorff," in Briggs and Calder (1990), 489–522.

Garraty, J. A., and M. C. Carnes. (eds.) (1999) *American National Biography* (Oxford University Press).

Gulick, C. B. (1931a) "Goodwin, William Watson," in Johnson and Malone (1964), 4:411–13.

———. (1931b) "Greenough, James Bradstreet," in Johnson and Malone (1964), 4:588–89.

Halporn, J. W. (1999) "Women and Classical Archaeology at the Turn of the Century: Abby Leach of Vassar College," in A. B. Kehoe and M. B. Emmerichs (eds.) *Assembling the Past: Studies in the Professionalism of Archaeology* (University of New Mexico Press), 121–32.

Harrison, J. E. (1915a) "Scientiae Sacra Fames," in *Alpha and Omega* (Sidgwick & Jackson), 116–42.

———. (1915b) "Greek Religion and Mythology," *The Year's Work in Classical Studies* 10:71–80.

Harte, N. (1986) *The University of London 1836–1986: An Illustrated History* (Athlone Press).

Horowitz, H. L. (1993) *Alma Mater: Design and Experience in the Women's Colleges from Their Nineteenth-Century Beginnings to the 1930s*, 2nd ed. (University of Massachusetts Press).

James, E. T. (ed.) (1971) *Notable American Women, 1607–1950: A Biographical Dictionary* (Belknap Press).

Johnson, A., and D. Malone. (eds.) (1964) *Dictionary of American Biography* (Scribner).

Kopff, E. C. (1994) "Ferguson, William Scott," in Briggs (1994), 172–74.

Larsen, J. A. O. (1932) Review of Macurdy 1932, *Classical Philology* 27:315–16.

Lloyd-Jones, H. (1996) "Jane Ellen Harrison, 1850–1928," in Shils and Blacker (1996), 29–72.

———. (2004) "Harrison, Jane Ellen," in Matthew and Harrison (2004), 25:504–7.

MacCracken, H. N. (1950) *The Hickory Limb* (Scribner).

Macurdy, G. H. (1905) *The Chronology of the Extant Plays of Euripides* (New Era; repr. Haskell House, 1966).

———. (1925) *Troy and Paeonia, with Glimpses of Ancient Balkan History and Religion* (Columbia University Press).

———. (1927) "Correspondence," *Classical Review* 41:157–58.

———. (1932) *Hellenistic Queens: A Study of Woman-Power in Macedonia, Seleucid Syria, and Ptolemaic Egypt* (The Johns Hopkins University Press; repr. Greenwood Press, 1975; AMS Press, 1977; Ares Publishers, 1985).

———. (1937) *Vassal-Queens and Some Contemporary Women in the Roman Empire* (The Johns Hopkins University Press; repr. Ares Publishers in *Two Studies on Women in Antiquity*, 1993).

———. (1940) *The Quality of Mercy: The Gentler Virtues in Greek Literature* (Yale University Press).

———. (1942) "Apollodorus and the Speech against Neaera (Pseudo-Dem. LIX)," *American Journal of Philology* 63:257–71.

———. (1944a) "Had the Danaid Trilogy a Social Problem?" *Classical Philology* 39:95–100.

———. (1944b) "Prologue to a Study of the Tragic Heroine," *Classical Weekly* 37:239–40.

Mahaffy, J. P. (1895) *The Empire of the Ptolemies* (Macmillan).

Matthew, H. C. G., and B. Harrison. (eds.) (2004) *The Oxford Dictionary of National Biography* (Oxford University Press).

McManus, B. F. (1997) *Classics and Feminism: Gendering the Classics* (Twayne).

———. (2007) "'Macte nova virtute, puer!': Gilbert Murray as Mentor and Friend to J. A. K. Thomson," in C. A. Stray (ed.) *Gilbert Murray Reassessed* (Oxford University Press), 181–99.

Pomeroy, S. B. (1994) "Macurdy, Grace Harriet," in Briggs (1994), 392–93.

Potter, D. (2004) "Tarn, William Woodthrope [sic]," in R. B. Todd (ed.), *The Dictionary of British Classicists* (Thoemmes-Continuum), 3:947–49.

Pounder, R. L. (1999) "Macurdy, Grace Harriet," in Garraty and Carnes (1999), 14:291–92.

Reinhold, M. (1994) "Greenough, James Bradstreet," in Briggs (1994), 233–34.

Reinhold, M., and W. W. Briggs. (1994) "Goodwin, William Watson," in Briggs (1994), 224–26.

Robinson, A. (2002) *The Life and Work of Jane Ellen Harrison* (Oxford University Press).

Schlesier, R. (1990) "Jane Ellen Harrison," in Briggs and Calder (1990), 127–41.

Schütrumpf, E. E. (1990) "Hermann Diels," in Briggs and Calder (1990), 52–60.

Shewan, A. (1927) Review of Macurdy 1925, *Classical Review* 41:37.

Shils, E., and C. Blacker. (eds.) (1996) *Cambridge Women: Twelve Portraits* (Cambridge University Press).

Solomon, B. M. (1985) *In the Company of Educated Women: A History of Women and Higher Education in America* (Yale University Press).

Stewart, J. G. (1959) *Jane Ellen Harrison: A Portrait from Letters* (Merlin Press).

Tarn, W. W. (1932) Review of Macurdy 1932, *Classical Review* 46:167.

———. (1938) Review of Macurdy 1937, *Journal of Roman Studies* 28:77–78.

"Tribute to Miss Macurdy" (1937), *Vassar Alumnae Magazine* 23:8–9.

Vicinus, M. (1985) *Independent Women: Work and Community for Single Women, 1850–1920* (University of Chicago Press).

Weigall, A. E. P. B. (1914) *The Life and Times of Cleopatra, Queen of Egypt: A Study in the Origin of the Roman Empire* (Blackwood).

Zwart, A. T. (1971) "Leach, Abby," in James (1971), 2:379–80.

Chapter 7

Baldwin, T. W. (1944) *William Shakespeare's Small Latine & Lesse Greek*, 2 vols. (University of Illinois Press).

Ball, R. J. (1994) "Highet, Gilbert Arthur," in W. W. Briggs (ed.) *Biographical Dictionary of North American Classicists* (Greenwood Press), 282–85.

Braden, G. (2004) "Plutarch, Shakespeare, and the Alpha Males," in Martindale and Taylor (2004b), 188–208.

Burrow, C. (2004) "Shakespeare and Humanistic Culture," in Martindale and Taylor (2004b), 9–27.

Bush, D. (1952) Review of Thomson 1952, *Shakespeare Quarterly* 3:375–77.

Carnochan, W. B. (1993) *The Battleground of the Curriculum: Liberal Education and American Experience* (Stanford University Press).

Cartledge, P. (1998) "Classics: From Discipline in Crisis to (Multi)Cultural Capital," in Y. L. Too and N. Livingstone (eds.) *Pedagogy and Power: Rhetorics of Classical Learning* (Cambridge University Press), 16–28.

Craig, H. (1953) "Review of Shakespeare Scholarship in 1952," *Shakespeare Quarterly* 4:115–24.

Cross, T. P. (1995) *An Oasis of Order: The Core Curriculum at Columbia College* (Office of the Dean, Columbia College), http://www.college.columbia.edu/core/oasis/ (accessed on 2 April 2007).

Farmer, R. (1767) *An Essay on the Learning of Shakespeare* (T. Longman).

Handford, S. A. (1959) "Prof. J. A. K. Thomson," *The Times*, 26 February, 14.2.

Hardwick, L. (2003) *Reception Studies*. Greece and Rome New Surveys in the Classics 33 (Oxford University Press).

Hardwick, L., and C. A. Stray. (eds.) (2007a) *A Companion to Classical Receptions* (Blackwell).

Hardwick, L., and C. A. Stray. (2007b) "Introduction: Making Connections," in Hardwick and Stray (2007a), 1–9.

Highet, G. (1949) *The Classical Tradition: Greek and Roman Influences on Western Literature* (Oxford University Press).

Howe, M. D. (ed.) (1942) *The Pollock-Holmes Letters. Correspondence of Sir Frederick Pollock and Mr Justice Holmes 1874–1932* (Cambridge University Press).

Hutton, J. (1950) Review of Thomson 1948, *Classical Philology* 45:65–66.

Jack, I. R. J. (1952) "Shakespeare's Use of the Classics," Review of Thomson 1952, *Times Literary Supplement*, 11 July, 450.

Jenkyns, R. (2007) "United Kingdom," in Kallendorf (2007), 265–78.

Kallendorf, C. (ed.) (2007) *A Companion to the Classical Tradition* (Blackwell).

Law, H. H. (1949) Review of Thomson 1948, *Classical Journal* 45:100–1.

Leech, C. (1953) "Shakespeare's Life, Times and Stage" [Review article], *Shakespeare Survey* 6:154–63.

Lindenberger, H. (1990) "On the Sacrality of Reading Lists: The Western Culture Debate at Stanford University," in *The History in Literature: On Value, Genre, Institutions* (Columbia University Press), 148–62.

Macurdy, G. H., and R. M. Weeks. (1936) "The Living Legacy of Greece and Rome," in *A Correlated Curriculum: A Report of the Committee on Correlation of the National Council of Teachers of English* (Appleton-Century), 138–47.

Marshall, C. (2000) "Shakespeare, Crossing the Rubicon," *Shakespeare Survey* 53:73–88.

Martindale, C. (2007) "Reception," in Kallendorf (2007), 297–311.

Martindale, C., and M. Martindale (eds.) (1990) *Shakespeare and the Uses of Antiquity: An Introductory Essay* (Routledge).

Martindale, C., and A. B. Taylor. (2004a) "Introduction," in Martindale and Taylor (2004b), 1–5.

———. (eds.) (2004b) *Shakespeare and the Classics* (Cambridge University Press).

Martindale, C., and R. Thomas. (eds.) (2006) *Classics and the Uses of Reception* (Blackwell).

McManus, B. F. (2007) " 'Macte nova virtute, puer!': Gilbert Murray as Mentor and Friend to J. A. K. Thomson," in C. Stray (ed.) *Gilbert Murray Reassessed* (Oxford University Press), 181–99.

Murray, G. (1927) *The Classical Tradition in Poetry: The Charles Eliot Norton Lectures* (Harvard University Press).

Nuttall, A. D. (2004) "Action at a Distance: Shakespeare and the Greeks," in Martindale and Taylor (2004b), 209–22.

Porter, J. (2007) "Reception Studies: Future Prospects," in Hardwick and Stray (2007a), 469–81.

Schein, S. (2007) " 'Our Debt to Greece and Rome': Canon, Class and Ideology," in Hardwick and Stray (2007a), 75–85.

Simpson, P. (1955) "Shakespeare's Use of Latin Authors," in *Studies in Elizabethan Drama* (Clarendon Press), 1–63.

Suits, T. A. (1990) "Gilbert Highet," in W. W. Briggs and W. M. Calder (eds.) *Classical Scholarship: A Biographical Encyclopedia* (Garland), 183–91.

Swanson, R. A. (1957) Review of Thomson 1956, *Classical Journal* 52:370–71.

Thomson, J. A. K. (1914) *Studies in the Odyssey* (Clarendon Press).

———. (1915) *The Greek Tradition: Essays in the Reconstruction of Ancient Thought* (Allen & Unwin).

———. (1920) "The Religious Background of the *Prometheus Vinctus*," *Harvard Studies in Classical Philology* 31:1–37.

———. (1921) *Greeks and Barbarians* (Allen & Unwin).

———. (1926) *Irony: An Historical Introduction* (Allen & Unwin).

———. (1932) "Erasmus in England," in F. Saxl (ed.) *England und die Antike*, Vorträge der Bibliothek Warburg 9 (Teubner), 64–82.

———. (1935) *The Art of the Logos* (Allen & Unwin).

———. (1948) *The Classical Background of English Literature* (Allen & Unwin).

———. (1951a) *Classical Influences on English Poetry* (Allen & Unwin).

———. (1951b) "The Classical Tradition," Review of Highet 1949, *Classical Review* n.s. 1:42–45.

———. (1952) *Shakespeare and the Classics* (Allen & Unwin).

———, trans. (1953) *The Ethics of Aristotle: The Nicomachean Ethics* (Allen & Unwin).

———, trans. (1955) *The Ethics of Aristotle: The Nicomachean Ethics* (Penguin Classics).

———. (1956) *Classical Influences on English Prose* (Allen & Unwin).

———. (1957) "Gilbert Murray 1866–1957," *Proceedings of the British Academy* 43:245–70.

Thomson, J. A. K. (1962) "Introduction: Homer and His Influence," in A. J. B. Wace and F. H. Stubbings (eds.) *A Companion to Homer* (Macmillan), 1–15.

Thomson, J. A. K., and A. Toynbee. (eds.) (1936) *Essays in Honour of Gilbert Murray* (Allen & Unwin).

Thomson, J. O. (1953) Review of Thomson 1952, *Modern Language Review* 48:68–69.

Wilson, J. D. (1957) "Shakespeare's 'Small Latin'—How Much?" *Shakespeare Survey* 10:12–26.

Chapter 8

Bacon, H. (1980) "Edith Hamilton" (306–8) and "Lucy Donnelly" (499–500) in B. Sicherman and C.H. Greene (eds.) *Notable American Women: The Modern Period* (Harvard University Press).

Ball, R. J. (1994) "Highet, Gilbert Arthur," in W. W. Briggs Jr. (ed.) *Biographical Dictionary of North American Classicists* (Greenwood Press), 282–85.

Beirne, R. R. (1970) *Let's Pick the Daisies: The History of the Bryn Mawr School 1885–1967* (The Bryn Mawr School).

Benario, H. W. (1994) "Hadas, Moses," in Briggs (1994a), 244–45.

Beran, M. K. (1998) *The Last Patrician: Bobby Kennedy and the End of American Aristocracy* (St. Martin's Press).

Briggs, W.W. Jr. (1994a) *Biographical Dictionary of North American Classicists* (Greenwood Press).

————. (1994b) "Gildersleeve, Basil Lanneau," in Briggs (1994a), 213–18.

————. (2002) "Foreword" to M. Reinhold *Studies in Classical History and Society* (Oxford University Press).

Brown, J. M. (1944) *Many a Watchful Night* (Whittlesey House).

————. (1963) "The Heritage of Edith Hamilton: 1867–1963," *Saturday Review*, June 2, 16–17.

Cairns, Huntington. (1993) *A Register of His Papers in the Library of Congress, prepared by G. Batts and F. D. Mathiesen. Revised and expanded by M. McAleer with the assistance of K. A. Kelly and S. McCoy* (Manuscript Division. Library of Congress. Washington, D.C.).

Casazza, J. (2003) "Taming the Savageness of Man: Robert Kennedy, Edith Hamilton, and Their Sources," *Classical World* 96:197–99.

Clack, J. (1994) "Robinson, Edward Anthony," in Briggs (1994a), 532–33.

Cleary, M. (1994) "Bulfinch, Thomas," in Briggs (1994a), 72.

Cottrell, R.C. (1992) *Izzy: A Biography of I. F. Stone* (Rutgers University Press).

Eugenides, J. (2002) *Middlesex* (Farrar, Straus & Giroux).

Evans, P. (2004) *Nemesis: Aristotle Onassis, Jackie O., and the Love Affair That Brough down the Kennedys* (HarperCollins Publishers).

Fowler, R. J. (1990) "Gilbert Murray," in W. W. Briggs Jr. and W. M. Calder III (eds.) *Classical Scholarship: A Biographical Encyclopedia* (Garland Publishing), 321–34.

Graves, R. P. (1995), *Robert Graves and the White Goddess, 1940–1985* (Weidenfeld & Nicolson).

Hallett, J. P. (1996–1997), "Edith Hamilton (1867–1963)," *Classical World* 90:107–47.

Hamilton, Alice. (1943) *Exploring the Dangerous Trades* (Little, Brown).

Hamilton, Andrea. (2004) *A Vision for Girls: Gender, Education and the Bryn Mawr School* (The Johns Hopkins University Press).

Hamilton, E. (1957) "The Classics," *Classical World* 31:29-32.

———. (1963) *The Greek Way*. With a new introduction by C. M. Bowra (Time Inc.; repr. by arrangement with W.W. Norton).

———. (1964) *The Ever-Present Past* (W. W. Norton).

Hamilton, E., and H. Cairns. (eds.) (1961) *The Collected Dialogues of Plato*. Bollingen Series (Princeton University Press).

Edith Hamilton Collection (C0253), Manuscripts Division. Department of Rare Books and Special Collections, Princeton University Library.

Hamilton Family Papers (MC 278-786-13), Schlesinger Library, Radcliffe Institute for Advanced Study, Harvard University.

Heymann, C. David. (1989) *A Woman Named Jackie* (Signet Press).

Horowitz, H. L. (1994) *The Power and the Passion of M. Carey Thomas* (Alfred A. Knopf).

Katz, E. (2001) *The Film Encyclopedia*, 4th ed., rev. F. Klein and R. D. Nolen (Harper Perennial).

John F. Kennedy Presidential Library and Museum: Historical Resources, http://www.jfklibrary.org/Historical+Resources/Archives/Reference. News Conference 63, State Department Auditorium, Washington, D.C., 31 October 1963, 4:00 pm.

Kennedy, M. T. (ed.) (1998) *Make Gentle the Life of This World: The Vision of Robert F. Kennedy* (Harcourt, Brace).

Lindquist, E. N. (1990) *The Origins of the Center for Hellenic Studies* (Princeton University Press).

McKay, A. G. (1994) "Murray, Robert Duff, Jr," in Briggs (1994a), 434–35.

Mellon, P. (1963) n.t. In *Addresses Delivered at the [Dedication of the] Center for Hellenic Studies* (Harvard University), 27–30.

Mellon, P., with J. Baskett. (1992) *Reflections in a Silver Spoon* (William Morrow).

Murnaghan, S. (2005) "Myths of the Greeks." Paper delivered at the 136th meeting of the American Philological Association, Boston, 9 January.

Olson, K. (1974) *The G.I. Bill, the Veterans, and the Colleges* (University of Kentucky Press).

Patner, A. (1988) *I. F. Stone: A Portrait. Conversations with a Nonconformist* (Doubleday).

Reid, D. F. (1967) *Edith Hamilton: An Intimate Portrait* (W.W. Norton).

————. (1969) *A Treasury of Edith Hamilton* (W.W. Norton).

Harry Fielding Reid Papers. Ms. 367. Special Collections. Milton Eisenhower Library, The Johns Hopkins University.

Schlesinger, A. M., Jr. (1965) *A Thousand Days: John F. Kennedy in the White House* (Houghton Mifflin).

————. (1979) *Robert Kennedy and His Times* (Houghton Mifflin).

Seymour, M. (1995) *Robert Graves* (Henry Holt).

Sicherman, B. (1984) *Alice Hamilton: A Life in Letters* (Harvard University Press).

————. (1991) "Edith Hamilton," in E. Foner, and J. A. Garraty (eds.) *The Reader's Companion to American History* (Houghton Mifflin).

Smith, M. S. (1982) *Robert Graves: His Life and Works* (Holt, Rinehart & Winston).

Stevens, G. (1974) *Speak for Yourself, John. The Life of John Mason Brown, with Some of His Letters and Many of His Opinions* (Viking Press).

Stray, C. A. (2004) "Sir Richard Livingstone," in R. B. Todd (ed.) *Dictionary of British Classicists* (Thoemmes-Continuum), 2:585–87.

Thomson, G. P. (1966) "Autobiography." (Unpublished).

Thomson, J. J. (1936) *Recollections and Reflections* (G. Bell & Sons).

White, J. B. (1970) "The Hamilton Way," *Georgia Review* 24:132–57.

Index